Lucretius on Death and Anxiety

Lucretius on Death and Anxiety

POETRY AND PHILOSOPHY
IN *DE RERUM NATURA*

Charles Segal

PRINCETON UNIVERSITY PRESS
PRINCETON, NEW JERSEY

Library of Congress Cataloging-in-Publication Data

Segal, Charles, 1936–
Lucretius on death and anxiety : poetry and philosophy in De rerum
natura / Charles Segal
p.   cm.
Includes bibliographical references.
1. Lucretius Carus, Titus. De rerum natura. 2. Death—History.
3. Anxiety—History. I. Title.
B577.L63D4375   1990   871'.01—dc20   90-32000   CIP

ISBN 0-691-06826-7 (alk. paper)

Publication of this book has been aided by the Whitney Darrow
Fund of Princeton University Press

This book has been composed in Linotron Sabon

To the memory of Craig Manning

June 26, 1935–February 10, 1986

CONTENTS

PREFACE

LUCRETIUS'S great poem *On the Nature of Things*, the longest sustained, non-hostile exposition of Epicurean philosophy to survive the collapse of pagan culture, aims at helping mankind by promoting spiritual tranquillity. Yet the work exhibits what for the modern reader is a shocking vividness in describing the process of dying. This study explores this contradiction, if contradiction it is. I am particularly concerned with the ways in which Lucretius's poetic expression and changing levels of style enable him to present fears about death that are not always stated explicitly or articulated fully in the formal logic of his argument. His approach to the fear of death, although informed at every point by Epicurean physics and psychology, has a weight and precision of detail that are nowhere to be found in Epicurus's extant writings. Consciously or not, Lucretius uses the expressive resources of poetry to supplement the abstractness, distance, and generality in the philosophy. This concern for emotional expressiveness and the maximum impact on the reader also accounts, at least in part, for the detailed descriptions of physical injury in books 3 and 5 and for the puzzling ending of the poem, an account of the great plague at Athens in 430 B.C.

From Constant Martha on, the fear of death forms a chapter or major section of nearly every book on Lucretius. Such discussions necessarily concentrate on the third book. The involving satirical vigor of the concluding diatribe (*nil igitur mors est ad nos*, "Death then is nothing to us," 830–1094) has tended to overshadow the less attractive-looking first two-thirds of the book, which, surprisingly, has not been carefully studied, especially from the point of view of language and style. It has, however, both a poetic and philosophical force that is distinctively Lucretian. Taken together with the accounts of the death of worlds in books 2 and 5 and the account of the plague in book 6, it offers a particularly rich field

for examining how the poet's language gives form to the emo-
tionally charged atmosphere that surrounds the fear of death.
Lucretius's concern with the soul's survival in the afterlife
may seem less pressing to our time than to ages more commit-
ted to Christian dogma. Dante placed Epicurus among the
heretics of Inferno and doubtless would have placed his disci-
ple there too had he known the poem. But Lucretius does have
something important to tell us about a fear that is an inevita-
ble concomitant of our being both mortal and intelligent. The
range and nuance of feeling and the images and associations
that only poetry can evoke enable him to explore dimensions
of the fear of death that the prose writings of Epicurus could
not touch.

As my primary aim is the elucidation and interpretation of
the texture of Lucretius's poetry in relation to the philosophi-
cal content, I shall not go into detail on his sources or on his
physiological theories, subjects that have been fruitfully dis-
cussed in the recent work of Pigeaud and Schrijvers (in the
Fondation Hardt volume on Lucretius). Although my princi-
pal concern is Lucretius's poetic expression, there are also im-
plications for attitudes toward death in classical antiquity.
This large and important topic lies beyond the modest limits
of this study, but I have briefly sketched some possible direc-
tions in the closing chapter.

The nature of Lucretius's argument and of my own analysis
has sometimes necessitated discussing the same passage in dif-
ferent contexts and from different perspectives. I apologize for
the occasional overlap. The text of Lucretius is generally cited
from Bailey's third edition, with commentary (Oxford, 1947).
Fragments of Epicurus are cited from Usener, occasionally
from Arrighetti. The *Letters* are cited from H. S. Long's Ox-
ford text of Diogenes Laertius, *Vitae Philosophorum* (Oxford,
1964), volume 2, which is abbreviated as D.L. In citing Greek,
I have generally transliterated individual words but not whole
phrases or sentences. Translations are my own unless other-
wise indicated, and they aim at reasonable fidelity to the orig-
inal rather than elegance.

ACKNOWLEDGMENTS

THIS STUDY owes much to two graduate seminars on Lucretius that I taught at Brown University and an undergraduate course at Princeton University on death in literature. I recall with pleasure and thanks my students' curiosity, questions, and interest. A sabbatical leave from Brown University and a Fellowship from the National Endowment for the Humanities in 1985–86 provided the precious leisure in which I could reread and rethink Lucretius. During this time I benefited greatly from the hospitality, personal associations, and library resources of the American Academy in Rome, the American School of Classical Studies in Athens, and the Institute for Advanced Study in Princeton. For research support in the later stages in the work and aid in the preparation of the manuscript I am indebted to Princeton University and to the Center for Advanced Study in the Behavioral Sciences, Palo Alto, California, where funding was provided by the National Endowment for the Humanities (#RA-20037-88) and the Andrew W. Mellon Foundation. To all of these institutions I am deeply grateful. I also thank my colleagues in the Department of Classics at Princeton University for collegial interest and advice.

Several friends and colleagues discussed Lucretian and Epicurean problems, commented on parts of the manuscript, or generously provided copies of publications. I particularly thank David Furley, Charles Garton, David Konstan, and Martha Nussbaum. Joanna Hitchcock of Princeton University Press gave her usual sound advice and warm encouragement. I owe many improvements in accuracy and consistency to Sherry Wert's careful copyediting. I am indebted to the anonymous readers of the Press for detailed and helpful criticisms. Ronnie Hanley and Andrew Keller of Princeton University retyped much of the work and valiantly struggled with word processors and their problems. Sharon Ray helped with the index, and Sterling Bland coordinated final details at the Press.

Finally, and most important, I thank my wife, Nancy Jones, for being a keen and supportive discussant of nearly every aspect of the book, *praepandens lumina menti.*

A version of Chapter 9 originally appeared in *Ramus* 15 (1986): 1–34; it has been thoroughly revised and recast for this volume. I thank the editors of *Ramus* and Aureal Publications for permission to reuse this material here. I have elaborated on some of the matters involving literary history found in Chapter 8 in my article on the Second Proem in *Harvard Studies.* In both cases, readers are referred to these works for further details and bibliography.

.   .   .

I dedicate this work to a gifted and erudite scholar whom *mors immatura* cruelly carried off just as his efforts and ability were beginning to bear fruit and he was nearing the completion of the Ph.D. program in Classics at Brown University. Despite heavy obstacles of poverty and illness, Craig Manning achieved distinction as a teacher and budding scholar. In his unassuming manner he conveyed his intellectual intensity, his enthusiasm, his love of scholarship, and his breadth of knowledge. He carried his great learning lightly. He gave generously to his students, friends, and fellow graduate students. He will be long remembered and sorely missed.

Lucretius on Death and Anxiety

—Are you afraid of Death?
—Not of death but maybe what leads to it.
—Doesn't life lead to it?
—I'm speaking of sickness, accident—being
incapacitated; unable to run my life; that can be worse
than death. I'm afraid of the unexpected. What I can
expect I can deal with.
—Bernard Malamud, *Dubin's Lives*

The extreme of the known in the presence of the
extreme
Of the unknown.
—Wallace Stevens, "To an Old Philosopher in Rome"

Should I have died less cheerfully before having read
the *Tusculans*? I think not. And now that I find myself
close to death, I feel that my tongue has grown richer,
my courage not at all.
—Montaigne, "Of Physiognomy"

Chapter 1

LUCRETIUS'S ADEQUACY TO THE FEAR OF DEATH: LOGIC, POETRY, AND EMOTION

FOR LUCRETIUS, death both is the greatest anxiety and embodies the greatest mode of anxiety. In one of the highest tributes that one ancient poet offers to another, Virgil seems to recognize this fact. Applying Lucretius's own encomium on Epicurus to the poet himself, Virgil congratulates his predecessor not only on "knowing the causes of things"—that is, explaining the workings of nature in a rational, scientific way—but also on trampling underfoot "all fears, and the doom against which no prayer avails, and the roar of greedy Acheron" (*Georgics* 2.490–92):

> felix qui potuit rerum cognoscere causas
> atque metus omnes et inexorabile fatum
> subiecit pedibus strepitumque Acherontis avari.

The young Virgil was both an Epicurean and a reader of Lucretius (as we see from *Eclogue* 6.31–40); and when he turns in the next lines of the *Georgics* from fear to his own delight in the gods of the countryside and the pastoral demigods Pan, Sylvanus, and the Nymphs, he perhaps implies that Lucretius's heavy toil has freed him to enjoy this happier side of nature (*Georgics* 2.493–94):

> fortunatus et ille deos qui novit agrestes,
> Panaque Silvanumque senem Nymphasque sorores.

(Happy too is that man who knows the gods of the country, Pan and old Silvanus and the sister Nymphs.)

Be this as it may, Virgil clearly understands that the central theme of the *De Rerum Natura* is the struggle against anxiety and particularly anxiety toward death.[1]

This insight of Lucretius's greatest reader also underlies the present study. Few poets in Latin deal more powerfully with death. Few also so beautifully convey their joy in the vital energies of the world as these pervade even the tiniest movements in nature. What then is the relation between Lucretius's philosophy and the extraordinary expressiveness of his poetry? Studies of Lucretius over the last quarter-century have shown that his poetic style is not merely the honey that coats the bitter taste of philosophy, in his own rather self-deprecating figure (1.936–50), but itself is an essential element in his argument. It remains, however, to integrate his poetry of death and war into the overall appreciation of his poetry of life and happiness, and that is the task of the present book.

From Statius and Saint Jerome on to Tennyson and our own time, Lucretius has fascinated readers at least as much for his contradictions as for his consistencies. An exponent of a philosophy whose goal is serenity, he exults in emotional intensity, what Statius called *docti furor arduus Lucreti*, "the steep madness of learned Lucretius" (*Silvae* 2.7.76). Committed to the ideal of peace in the soul, he writes extraordinarily detailed accounts of violence. War is the basis of many of his most powerful images, including one of the poem's controlling metaphors, the battle between life and death.[2] Closely following Epicurus, he advocates a calm objectivity and impersonality in viewing death; yet he has a vivid sympathy for birth, nurture, and growth. Scornful of conventional beliefs in the gods, Lucretius will appear to many readers to be in some

[1] Among the fullest general studies of death in Lucretius are Martha, *Le poème*, ch. 5, esp. 132ff.; Sikes, *Lucretius*, 125ff.; Logre, *L'anxiété*, 185–215; Boyancé, *Lucrèce*, ch. 6, esp. 145ff.; Perelli, *Lucrezio*, ch. 2, esp. 115ff.; Schmid, "*Lucretius Ethicus*"; and Stork, *Nil igitur mors est*, which has a useful introduction on the general importance of the fear of death in Lucretius (pp. 1–5).

[2] See, for instance, 2.573–76; in general, Klingner, "Lucrez," 203; Minadeo, *Lyre of Science*, chs. 2 and 3, passim.

sense a religious spirit. One will think immediately of his celebration of the blessed abode of the gods and his awe at the vision of infinity in the proem of book 3 or his description of the majesty of the heavens in book 5, with its "solemn constellations of the sky's night-wandering torches and the flames that fly" (5.1188–93).

Like other Hellenistic philosophers, Epicurus aims at achieving a godlike invulnerability.[3] Lucretius, on the other hand, has the Roman concreteness about the practical realities of life and a poet's appreciation of the rich and disturbing physicality of the world around us. The philosopher George Santayana long ago put his finger on the weakness in Epicurus's treatment of the fear of death. Epicurus, he suggested, did not confront "the radical fear of death," of which the driving force is the love of life:

> Epicurus, who feared life, seems to have missed . . . the primordial and colossal force he was fighting against. Had he perceived that force, he would have been obliged to meet it in a more radical way. . . . The love of life is not something rational or founded on experience of life. It is something antecedent and spontaneous. It is that Venus Genetrix which covers the earth with its flora and fauna. It teaches every animal to seek its food and its mate, and to protect its offspring; as also to resist or fly from all injury to the body, and most of all from threatened death.[4]

Modern interpreters may demur at this certainty about Epicurus's fear of life, but few will disagree on Lucretius's enthusiasm for Venus Genetrix and all that she embodies. Indeed, the rhetoric of this passage seems itself inspired by Lucretius's own opening invocation to Venus, *Aeneadum genetrix*.

Other tensions may be due to unresolved issues within Epicureanism itself. As Martha Nussbaum observes, the Epicurean voice of nature urges us to accept the limits of our mor-

---

[3] See Mitsis, *Epicurus' Ethical Theory*, Introduction, esp. p. 2; Nussbaum, "Mortal Immortals."

[4] Santayana, "Lucretius," 52.

tality; but another voice, ultimately echoing the Platonic and Aristotelian praise of the life of the intellect, confers on the wise man an aura of quasi-religious transcendence, albeit within this life.[5] Thus Epicurus ends his *Letter to Menoeceus* (D.L. 10.135) with the exhortation to meditate on his precepts day and night, for in this way "you will never suffer disturbance sleeping or waking, but you will live as a god among men; for one who lives amid eternal goods is not like a mortal creature."

On the one hand, Epicurus would have us accept the material basis of our life in this fragile world of continual atomic dissolution and renewal. On the other hand, he has us look to the gods, in their serene and remote indifference, as eternal models of the highest peace, as we see them in the proem to Lucretius's third book. To put the contrast a little differently, as a creation of impersonal physical processes, life is of no particular concern to the universe; but from the point of view of the human consciousness that it brings into being, it is indeed of the highest value.[6] This tension, as one would expect, is strong in Lucretius, with his passionately engaged vitalism; and one of its manifestations, as we shall see, is an approach to death that is more personal and emotional than anything in Epicurus's extant writings.

If, in certain areas, Lucretius has his own way of interpreting Epicureanism, this does not mean that he is deeply divided against himself. Epicurean science does for him something analogous to what the heroic tradition does for Homer. As in the case of the Homeric simile, the unifying frame of a larger system encourages and legitimizes observations of everyday experience without the loss of poetic elevation or purpose. Lucretius drew from Epicurus an expansive overview of nature at once systematic and morally engaged, enthusiastic and precise, all-encompassing, yet attentive to the smallest detail.[7]

While the ethics of Epicurus gave him a high moral aim—

[5] See Nussbaum, "Mortal Immortals, 324–27."
[6] See DeLacy, "Process and Value," passim.
[7] For indications of some of Lucretius's indebtedness to Epicurean science along these lines, see Klingner, "Lucrez," 191.

nothing less than saving mankind from suffering and unhappiness—the physics provided a model of nature both grand in its infinity and intelligible to human reason. Because of the unity of the atomic processes that are the same for every phenomenon of the world, all of nature can be perceived in its permanence, coherence, and interconnectedness.[8] Thus the human body and the universe are linked by their common origins in the movements of atom and void, and their different lives and deaths illuminate one another.[9]

Through Epicurean physics, Lucretius becomes sensitized to a range of phenomena that had rarely found its way into the high style of Latin hexameter poetry: the specks of dust in a sunbeam, or the iridescence in a pigeon's feathers, or the splendor of a peacock's tail, or clothes drying, or the reflected light from an awning in the theater, or the sensation of cold on the teeth. His zeal to prove and explain the workings of the invisible atomic world leads him to daring analogies and elicits brilliant observations of nature. The notion of infinity, whether of worlds, size, or number, stimulates his visual imagination. Thus we have accounts of elephants and wild beasts in battle, cloud formations and comets, seashells and the sloughed skins of snakes or cicadas. He can convey the grandeur of space and the vastness of time as almost no other Latin poet. He heroizes Epicurus for his journey to the flaming walls of the world (1.69–77), but he himself repeatedly looks at the infinite reaches of space and conveys his awe at the breadth and power of the vision, whether in a general reflection on the "deep and vast immensity" that lies open before him or in his personal response of "divine pleasure and shivering awe" at Epicurus's uncovering of nature's secrets (1.957, 3.28–30).

The world for Lucretius is a place of marvels. His wonder even borders on a sense of the sacred. Venus, personification of the life force that he so admires, has a "sacred body" as she covers Mars in her embrace (*corpore sancto*, 1.38). Sicily holds among its volcanic fires and subterranean roars "noth-

---

[8] See Santayana, "Lucretius," 27–29; now Schiesaro, *Simulacrum*, 17–48.
[9] See below, Chapter Five.

ing more glorious nor more sacred and wondrous and dear"
than the philosopher Empedocles (*nec sanctum magis et
mirum carumque*, 1.729–30). Democritus's principles,
though sometimes erroneous, are "holy" (*sancta viri senten-
tia*, 3.371). His own words, he claims, are poured forth with
"more holiness and far greater certainty of truth" than those
of the Pythian priestess on Apollo's tripod at Delphi (5.110–
12; cf. 1.736–39).

Is it surprising, then, that a poet with so developed a sense
for the marvels, variety, and sanctity of life would feel toward
death something less than the cool indifference counselled by
Epicurus? Lucretius counselled this too, and believed his
counsel (so far as one can tell). But one to whom life mattered
with the intensity and passion that Lucretius everywhere ex-
hibits might well appreciate the ordinary man's anxieties and
fears. He may well have sympathized with that "radical fear
of death" which, as Santayana suggests, stems from a keen,
delighted, and passionate love of life.

We must not here fall into the appealing abyss of the "anti-
Lucretius in Lucretius," the poet inwardly divided against
himself and his doctrine. Even if he did not find in Epicurus's
writings his own enthusiasm for life and living things, he
found many other things. The poet who could find in the
"hoped-for pleasure of sweet friendship" the inducement to
stay awake for the long night vigils of poetic toil (1.140–45)
would have reponded to the jubilant, almost evangelical cele-
bration of friendship by his Master: "Friendship goes dancing
around the world, announcing to us all to awaken to blessed-
ness." [10] He would have admired Epicurus's deathbed provi-
sion for his disciple's children. Thrilling to the awesome divin-
ity of Epicurus's intellect, he would have been deeply touched
by the closing sentence of the *Epistle to Menoeceus* on the
quasi-divine life of the wise man, cited above.[11]

[10] *Sententiae Vaticanae* 52; cf. *Kyriai Doxai* 27. For the importance of
friendship in Epicurus's thought, see Frischer, *The Sculpted Word*, 75–76,
with further references; also Clay, "Epicurus' Last Will," 254–55.

[11] On the godlike life of the wise man, see Frischer, *The Sculpted Word*,
77–79, with the references there cited. We may note too the almost cultic

For all of his own passion and appreciation of the irrational, Lucretius fully shares Epicurus's belief in the power of reason to explore the dark places of man's nature and nature's irrationality. In human life he identifies "a certain hidden force," *vis abdita quaedam*, that, like religious superstition, "crushes human affairs" and mocks man's pretensions to power and authority (5.1233–35). This "hidden force" belongs to the uncontrollable violence of nature, storms, earthquakes, tidal waves, and other disruptive phenomena of nature that Lucretius analyzes in book 6. But such a force operates in human life too, and particularly in the areas of love, death, and war—the areas of Freud's *eros* and *thanatos*.

Victorian interpreters have often yielded to the temptation of a biographical view and attributed Lucretius's absorption with death to a deep pessimism or a morbid personality. Tennyson's portrait of a great but gloomy mind struggling with incipient madness remains impressed on the English-speaking world. In the same spirit Constant Martha apostrophized, "O most sincere of poets, contemplating the force of your genius in the greatness of your ruin."[12] For Santayana, Lucretius is a poet of "profound melancholy." [13] Among more recent scholars, E. E. Sikes, for example, regards Lucretius as personally "obsessed" with death.[14] To the psychiatrist Logre, Lucretius's apparently welcoming attitude toward death and his unconcern with the physical pain attending it are the perfect symptoms of a suicidal personality.[15] Luciano Perelli, who lays great stress on the mood of anxiety throughout the poem, sees an unconscious contradiction between Lucretius's ratio-

---

veneration of the Master, on which see ibid., 205ff., and Clay, "Cults of Epicurus," passim.

[12] Martha, *Le poème*, 172.

[13] Santayana, "Lucretius," 46.

[14] Sikes, *Lucretius*, 126.

[15] Logre, *L'anxiété*, 214–15. See also Lortie, "Crainte anxieuse," 51ff., who quotes Père Sertillanges, *Le problème du mal* (Paris, 1948), 151, to the effect that Lucretius "avait tellement peur de l'Achéron que par contraste l'anéantissement lui paraît une délivrance" (Lortie, "Crainte anxieuse," 62).

nal, Epicurean view of death as liberation and the "obsessive form" that death assumes within the work. This obsession, he suggests, negates or at least obstructs the poet's explicit attempt to reassure his audience and instill a serene acceptance of death as part of the ἀταραξία, or freedom from disturbance, that is among the gifts of his espoused doctrine.[16]

The dark strain is perhaps not to be denied; yet it is not death alone that absorbs Lucretius, but the struggle between life and death.[17] If he shows us the destruction of our world and our selves, he also reminds us of the indestructibility of the atoms that will combine into new worlds. If he depicts the aggressive violence and self-destructiveness of mankind, his aim is to provide the medicines of reason and understanding that can turn us to a better use of our lives.

That man is educable by rational instruction is the underlying assumption of Lucretius's poem. He drew from the Master the optimistic belief that philosophy could revolutionize our lives and bring us almost godlike happiness (cf. 3.319–22).[18] Epicurus's own godlike divinity is both a model and an incentive (cf. 3.3–30, 5.7–12 and 49–57). But man is also subject to irrational fears and hopes and may "wander" or stray from the path of reason (2.9–10). Hence the repeated pleas to the reader to exert himself and join with the poet in the battle against the darkness of ignorance and superstition. In following in the footsteps of his master and alleviating human suffering by bringing reason where unreason was, he is also following the humane tradition of θεραπεία, the healing of souls in Greek philosophy. But as a poet he is also keenly aware of how deep-seated is the irrational in us all; and he possesses a unique power of imagination and visual representation in exposing that irrationality.

---

[16] Perelli, *Lucrezio*, 102: "Se dunque nelle intenzioni del poeta il tema della morte viene introdotto come desiderio di liberazione dal timore della morte, poeticamente il pensiero della morte assuma una forma ossessiva che annulla le intenzioni serenatrici." See also pp. 51–52 and 115ff.

[17] See Minadeo, *Lyre of Science*, chs. 2 and 3; Klingner, "Philosophie und Dichtkunst," 150ff.

[18] See most recently Mitsis, *Epicurus' Ethical Theory*, 148–49.

Epicurus posits an intimate relation between the sufferings of the body and of the mind that follows from the continuum of the physical processes, extending from the visible to the invisible. Epicurus's great predecessor, Democritus, drew an explicit parallel between the healing of bodily ills and healing the soul (68 B31 and B288 Diels-Kranz). Epicurus, perhaps intentionally, echoes his words (frag. 221 Usener). Before Democritus, Greek tragedy explored medical analogies for emotional or psychological disturbances. Lucretius himself assumes the doctor's role when he would apply the honey of poetry to the wormwood medicine of his doctrine (1.936–38, repeated in 4.11–13). He may be drawing as much upon the literary tradition as on the atomic theory (cf. the similar metaphor in Plutarch's *On the Education of Children* 18.13D). But he is firmly within the tradition of atomism, at least as far as Democritus and Epicurus are concerned, in this shading over of his argument in book 3 from the physiological bases of the soul's maladies to ethical and psychological concerns. Alongside the proofs of the soul's physical weaknesses and therefore mortality, according to the atomic theory, there is much in the first part of book 3 that belongs to the ancient "medicine of the soul," the Democritean ἰατρικὴ ψυχῆς.

Lucretius's treatment not just of death but of the *fear* of death brings together the two strongest directions in the *De Rerum Natura*: the ethical-emotional θεραπεία of the soul through Epicurean science and the poetic tradition that offers wisdom and consolation in the face of man's greatest fear and worst ill. The latter is rooted in the compassion for the mortal condition as a whole in both epic and didactic hexameter poetry, where the subjection to mortality constitutes the defining characteristic of the human race.[19] The combination of common-sense argumentation, the "hard" evidence of Epicurean science, and the humane wisdom and authority of an ancient poetic tradition enables him to meet diverse anxieties at many levels and for many different kinds of readers.

[19] For example *Iliad* 9.319–20, 12.322–28; *Odyssey* 11.34–41, 218–22; Hesiod, *Works and Days* 100ff. and *Theogony* 603ff.

For Lucretius, as an Epicurean thinker, death is a scientifi-
cally understood process, the dissolution of atoms. But death
has another, darker side, hidden in the shadows: the fear of
the painful process of dying through massive physical injury
and fears about annihilation, the total extinction of one's self,
dissolution into nothingness. These are not confronted di-
rectly in book 3, but do appear, powerfully, in the account of
the plague at Athens in book 6. Some of those fears, however,
are already anticipated in the imagery, if not in the overt ar-
guments, of book 3. My analysis will try to show how the
language of book 3, and especially the metaphorical descrip-
tions of death, even within the framework of the scientific ra-
tionality of the atomic process, convey its other side, the dark
fears that are hidden in the shadows and need to be brought
forth into the light in order to be grappled with and overcome
(cf. 1.146–48).

One way to bring these fears into the light without seeming
to countenance them is to present them through figurative lan-
guage, chiefly imagery. In this way Lucretius is able to ac-
knowledge their emotional reality but also to keep them under
the control of Epicurean rationalism and the "truth" of the
atomic processes. Inevitably a certain tension develops in
places between the poetry and the scientific philosophy. This
tension, however, is not so much a contradiction as an inevi-
table result of the crossing of complementary currents in Lu-
cretius's work: a poet's interest in conveying the raw power of
the terror and horror that death inspires in us as human ex-
perience, and a moralist's concern to eradicate such fears and
enable us to accept with tranquillity the inevitable end.

Book 3 is concerned primarily with two aspects of the fear
of death: anxiety about what happens to our bodies after we
die, and the folly of those who believe the traditional myths
about the afterlife, especially the punishment of the soul in the
Underworld.[20] As observers from antiquity to the present have
pointed out, however, this most systematic attempt in the

---

[20] For the closing section of book 3, see Conte, "Trionfo della morte";
Stork, *Nil igitur mors est*; and Wallach, *Lucretius and the Diatribe*.

poem to eradicate the fear of death neglects the two powerful anxieties noted above, the fear of suffering in the process of dying and the instinctive fear of annihilation.[21]

These omissions are all the more striking since some Epicureans did in fact pay attention to at least the first item, pain attendant on the process of dying.[22] Diogenes of Oenoanda, for example, clearly recognized the suffering of a long terminal illness (frag. 376, cols. 2 and 3, Chilton). Lucretius's contemporary, the Greek poet and Epicurean philosopher Philodemus, also mentions the fear of a slow and painful death by prolonged illness (*De Morte* 5.9ff. and 28.14ff.), but argues that the soul's separation from the body in death is not necessarily a painful process (8.1–9.12). He is sympathetic to men who would prefer to die in battle and, like Montaigne, observes that in many cases a long terminal illness is no more painful than death in battle (28.20–32). Presumably, however, it can also be no less painful.

Experience will not necessarily have borne out Epicurus's optimistic view that prolonged pain in serious illness will be endurable and intense pain of only brief duration (*Kyriai Doxai* 4); and Lucretius's contemporary, Cicero, makes this criticism at length (*De Finibus* 2.28.93–30.96). Against Epicurus's consoling thought that the memory of past happiness helps us in times of physical pain, Plutarch objects that such thoughts are of little avail amid the writhings and convulsions of the body gripped by mortal illness (*Non Posse Suaviter Vivi Secundum Epicurum* 18.1099E). Cicero makes a similar point in the *Tusculan Disputations*, observing that such a tactic is of no more help than it would be to remind a man suffering from

[21] This point is made in Giussani's excursus to book 3, *T. Lucretius Cari* (1897), 3:140–41; see also Perelli, *Lucrezio*, 101–2.

[22] Epicurus himself recognized that grief at death is a natural reaction and is preferable to insensitivity: Plutarch, *Non Posse Suaviter Vivi Secundum Epicurum* 1101A–B (frag. 120 Usener). Unfortunately Epicurus's *On Diseases and Death* (frag. 18 Arrighetti) is not extant; see Gigante, " 'Philosophia Medicans,' " 55. See also Santayana, "Lucretius," 52 for a criticism of Epicurus's inattention to the process of dying. He cites Francesca's "Il modo ancor m'offende," of Dante, *Inferno* 5.

extreme heat that he once swam in the cold rivers of his native Arpinum (5.26.74). Cicero is probably reflecting the common-place view of his time when he quotes Epicharmus: *emori nolo, sed me esse mortuum nihil aestimo* ("I do not want to suffer death, but to be dead I consider as nothing," *Tusc. Disp.* 1.8.15).[23] Such concerns with the process of dying surface in other Roman writers of the period or shortly after, like Tibullus and Propertius.[24]

In his polemical treatise, *Non Posse Suaviter Vivi Secundum Epicurum*, Plutarch argues at length that Epicurus does not address the real fears about death. These concern not the afterlife but rather the loss of consciousness, "oblivion, ignorance, and darkness" (λήθη, ἄγνοια, σκότος, 10.1093A). Returning to this point near the end of his treatise, Plutarch maintains that the terror of non-being is far more powerful than the myths about Hades (26.1104C). "The face of death that all men fear as terrifying and grim and dark is that of loss of sensation, oblivion, and ignorance" (ἀναισθησία, λήθη, ἄγνοια, 26.1104E). For this reason, Plutarch goes on, men feel disturbance and malaise about expressions like "he has been destroyed" and "he is no longer" (οὐκ ἔστι). Instead of removing the fear of death by his *Tetrapharmakon*, including the maxim that "What has no sensation is nothing to us" (*Kyriai Doxai* 2), Epicurus only confirms it, for he virtually demonstrates its power: such a "dissolution into the absence of thought and sensation" (τὴν εἰς τὸ μὴ φρονοῦν μηδὲ αἰσθανόμενον διάλυσιν) is the very thing that our nature fears (27.1105A).

In describing our terror at the vast nothingness of our non-

---

[23] Sikes (*Lucretius*, 132) remarks, "The ordinary man does not, perhaps, fear death in the abstract so much as the painful process of dying." Kenney (*Lucretius III*, 32–33) quotes Byron on Juvenal 10: "I should think it might be read with great effect to a man dying without much pain" and also Cornford, "I do not know how common the horror of death may be among normal people; but, where it exists, is it not often the prospect of extinction that horrifies them?"

[24] Michels, "Death," 175, notes that by contrast to Lucretius, Propertius is deeply involved with the process of dying.

being, Plutarch in fact uses some of the same imagery as Lucretius does (as we shall see) when he deals with the soul's dissolution. Plutarch remarks that Epicurus's sayings in effect leave us "immersed in non-being from which we can never emerge" (30.1106E). It is the very infinity (ἀπέραντον) and unchanging continuation of this condition that is so terrifying: "Our soul is poured forth into a yawning ocean of infinity" (30.1106F). Epicurus's consolation for death, in Plutarch's view, removes our only hope: "For if, as Epicurus says, death takes place also with pain, the fear of death is entirely inconsolable since it leads us to the loss of good things through a path of suffering" (30.1107A).

Epicurus himself seems more concerned with overcoming infinite desires than with the fear of the infinite void after death; and in fact most of his warnings against the "unlimited" are directed at desire.[25] If we limit infinite desire by what is "necessary" (τὸ ἀναγκαῖον), we can achieve that autonomy or self-sufficiency (αὐτάρκεια) through which we approximate the calm of the gods (fragment 458 Usener = Porphyry, *De Abstinentia* 1.54). Epicurus's fullest advice on this subject is a brief passage in the *Letter to Menoeceus* (D.L. 10.124):

Death is the cessation of sensation. Whence the true knowledge of the fact that death is nothing to us renders enjoyable the mortal part of life, not adding limitless time (ἄπειρον προστιθεῖσα χρόνον) but rather taking away the longing for immortality. For there is nothing terrifying in living to one who has genuinely grasped the fact that there is nothing terrifying in not being alive.

The failure to understand this limit of desires and of time may also be the reason why men amass wealth and power, with the resultant crimes to which Lucretius refers at the beginning of his discussion of the fear of death (3.59–77).[26]

[25] See, e.g., *Kyriai Doxai* 10 and 15; in general, see Schmid, "*Lucretius Ethicus*," 137ff.
[26] Schmid, "*Lucretius Ethicus*," 139ff., makes an interesting and convincing case for linking this passage with the Epicurean warning against unlimited desires. See also Miller, "Art of Dying," 172. We may compare also *Kyriai*

Epicurus's rationalism, however, seems not to have explored the possibility that men could fear this very infinity of non-being. According to a passage in Porphyry (frag. 458 Usener), he may have paired the insatiable desire for "life, wealth, and property" with "fearing the terror associated with death as limitless" (τὸ κατὰ τὸν θάνατον δεινὸν ὡς ἀπέραντον).[27] Porphyry seems to be expounding Epicurus's thoughts on death in the *Letter to Menoeceus* cited above and not elaborating theories of his own. But even if he is transmitting Epicurean doctrine, he implies not that infinity itself is the source of fear but rather that the issue is the extension of our desires to the limitless time beyond our death. We fear that we will somehow be deprived of these goods for infinite time (cf. Lucretius 3.900ff.).

In urging us toward the prospect of a livable happiness, Epicurus, like Lucretius, is aware of the fragility of our being, of the dangers surrounding life on every side, and of the changing, ephemeral nature of our circumstances.[28] Philodemus reflects this spirit of practicable, manageable happiness when he remarks, "The sensible man, having determined that he can obtain everything conducive to the autonomy for a happy life, walks about, for the rest prepared for burial, and he enjoys the single day as if it were a lifetime" (*De Morte* 38.14–19). It is the marring of lived life that is pitiable, he suggests, not death per se (*De Morte* 33.30ff.); and Lucretius would doubtless agree (cf. 3.59ff., 978ff.).

To Plutarch's arguments about the fear of infinity, then, Epicurus could answer, as others had before him, that such fears are based on false assumptions about "goods" and about the afterlife, since both will matter to us as little after our death as they did before our birth.[29] There is, however, something not

---

Doxai 19: "Infinite time and time that is limited hold the same pleasure, if one measures the limits [of pleasure] by rational accounting."

[27] On these relationships, see Schmid, "*Lucretius Ethicus*," 150–53.

[28] Cf. Epicurus, *Kyriai Doxai* 7; Lucretius 5.218–34, 1120–30.

[29] Cf. Lucretius 3.870–903 and 972–77; also Pseudo-Plato, *Axiochus* 365D, 370A. See Puliga, "*Chronos e Thanatos*," 252–53; also Furley's study

entirely rational about the fear of death that Epicurus's *Tetra-pharmakon* seemed to some not to have addressed. When in the *Letter to Menoeceus* Epicurus does acknowledge death as "the most terrifying of evils" (τὸ φρικωδέστατον τῶν κακῶν, D.L. 10.125), it is only in the context of asserting that it is "nothing to us." There remains the very troubling tension that many people, both ancients and moderns, continue to feel between our finitude and the infinity of our future non-being. The proof, based on the soul's mortality, that we do not experience infinity after death does not necessarily eliminate our anxiety about an infinite void stretching before us.

Plutarch's criticisms were written a century and a half after Lucretius; but, as the discussions in Cicero and Philodemus noted above indicate, they may reflect objections voiced by philosophical opponents over a long period. Lucretius may or may not have known of these counter-arguments to his Master's thought. As a poet, he probably had an intuitive sensitivity to this more emotional dimension of his contemporaries' fears about death; and this awareness is reflected, as I shall argue, indirectly in the language of book 3. If Plutarch's images of the terrifying infinity of the sea of non-being and of immersion, for example, appear repeatedly in Lucretius,[30] it is not because the Roman writer is necessarily using a common source anterior to both himself and Plutarch, but because as a poet he is keenly aware of the terrors that haunt the human mind.

Lucretius's emphasis on the fears about the afterlife presents still another problem. These anxieties seem not to correspond to the actual concerns of his day. Funeral inscriptions and other indications of popular attitudes, studied by scholars as diverse as Franz Cumont, Tenney Frank, and Richmond Lattimore, suggest that in fact the belief in an afterlife played

---

of the "mirror of the past" argument in Lucretius 3.832ff.: Furley, "Nothing to Us?" 76ff.

[30] See, for example, Lucretius 3.829, discussed below, Chapter Four. Rambaux, "La logique," 216–18, however, tries to show that Lucretius's argumentation often follows the structure of an implicit dialogue, answering the objections of an imaginary interlocutor.

a relatively small role in contemporary anxieties about death.[31] Within the Greek world the lightness with which men treat such fears of the afterlife forms another of Plutarch's objections to the efficacy of Epicurus's philosophy. For most men, he says, the fears of Hades belong to "the mythical" (τὸ μυθῶδες, *Non Posse Suav. Vivi* 26.1104C). "Not very many men fear those things, as they are the teachings of mothers and nurses and fabulous tales, and those who do fear them believe that mystic initiations and purifications help us against them" (27.1105B).

Cicero is, once more, a useful witness for contemporary attitudes. His interlocutor in the first book of the *Tusculan Disputations* regards death as an unmitigated evil, not because of the punishments of Hades (which are dismissed as old wives' tales, 1.6.10 and 1.21.48), but because the dead are "nothing," *miseros ob id ipsum quidem quia nulli sint* (1.6.11). The misery of death consists in lacking the light of life: *omnes denique miseros, qui hac luce careant* (1.6.12). For a creature that has once enjoyed life, non-being is itself the greatest suf-

---

[31] Franz Cumont, *Afterlife in Roman Paganism* (New Haven, 1922), 17ff.; Tenney Frank, *Life and Literature in the Roman Republic*, Sather Classical Lectures 7 (Berkeley, 1930), 234–35; Richmond Lattimore, *Themes in Greek and Roman Epitaphs* (Urbana, Ill., 1942), 59ff. Paul Veyne, ed., *A History of Private Life*, vol. 1, *From Pagan Rome to Byzantium*, trans. Arthur Goldhammer (Cambridge, Mass., 1987), 219–23, also stresses the relative unimportance of afterlife in Roman concerns with death. Funeral rites, he suggests, may have been more important as a means of consolation than to allay fears of the hereafter. The real subjects of fear, he argues, were the gods. Lucretius's concern with the fear of death, then, is to be explained in part by the fact that "paganism, a religion of festival, had an ethical component, which aroused anxieties that it could not allay because it was not a soteriological religion that could reassure the faithful by organizing their lives in this world on the pretext of securing salvation in the next" (p. 223). To find out how best to live in this world, then, one had to turn to the philosophers. Hopkins, *Death and Renewal*, 226–35, makes the sensible and important point that pagan antiquity contained a wide variety of not necessarily consistent and in fact often contradictory views of the afterlife that could exist side by side, and that it could tolerate a wide range of discrepancies between formal beliefs (especially as verbalized and formalized in philosophy and literature) and practices in the family cults and other forms of popular religion.

fering: *nam istuc ipsum, non esse, cum fueris, miserrimum puto* (1.6.12).

It is, then, arguable that Epicureanism appealed to Lucretius and his contemporaries not because it allayed fears of an afterlife but because it addressed the problem of anxiety, including the free-floating anxiety about pain and death. Epicurus's doctrine, through its materialist psychology, brings these fears into the open and gives them a concrete focus in the body and its suffering. Once brought forth into the light, as Lucretius repeatedly tells us, the hidden, unavowed, and unspeakable dread loses some of its terror (cf. 1.146–48 and elsewhere). The ancient θεραπεία of the soul, in this respect, is not so far from modern psychotherapy, perhaps because the needs of the soul have changed relatively little over the last two millenia.

For Lucretius, the depressive reaction to the approach of death is the most painful and pitiable part of dying.[32] In describing the plague in book 6, he singles out this experience as follows: *illud in his rebus miserandum magnopere unum / aerumnabile erat* ("In these circumstances that one thing was greatly to be pitied and painful in great degree," 6.1230–31). A few lines later he praises as "best man" the active, energetic person who yielded to pity for the afflicted and tended the dying, often at the price of his own lonely and untended end (6.1239–46). Lucretius's restraint (or the possibility of a lacuna after 1246) suppresses the details of what kind of death the "worst man" (in contrast to "each best man," *optimus quisque* of 1246) might have, but presumably this is implied in those who perished *vitai nimium cupidos mortisque timentis* ("excessively desirous of life and fearful of death," 1240). The worst death, then, would be to die gripped by the terror of dying, clinging to life, and yet helpless before the power of the disease.[33]

---

[32] On Lucretius's transformations of Thucydides' narrative of the plague in the direction of greater emphasis on the emotional responses to death (especially sadness and depression), see Commager, "Lucretius' Interpretation," 105ff.

[33] The importance of fear in defining the horror of such a death would be

This desperation in the face of death as a physical reality supplements the earlier discussion of book 3 in one important detail. There Lucretius criticizes men who acknowledge that illness and dishonor are more frightening than death but nevertheless cling to life even amid the most dreadful circumstances, surrendering to the superstitions about prayers and offerings to the gods (3.41–54). In such circumstances of adversity, he adds, a man's true feelings become visible: *eripitur persona, manet res* ("The mask is torn away, the actuality remains," 3.58). The fear of death here appears only in very general terms as the final test of a man's character, as it was traditionally in Greek literature. In book 6, however, this test by confrontation with death reveals its full force, with unsparing horror.[34]

Near the end of the introductory discussion of death in book 3, Lucretius notes the paradox that men sometimes fear death so violently that they inflict it upon themselves, forgetting that this very thing is the source of their anxieties (3.78–82). Book 6 documents the physical reality of this terror, again with precise psychological details. The victims of the plague, perceiving its advance to their genitals, "heavily fearing the threshold of doom, live deprived by iron of their manly part; and some without hands and feet nevertheless remain in life" (6.1208–11). To such an extent, Lucretius concludes, did the sharp fear of death advance upon them (6.1212). The language is strong, and it also echoes the generalizations about the fear of death at the beginning of book 3 (cf. *Tartara leti,* "the Tartarus of doom," 3.41, and *limina leti,* "thresholds of doom," 6.1208; *denique vivunt,* "they still live," 3.50, and *manebant / in vita tamen,* "yet they remain in life," 6.1210–11). Instead of killing themselves because they fear death—which is Lucretius's rhetorical and hypothetical *reductio ad absurdum* in 3.78ff.—real men in the historical past, when

---

in accord with the Epicurean emphasis on anxiety: see Konstan, *Some Aspects,* 19ff., esp. 22, and 55–58; also Frank (above, note 31), 235–36.

[34] On the relation between the fear of death in books 3 and 6, see Stork, *Nil igitur mors est,* 157–58, and Bollack, *Raison,* 459ff.

gripped by the actuality of such mortal fear, chose to mutilate themselves in order to stay alive.

Lucretius's association of mutilation with the sharpest attack of the fear of death in this passage of book 6 offers an important clue to his treatment of the anxiety about death in book 3. Book 3, as we shall see, is remarkable for its detailed descriptions of bodily mutilation. This insistence on mutilation and related bodily suffering, I suggest, is a displaced form of the real fear of death, one of the fears that in fact most frequently occurs in actual life. Only at the very end of his poem, and under the shelter of historical distance, does Lucretius acknowledge this fear in its raw power and instinctive terror.

The fear of mutilation or dismemberment constitutes what psychologists label a "primary boundary anxiety," an anxiety about the invasion, transformation, or deformation of one's corporeal being.[35] Such concerns about the integrity of one's body exist, to a greater or lesser degree, in all of us and are closely related to our feelings of security and our basic instincts for survival. The fear of death is a heightened form of such boundary anxieties, for it is often accompanied by the terror of total self-annihilation, the dissolution of one's personal identity into an infinite, all-swallowing ocean of nonbeing, like that described by Plutarch as quoted above.

Ovid's *Metamorphoses* may suggest a helpful analogy: the violation of the body's form by changes of shape or substance. The realistic genre of narrative poetry produces something of the same frisson of terror as the accounts of death produce in Lucretius.[36] Such passages draw their power from anxiety

[35] The standard works are Seymour Fisher, *Body Consciousness* (Englewood Cliffs, N.J., 1973), and *Body Experience in Fantasy and Behavior* (New York, 1970). For applications to classical texts, see R. F. Newbold, "Boundaries and Bodies in Late Antiquity," *Arethusa* 12 (1979): 93–114, and "Discipline, Bondage, and the Serpent in Nonnus' Dionysiaca," *Classical World* 78 (1984–85): 89–98; also my essay, "Boundary Violation and the Landscape of the Self in Senecan Tragedy," *Antike und Abendland* 29 (1983): 172–87, reprinted in my *Interpreting Greek Tragedy* (Ithaca, N.Y., 1986), 315–36.

[36] See my "Ovid," 57–58.

similar to the fear of death: the helplessness, disorientation, self-alienation in seeing your familiar corporeal form change into something that is "not yourself," that is, watching and experiencing the end of what "you" are.

The least rational, and therefore most powerful, components of the fear of death appear in implicit rather than explicit forms, that is, in the recurrent images of primary boundary violation, such as mutilation and putrefaction. These surface as an explicit subject of the poem just at the point where Lucretius confronts those terrors of death which are suppressed in book 3: his account of the depression and anxiety of those who are caught in the process of painful dying in the plague. Here physical dissolution is not merely a value-free atomic process but a dreadful experience. The victims, day by day, watch the deteriorating changes going on in their own bodies.

Such a displacement of anxiety from one area (physical suffering and the violation or annihilation of bodily integrity) to another (the afterlife) is in fact consistent with Epicurean psychology, as David Konstan has pointed out, for the Epicureans recognized the fear of the Underworld as a displaced form of fear in this life.[37] Lucretius himself formulates the principle in 3.978ff. when he gives an allegorical interpretation of mythical sinners like Tantalus and Sisyphus: *sed Tityos nobis hic est, in amore iacentem . . .* ("This is Tityos for us, the one who lies sprawled in love," 3.992).[38] This form of displacement, however, operates at a relatively conscious level and follows a traditional technique of the allegorical interpretation of myth.[39] Lucretius's displacement of anxieties about death into images of violating the boundaries of the body is less explicit and less systematically articulated, but it is also a part of the therapeutic effect of the poem's argument.

[37] Konstan, *Some Aspects*, 25–27.
[38] This statement also forms a pendant to *nil igitur mors est ad nos* ("Death is nothing to us," 3.830).
[39] For such allegorizations, see Schrijvers, "Critique des mythes," passim; also Asmis, "Lucretius' Venus," 469–70; Kenney, *Lucretius III*, ad 978–1023 (pp. 222–23).

Another mode of displacement, admittedly remoter and more speculative, may be at work if Lucretius's details of putrefaction, mutilation, and other destructive attacks on the body reflect a concern with a generalized moral decay, of the sort that Sallust, for example, castigates in his *Catiline*. Lucretius too frequently touches on this kind of corruption, particularly at the beginning of the book that has the most extended treatment of bodily injury (3.59–78). More broadly still, this attention to the disintegration or disfigurement of the whole body may reflect feelings of disorientation at a time of turmoil and massive social and political change. There is perhaps no more immediate expression of disorientation than to lose the clear relation to one's own corporeal being or the sharp outline of one's own form in the world. The modern reader will think at once of Kafka's *Metamorphosis*.

Be this as it may, Lucretius regards the fear of death as akin to other harmful emotions precisely because it operates beneath the level of fully conscious rationality. It is therefore harder to uproot. Just as Lucretius, following Democritus, points out the illogic of inflicting death on oneself out of the fear of death (3.79-84),[40] so he also suggests that the fear of death is the underlying cause of misery in human life insofar as war, violence, and greed indirectly result from it when men, "driven by false terror," seek to accumulate wealth or power as a means of escaping death (3.58–78). [41] Later in the book he returns to the notion that the fear of death conceals, "beneath" itself, still another fear (3.870–78). When you see a man concerned about the fate of his body after death, you can

[40] Cf. Democritus 68 B203 and B297 (Diels–Kranz); see Bailey, *T. Lucreti Cari*, ad 3.79ff. (p. 1002) and also p. 1158 for further parallels.

[41] On this passage, see Farrington, "Meaning of *Persona*," 8–11; Desmouliez, "Cupidité," passim; Konstan, *Some Aspects*, 10ff., esp. 14, n. 32; Perelli, *Lucrezio*, 83–84; Jope, "Lucretius' Psychological Insight," 227–29; Schmid, "*Lucretius Ethicus*," 139ff. Richard C. Monti, "Lucretius on Greed, Political Ambition and Society: *de rer. nat.* 3.59–86," *Latomus* 40 (1981) 48–66, esp. 58ff., stresses social and historical factors behind Lucretius's analysis rather than psychological elements. Cicero, *De Finibus* 1.15.49, agrees with Lucretius 3.59ff. on the widespread crimes resulting from the fear of death. The idea is implicit in Epicurus, *Kyriai Doxai* 7.

be sure that another, irrational impulse lurks, in hiding, "beneath" the surface: *subesse / caecum aliquem corde stimulum, quamvis neget ipse* (3.873–74). With this analysis of a hidden psychological cause related to the fear of death we may compare the "hidden desire for honors" as a means of escaping death at the beginning of the book, in the passage discussed above (*honorum caeca cupido*, 3.59).

Lucretius uses a similar metaphor of subsurface irrationality in book 4, apropos of the "impure" (because irrational and therefore dangerous) pleasure of love. Lovers seek hard and even painful kisses *quia non est pura voluptas / et stimuli subsunt qui instigant laedere id ipsum / quodcumque est, rabies unde illaec germina surgunt* ("because the pleasure is not pure and there are goads beneath that prick them on to hurt that very thing, whatever it is, from which these seeds of madness arise," 4.1081–83). These hidden, emotionally harmful elements not only lurk "beneath" but also "rise up" or sprout, like an evil growth from a bad seed. Death and love are for Lucretius the areas of life that mankind handles with the least rationality.

The presence of something dark and hurtful "beneath" the surface in the passages cited above points toward Lucretius's grasp of something that we would call the unconscious.[42] This element forms a common ground connecting all the dangerous and disruptive passions. One healing technique of Epicurean philosophy is to reveal how one kind of fear can be a symptom or a pretense of another kind of fear "beneath" it (cf. 3.870–78). The process—akin to displacement in the technical Freudian sense—may also be reversed and applied to the first two-thirds of book 3. At the level of logical argumentation, the vivid accounts of mutilation, loss of consciousness, and putrefaction technically prove the mortality of the soul and

---

[42] For Lucretius's implicit recognition of the unconscious, see Logre, *L'anxiété*, 191–92 and 199, and Jope, "Lucretius' Psychological Insight," passim, who makes the good observation (p. 237) that as a materialist Lucretius was accustomed to account for the visible by the invisible and was therefore disposed to recognized hidden, unconscious motivations behind overt behavior, conscious decisions, and verbalized intentions or explanations.

thus dispel the fear of the afterlife; but the examples them-
selves are a displaced form of those primary boundary anxie-
ties that belong to the most powerful of the fears about dying.
Before analyzing these examples in detail, however, we must
consider some differences in the ways that Epicurus and Lu-
cretius present the process of dying.

Chapter Two

ATOMS, BODIES, AND INDIVIDUALS: DEATH IN EPICURUS AND LUCRETIUS

IF WE MAY INVOKE the terminology of the modern historian of death, Philippe Ariès, Lucretius in books 3 and 6 reaches beyond what Ariès calls "tame death." This is death as the end of life accepted more or less without anxiety, as "natural," divinely ordained, and attended by the comfort and solace of family, community, and religious observance.[1] Lucretius's accounts of death in book 3 and book 6 approximate what Ariès calls "the death of the self." This is a harsher and more anguished experience of death, marked by the uneasy awareness of the physical processes that destroy our identity. This view of death pictures not just the separation of the soul from the body (which is Epicurus's primary concern), but the ugly and painful deterioration and decomposition of the body.[2]

Epicureanism assuages some of these fears by urging our detachment from the dying body. But what happens if we cannot disengage and so remain more concerned with our body in the stages of dying than with the body after death? Lucretius's vivid corporeal imagery, both in book 3 and in book 6, I believe, addresses these latter concerns.[3] His argument is indirect and allusive, perhaps because he is aware that he is dealing with a subject generally avoided by the Master, or perhaps because he realizes that the material takes him into the areas

[1] See Ariès, *Hour of Our Death*, pt. 1, esp. 14ff.

[2] Ibid., pt. 2, esp. 110ff., on the "macabre" in the late Middle Ages. Here, Ariès observes, the "literary sources place as much emphasis on the decomposition during life as on that after death" (p. 123). Death itself brings no relief, but comes in pain (pp. 121–22). Death lies "in the inmost recesses of life" and belongs to "the bodily envelope of the rottenness within" (p. 121).

[3] On Lucretius's greater involvement with the body in general, see Klingner, "Lucrez," 209–10.

where poetry, with its tendency toward emotional engage-ment, least comfortably walks the same road as philosophy, with its aim of serene detachment. He prepares for this theme in book 2, further develops it in book 3, and completes it with the plague that ends the poem.

In coming to terms poetically with an experience analogous to what Ariès calls "the death of the self," Lucretius is not necessarily contradicting the teachings of Epicurus. Rather, he is supplementing them. In dwelling on the physical and mental suffering brought by death in books 3 and 6, he is practicing his own form of the Epicurean θεραπεία of the soul. His "therapy" lies in the emotive power of his poetic form. This approach corresponds to the uses that Socrates and Plutarch make of their eloquence in their efforts to overcome the fear or sadness of death in the pseudo-Platonic *Axiochus* and the *Consolation to Apollonius* respectively. (Plutarch, like Cicero in the *Tusculans*, also utilizes a wide array of the poets, in quotation and paraphrase.)

Although Epicurus acknowledges that "death is the most terrifying of evils" (φρικωδέστατον τῶν κακῶν, *Epistle to Me-noeceus*, D.L. 10.125), he de-emphasizes its somatic aspects by viewing it in strictly atomic terms, as the separation of the soul-atoms from the body and their return to the reservoir of atomic material in the universe. Lucretius largely uses this ap-proach, sometimes with his own rather more personalized ver-sion, as when he urges the necessity of making one's atomic material available to future generations (3.964–71).

In one fragment Epicurus deals, at least by implication, with the physical vulnerability of the body to death (frag. 339 Use-ner): "Against everything else we can obtain security, but as far as death is concerned, we mortals all inhabit an unwalled city" (πόλιν ἀτείχιστον). Epicurus's metaphor suggests the notion of the body as the fragile, physical vessel of the soul. This is a figure that Lucretius develops and utilizes at length in order to argue for the non-survival of the soul at death (e.g., 3.434–44, 554–57; cf. 3.936–37 and 6.17ff.). As Epicurus's fragment is shorn of its context, we cannot be sure that he is necessarily offering this point as consolation; he may be

merely stating our defenselessness against death. The con-
sciousness of the body is only vaguely implicit in his (negative)
metaphor of the "wall," and thus is still at a considerable emo-
tional distance from any detailed consideration of the body's
experience in death.[4]

Epicurus's de-somatizing approach doubtless helped to al-
lay the fear of death as the painful deterioration of limbs and
organs. Nevertheless, the issue of physical pain in the process
of dying was not entirely ignored in contemporary considera-
tions. Leaving aside accounts of death by torture or other ter-
rible suffering in Greek tragedy and history, Cicero and Plu-
tarch, as I mentioned above, attacked the Epicurean solution
of happy memories as a counter to the pain of terminal illness.
Elsewhere in the *Tusculans*, Cicero criticizes Epicurus for his
contradiction between admitting pain as the worst of evils and
yet claiming that the wise man will pay no attention to it.[5]
Considering the question of pain at the moment of death in
the first book, he may have in mind Epicurus's argument that
the soul's departure from the body, though sometimes painful
(*non fit sine dolore*), may be "without sensation and even
sometimes with pleasure" (1.34.82).

Epicurus's absolute division between the person alive and
the person dead, with no *tertium quid* in between,[6] may pro-
vide a logical answer to fear of the transition between life and
death, but it does not help against the fear of bodily pain in
dying. As Cicero observes, such an argument might hold for
one whom pain killed at its first arrival, but would not apply

[4] For a detailed discussion of walls and boundaries in relation to death, see
below, Chapter Five.

[5] Cicero, *Tusc. Disp.* 2.7.17–18, 2.18.44. See also *De Finibus* 2.27.88ff.
For a recent discussion of Cicero's criticisms of Epicurus's arguments about
pain, with further bibliography, see Mitsis, *Epicurus' Ethical Theory*, 24ff.,
esp. 26–27. We may add that Montaigne, an avid reader and quoter of both
Cicero and Lucretius, makes similar distinctions between fearing death and
fearing pain in his "Of Physiognomy," *Essays* 3.12 (Frame translation,
3:298): "For it may be believed that we are naturally afraid of pain, but not
of death for its own sake: it is a part of our being no less than life."

[6] *To Menoeceus*, D.L. 10.125; Cicero, *Tusc. Disp.* 1.34.82.

to many cases in common experience (*De Finibus* 2.28.93).[7]
In fact, such anxiety about a painful death is a theme of the
consolation literature (e.g., in Plutarch's *Consolation to Ap-
ollonius* 30.117C). Such concerns also explain why the stan-
dard exemplars of the happy death are Cleobis and Biton, who
die in their sleep.[8]

Where Epicurus does deal with the problem of what he calls
"excessive pain accompanying death" (frag. 448 Usener), his
solution is to invoke the *tetrapharmakon*, that death is noth-
ing to us, that we feel no pain after death, and that excessive
pain will have its built-in limits (*Kyriai Doxai* 1–4). Here he
quickly shifts the ground from the body in death to the non-
feeling of the soul once released from the body. Elsewhere he
urges that the wise man will be prepared for this moment by
his prior meditations on his end, that he will have the spiritual
resources (chiefly the memories of past goods) to set against
the present ills, and that he will then be able to laugh at great
pain.[9]

Epicurus himself seems to have met the last stages of his
own illness with a calm and fortitude worthy of his princi-
ples.[10] Yet he must have known that not everyone would pos-
sess his serene temper or inner strength. The extant writings,
of course, may convey only a small part of what the man him-
self communicated to his followers through his example and
his personality. Nevertheless, his most extended treatments of
death in the surviving works, both in the *Epistle to Menoeceus*

---

[7] On Epicurus's argument in D.L. 10.125, see Domenico Pesce, *Introdu-
zione a Epicuro* (Rome and Bari, 1981), 96–97.

[8] So Cicero, *Tusc. Disp.* 1.47.113; Plutarch, *Consol. ad Apoll.* 14.108F.
Crantor is widely assumed as a common source, but see also Ps.-Plato, *Axi-
ochus* 367C.

[9] See Epicurus (see frags. 138, 205, 292.16, 470, 490–91, 599, 600, 601,
603 Usener; *Kyriai Doxai* 40; Plutarch, *Non Posse Suav. Vivi* 3.1088B,
5.1090A, 23.1103D. For a succinct recent discussion of Epicurus's answers
to the problem of death, see Baltes, "Die Todesproblematik," 127–28. For the
importance of memory in the school of Epicurus, especially in the care and
even the worship of Epicurus, see Frischer, *The Sculpted Word*, 90ff., 246ff.;
Clay, "Cults of Epicurus," passim, esp. 11–12, 24–28.

[10] Epicurus, frag. 138 Usener; also D. L. 10.15–16, 22, 25.

(D.L. 10. 124–27) and in the *Epistle to Herodotus* (63–67) are at a level of abstraction and generality that would probably offer little comfort to the common man or woman. For all of his compassion for the emotional suffering of his fellow mortals, his emphasis is upon intellect, right reason, and accurate perception, not feeling. He views his task as a moralist as maximizing the value of the life that we have by stressing the positive things in our grasp. His physics and materialist psychology enable us to recognize what death is and what it is not, so that we can limit its power over our minds. By grasping the true nature of death as an atomic process, we obtain the victory of knowledge over the unknown.

Although the fragments contain some moralizing exhortations about meditating on death and meeting it with equanimity, as we have noted, Epicurus, as a systematic philosopher, fights death primarily at the atomic level. His follower, Philodemus, Lucretius's contemporary, adopts the same strategy. Philodemus acknowledges the objection that "all deaths occur with intense pain" because the close union between soul and body cannot be dissolved without violence (*De Morte* 8.1–15). His response moves almost immediately from the experience of "sharp pain" (μετ᾽ ἄκρων ἀλγηδόνων, 8.2) to the atomic nature of the soul, whose fine, rapidly mobile atoms pass unhindered through the spaces between the larger, coarser atoms of flesh and bone (8.13–20). Here lies the greatest difference from Lucretius. Lucretius is a poet, with a poet's feeling for the concrete, for the affective dimension of life, and for the close interrelation between the physical and the emotional areas of experience. Through his poetic sensibility, he is able to restore to Epicureanism an appreciation of the emotional impact of encountering death. For him, as for Epicurus, "death is nothing to us" (3.830; Epicurus, *Kyriai Doxai* 2; *Epistle to Menoeceus* 124). But in his forceful closure to book 3, with its lines on the paradox of "eternal death" (3.1091–94), death is also a physical and emotional reality of tremendous power.

Lucretius, to be sure, does not disagree with Epicurus's highly intellectual approach, and of course he repeats many of the Master's arguments. But he is willing to explore the darker

places of the soul, and he ventures more deeply into those
fears and experiences which Epicurus dismisses. He knows the
vis abdita quaedam, the hidden force of irrationality that mars
human affairs (5.1233ff.). It is revealing, then, to juxtapose
the intellectual tenor of Epicurus in the *Epistle to Menoeceus*
(124–27) and in the *Epistle to Herodotus* (63–67) with Lucre-
tius's detailed discussion of the *mortis signa*, the physical
symptoms that herald the approach of death in the account of
the plague with which he closes his poem (6.1182ff.).

In the *Epistle to Herodotus* Epicurus regards the body as an
agglomeration (ἄθροισμα) of atoms. He does not mention cor-
poreal details, and he defines death as "dissolution of the ag-
glomeration as a whole" (διαλυομένου τοῦ ὅλου ἀθροίσμα-
τος). Thereupon "the soul is dispersed and no longer has the
same powers nor is capable of movement, so that it does not
possess sensation either" (D.L. 10.65). Epicurus scarcely men-
tions the word "death" in the passage. In fact, the only time
he does is in the negative form of losing feelings and thought
(D.L. 10.63 *ad fin.*), so that "when the soul is gone [from the
aggregation], it does not have sensation" (10.64).[11]

Epicurus's concern here is admittedly with atomic psychol-
ogy, not ethics. But even the more ethically focussed discus-
sion in the *Letter to Menoeceus* maintains the same tone of
rationalistic generality. Epicurus exhorts Menoeceus to free
himself from the fear of death through knowledge and clear
definition:

> Grow accustomed to think that death is nothing to us, for every
> good and evil lies in sensation, and death is the deprivation of
> sensation. Thus the correct knowledge of the fact that death is
> nothing to us makes it possible to have profit from the mortal
> part of life, not adding limitless time, but taking away the desire
> for the absence of death. For nothing is terrible in being alive to
> the man who has genuinely grasped that there is nothing terrible
> in not being alive.   (D.L. 10.124–25)

[11] This negative mode of dealing with death is also criticized by Plutarch,
Non Posse Suav. Vivi 7.1091Aff. and 23.1103D–E.

The combination of the negative definition of death as non-being and the emphasis on the knowledge of death as non-sensation are characteristic of Epicurus's approach.[12]

The passage from Lucretius's account of the plague is too long to quote in full, but even a short extract will illustrate the difference in tone. Lucretius dwells on physical details for which there can be no place in Epicurus's highly intellectualized discussion. We may note in particular how the late stages of illness combine both the emotional states of "fear" and "depression" and the strictly physiological symptoms of ringing ears, heavy and uneven breathing, and sweating (6.1182–87):

> multaque praeterea mortis tum signa dabantur,
> perturbata animi mens in maerore metuque,
> triste supercilium furiosus vultus et acer,
> sollicitae porro plenaeque sonoribus aures,
> creber spiritus aut ingens raroque coortus,
> sudoris madens per collum splendidus umor.

(In addition, many marks of death were then given, the mind greatly disturbed in grief and fear, a gloomy brow, a wild and sharp countenance, the ears also troubled and full of sounds, thick or heavy breathing arising infrequently, glistening droplets of sweat dripping over the neck.)[13]

This close interaction of mental and physical responses is a consequence of the physical intertwining of *animus* and *anima* in the Epicurean materialistic psychology, as Lucretius makes clear in a related passage in book 3 (152–60). But Lucretius supplies what is missing in Epicurus (or at least in what we have of Epicurus): a confrontation with death not merely as the single moment of the separation of soul and body or the division between being and non-being, but as a gradual, terrifyingly concrete physical process. Its corporeal effects interact with our mental life and produce just those emotions which

---

[12] Other aspects of this important passage are discussed in Chapter Five.

[13] See Bright, "Plague," 616–17, who observes that this passage is without a Thucydidean basis.

Epicureanism seeks to combat: disturbance of mind (the opposite of ἀταραξία), fear, and depression: *perturbata animi mens in maerore metuque* ("the mind greatly disturbed in grief and fear," 6.1183).

The transition from the emotions of 1183 to their visible manifestation in the "saddened brow" and "wild and intense face" in 1184 shows how powerful a hold the emotions consequent upon terminal illness have over our spirits. In book 3, Lucretius is equally clinical in observing the changes in the face (*vultus*) at "the final moment," when soul leaves body (3.592–96):

> quin etiam finis dum vitae vertitur intra,
> saepe aliqua tamen e causa labefacta videtur
> ire anima ac toto solvi de corpore velle
> et quasi supremo languescere tempore vultus
> molliaque exsangui trunco cadere omnia membra.

(But even when the soul moves about within the limits of life, often from some cause weakened it seems to want to depart and to be released from the whole body, and the countenance seems to grow faint as if at the final moment, and all the limbs, grown soft, collapse in the bloodless trunk.)

Here in book 6, however, the significance of the facial expression is more psychological and more intimately related to the fear of losing life, as this fear can now be confronted more openly.

This interrelation between the somatic and the psychological in anxiety about death was also part of the philosophical tradition prior to Lucretius. In the pseudo-Platonic *Axiochus*, which is probably influenced by Epicureanism, a young man is concerned about the depressive symptoms of his father, whom Socrates finds "very much in need of encouragement, restlessly going up and down and letting forth groans amid tears and the smiting of hands" (365A). Lucretius's analysis of the plague, *mutatis mutandis*, agrees with Plutarch's anti-Epicurean arguments on the emotional disturbances consequent on extreme pain (*Non Posse Suav. Vivi* 18.1099E). Lucretius seems to recognize more fully than his Master the emotional state of a lingering death, when disturbance of mind, sadness, and fear dominate the entire field of the sufferer's consciousness (6.1183–84). A man or woman in such a condition would not easily follow Epicurus's advice and summon up the memories of past joys to outweigh the present pain. "I can neither concentrate on poetry nor enjoy poetry," Wallace Stevens wrote in his last letter—and he was still able to write letters.

Lucretius has already offered us an alternative to this hopeless scene of book 6, namely the serene, philosophical deaths of Democritus and Epicurus at the end of book 3, to be discussed in Chapter Eight (3.1039–44). This is doubtless the form of death that Epicurus envisaged for the wise man, as the fragments cited above suggest. Such an end stands in the tradition of philosophy's greatest paradigm of serenity and peace in the face of death, the Socrates of the *Crito* and *Phaedo*. Here the presence of the great thinker excludes grief, fear, and pain. While the friends around him are broken up with sobbing and weeping, Socrates himself remains calm, reasonable, and cheerful (see *Phaedo* 58E–59A, 116A–118E, especially 117D–E). He even makes a joke about drinking the poison (117B), as if anticipating the Epicurean sage who laughs at his pain. The numbness creeping up his legs, too, is a matter of terse, objective observation, not terror (117E–118A).

Lucretius's equivalent to such a scene, namely 3.1039–44, is very brief, and also three books away from the scenes at the end of book 6. He perhaps intended to contrast the experiences of death for the unenlightened and for the wise man (a point to which we shall return at the end of this chapter). Whatever his exact purpose, and whether or not he is drawing on a still-undiscovered portion of Epicurean teachings, his treatment of death in this powerful finale of the poem, as also in some anticipatory passages in book 3, makes the pain of dying far more real than it is in his Master's treatment. He brings the *Epistle to Menoeceus* down to earth.

Where he follows the Master more closely, Lucretius has a number of strategies for reproducing the de-individualizing approach to death. In the proem of book 2, for instance, he establishes the removed perspective of the sage who looks out from his lofty tower of wisdom to "another's great suffering" on the raging sea. In book 3 he gives us the perspective of Natura herself, the impersonal world-process speaking as a kind of *deus ex machina*. In the closing section of book 4 he himself assumes a similar voice, speaking as the knowing, ironical observer of other men's follies in love.

Correspondingly, in treating death throughout the poem, Lucretius generally avoids viewing it as part of the life story of an individual.[14] Death is merely the dissolution of what Epicurus calls an ἄθροισμα, an agglomeration of atoms; as such it is to be regarded with the cool detachment that all atomic processes invite. Lucretius's "distant views" at the beginning of book 2 are a poetic equivalent for this removed atomic perspective (especially by contrast to the old farmer who laments the earth's declining fertility at the end of book 1); and it is continued in the spatial and temporal perspectives on early man in book 5 and on the Athenian plague in book 6.

Knowing "the nature of things" is what enables the wise man to take this long view and thereby attain the true *voluptas*

---

[14] The closest Lucretius comes to such an implicit life story is perhaps the admiral, with his "strong legions and elephants," caught in the storm of 5.1226–32. But even here there is nothing to take us beyond this single moment except the general reflection on the irrationality of ambition in the following lines. By contrast, we may compare the way in which Henry David Thoreau personalizes and individualizes the anonymous victims of a shipwreck off the Massachusetts coast in the opening chapter of his *Cape Cod* (1857). He immediately supplies personal histories, as in the case of "one livid, swollen, and mangled body of a drowned girl,—who probably had intended to go out to service in some American family," or a "woman who had come before, but had left her infant behind for her sister to bring . . . and saw in one [box] . . . her child in her sister's arms, as if the sister had meant to be found thus." Even his sentimental Christian moralizing (which begins with a thought that Lucretius might have endorsed) gives these corpses a life, a set of goals and hopes, and a final journey: "Why care for these dead bodies? They really have no friends but the worms or fishes. Their owners were coming to the New World, as Columbus and the Pilgrims did,—they were within a mile of its shores; but, before they could reach it, they emigrated to a newer world than ever Columbus dreamed of. . . ."

of serenity, like the godlike Epicurus and the gods them-
selves.[15] Epicurus's "forceful strength of intellect" brings him
to the "flaming walls of the world" and allows him to "tra-
verse the measureless universe" (1.72–77). Instead of being
crushed by religion, which seems to look down on us from its
unassailable power in the heavens, he lifts "us to the heavens"
in a spiritual victory. The superstitious practices and beliefs of
religion are "in their turn crushed beneath our feet" (1.62–67,
78–79).[16]

The peace of this removed perspective, however, is not
without a certain ambiguity.[17] The gods enjoy this distance
without the struggle and effort of the philosopher, "for nec-
essarily the entire nature of the gods must enjoy immortal life
in the highest peace, removed from our affairs and far dis-
joined from them" (1.44–46, repeated at 2.646–48). To be
thus *semota ab nostris rebus seiunctaque longe* ("removed
from our affairs and far disjoined from them") is to be a god.
But as a mortal, one is, by definition, living in the midst of
"our affairs." "We" can be "removed" from "our affairs"
only partially or metaphorically.

As a poet, moreover, Lucretius is inevitably heir to a tradi-
tion of personalizing human suffering. We need only compare
the serene distance of the storm-watcher in the proem of book
2 with Homer's detailed picture of Odysseus spitting out salt
water as his clothes drag him down amid the waves (*Odyssey*
5.321–23) or, closer to Lucretius's own time, with the an-
guished cry that Virgil gives his Aeneas as his ships are whirled
about and broken up in the storm (*Aeneid* 1.84–103). Lucre-

[15] See DeLacy, "Distant Views," passim, esp. 50–51; also Clay, *Lucretius and Epicurus*, 219–20.

[16] So too the poet-philosopher can appreciate the beauties of the heavens (cf. 5.1204–6, 1216; also 3.18ff), but ordinary mortals, because they do not know the causes of celestial phenomena, have their minds "contracted by fear of the gods" (5.1218–19; cf. 5.1188–93) rather than expanded to the wide horizons that Epicurus reaches.

[17] See, for instance, DeLacy, "Distant Views," 55: "As for Lucretius him-self, throughout the poem he strives for the distant view. He is not always successful, especially when he is looking at the joys and suffering of man-kind."

tius the poet cannot and does not maintain the distance of Lucretius the Epicurean, although, as we shall see, he is not necessarily less of an Epicurean for abandoning this distance.

The Epicurean philosopher finds it "sweet" to "look down on the great struggles of war drawn up over the fields, without your share in the danger" (2.4–6). Yet the next book does in fact place us in the wild fury of the battlefield, amid the slashed limbs and the warm, spurting blood (3.642–53). Such a passage radically changes our perspective from that of remote observer to that of engaged participant. We are there beside the man who "cannot feel the pain because of the swiftness of the hurt" (3.645), the man who "does not grasp the loss of his left hand" (3.649) or who "climbs, presses on" or tries to get up despite the severed foot on the ground beside him (3.651–53).

Even as we see such a scene from close up, however, we realize that it also exemplifies the folly, violence, and wastefulness of war, the deadly struggles of ambitious men for the wealth and power that truly poison life.[18] Epicurean doctrine enables us to keep our distance from such conflicts, just as it enables us to look on the "eternal conflict" (*aeternum certamen*) of the atoms with untroubled heart because we understand the true goal and meaning of the world (2.118–20, 573–74). In like manner, we ought to be able to look with calm, uninvolved understanding on men's destruction and pollution of life in their "conflicts to reach the highest honor" (*certantes*, 5.1124) or on the final "quarrel" of men over bodies empty of life (*rixantes*, 6.1286). But in fact we are not gods, and we cannot become quite so "far disjoined" as they from

---

[18] Cf. 2.40–54, 3.59–84, 5.1117–35. On the negative meaning of war throughout the poem, see below, Chapter Nine. Clay, *Lucretius and Epicurus*, 220–21, also points out the contrast between the helplessness of "your legions" in 2.40 (addressed to Memmius) and the distance appropriate to the Epicurean view of such violence in the removed perspective on war in 2.323–32. It is also instructive to compare the admonition to Memmius with the broader, less personal reflection on the folly of war and military power in 5.1226ff. The latter passage implicitly generalizes the "legions" of Memmius to any military force.

what remain "our affairs" (2.646–48, *supra*). Lucretius does
not overtly articulate this tension between philosophical de-
tachment and human involvement, but it remains implicit in
his poetic practice and, as we noted above, imbedded in the
poetic tradition in which he works.

Book 5 dramatically illustrates this shift of perspective and
its ambiguities. In describing the life of early man, Lucretius
changes from the "human race" viewed externally in the fields
of far-off time (5.926–32), to *unus quisque* (5.990), the hu-
man individual, primitive though he is, who is caught by wild
beasts and "fills the forests and mountains with his groaning
as he sees his living flesh being buried in a living tomb"
(5.990–93). By shifting our vision to the individual human
sufferer and making our point of view coincide with his as he
"sees" his own horrible death being accomplished (5.993),
Lucretius puts us empathetically in that time and place. At the
same time, he does not allow us to remain long in this mood
of involved identification, for he at once forces us to take the
long view of his philosophical anthropology. Here we see that
the sufferings of that remote time, terrible as they were, are
still less than through war, greed, and malice (5.999–1010).
As our eyes adjust to this longer perspective, the suffering of
early man recedes into the temporal distance of "then" versus
"now" (*tum . . . tum, nunc . . . nunc*, 1006–10).[19]

In like manner, the plague at Athens in book 6 is removed
in both place and time; and Lucretius's transition underlines
the geographical remoteness (6.1103ff., 1138ff.). With the
cool eye of the clinician, Lucretius gives a scientific account of
the "force of the disease" in atomic terms (6.1090ff.; cf. *se-
mina vitalia*, "life-giving seeds," in 1093–94). The perspective
is, once more, that of the distant observer of skies, clouds, air,
wind, rivers, crops, and pastures (6.1096–1138). There are no
individuals, only "the race of men," here joined with the
"herds of cattle" in common subjection to a physical process,

---

[19] This ambiguity between removed perspective and sympathetic involve-
ment is also related to that between historical description and moral exem-
plar, a tension that runs throughout the culture history of book 5: see below,
Chapter Nine.

in this case the "force of disease": *coorta / morbida vis hominum generi pecudumque catervis* (6.1091–92). The only personal subjects come when the philosopher-poet looks down on unnamed, generalized people (e.g., *quicumque*, "whoever") who change their abode (6.1104–5). When Lucretius does finally use the first-person plural, "we," it is in the verses that lead directly into the Athenian plague; and his aim is to emphasize the universality of human helplessness in the face of nature's power (6.1133-37).

With this transition, Lucretius re-introduces the human subject. The disease moves from Egypt to Attica and then into the city of Athens. Like a beast or a monstrous incubus, it now "drains the city of its citizens (*civibus*) and weighs upon the entire people of Pandion" (*populo*, 6.114–43). Not only does Lucretius now turn from the heavens to human subjects; he also brings us down to the specific, corporeal effects of disease within the human body. In fact, he begins the account of the plague not so much with the Athenians themselves as with the afflicted parts of their bodies, listing the various symptoms in head, eyes, throat, tongue, chest, heart, and so on (6.1145–46).[20]

Lucretius does little to soften the abruptness of this shift from the "air, fields, and plains" and from the remote geographical terms (Egypt, Cecrops, Pandion) to the individual organs of the body (compare 6.1138–43 with 1145–53). The very harshness of the transition calls attention to the poet's reinterpretation of the Epicurean peaceful death. Lucretius is here doing what Epicurus does not: he has moved from death as an atomic process to death as the suffering of individual human bodies. To this end, he changes his perspective from

---

[20] On the medical logic and physiological clarity of Lucretius's list and progression of the symptoms in the body, see West, "Two Plagues: Virgil, *Georgics* 3.478–566 and Lucretius 6.1090–1286," in David West and Tony Woodman, eds., *Creative Imitation and Latin Literature* (Cambridge, 1979), 77–80; see also Bright, "Plague," *passim*. West also offers a detailed analysis of the rhetorical transformation of Lucretius's symptomology in Virgil's plague from the *Georgics* passage. I shall discuss other aspects of the plague, from different points of view, in Chapters Six, Seven, and Ten, below.

impersonal nature to the feeling human subject, albeit still en
masse. This concentration on the felt suffering of human vic-
tims rather than on the diagnosis of symptoms also marks Lu-
cretius's difference from his immediate source, Thucydides.[21]

Lucretius the philosopher, overseeing the entire world,
knows that atoms bearing life and death fly about randomly
through the winds and clouds. Lucretius the poet places us in
the midst of the stricken city, in fact within the very bodies of
the human sufferers. In this closer, more empathetic perspec-
tive we become aware of the fear that rises almost tangibly
around us, in the futile and frightened murmuring of the heal-
ing art (*mussabat tacito medicina timore*, 6.1179). Here too,
as in the account of early man in 5.993ff., the climax of the
terror is the individual's subjective reaction, when "each one
sees himself entangled in disease," with death ahead of him;
and the result is grief and depression (6.1231ff.).

The individualizing phrase in 6.1231, *se quisque videbat*
("each one was seeing himself"), reminds us of the equally
particularized *unus quisque* in 5.990. The phrase recurs near
the end of book 6, where "the grief of present circumstances"
has subdued the human spirit entirely (6.1278), and "each and
every one" (*unus quisque*) has surrendered to the depressive
and irrational effects of death and its terrors (cf. *maestus*,
"sad," "depressed," 6.1280). Irrationality breaks forth in the
self-destructive form of misdirected aggression and energy as
men join in bloody fights to bury bodies that are empty of life,
the vignette on which the poem ends (6.1280–86).[22]

These closing scenes show men at the furthest remove from

[21] See Clay, *Lucretius and Epicurus*, 263; also Commager, "Lucretius' In-
terpretation," and Bright, "Plague," passim.

[22] Although Lucretius is closely following Thucydides here (2.52.4), he has
added the violent details of the "vast shouting" and the "quarreling with
much blood" to the severe Greek account, vivid but noteworthy for its utter
bareness of adverbial or adjectival modifiers. The passage in Thucydides is,
literally, as follows: "Some, putting corpses of their own on the pyres belong-
ing to others, anticipating those who had heaped up [the pyres], lit them,
while others, throwing [the body] that they were carrying on top of another
body already burning, went away." On the motif of blood (*multo cum san-
guine*) in connection with war and violence, see below, Chapter Nine.

Epicurean ἀταραξία and ἡδονή, the serenity and joy that constitute the happy life. Such men commit a double error: they are wrongly anxious about their own deaths, and they misunderstand the value of the body, both their own and others'. They fight bloodily for the wrong kind of *corpora* (6.1286). Lucretius, however, does not merely castigate their error. He enters into it sympathetically, dramatically; and he thereby makes us his readers feel, in our own skin, what it is to fall prey to uncontrollable anxiety when death's touch is upon us, when we too "are given over to death-and-disease" and see ourselves "entangled" in the nets of a disease that condemns us to certain death (cf. *morbo mortique dabantur*, 6.1144; *ubi se quisque videbat / implicitum morbo morti damnatus ut esset*, 6.1231–32).

When this account is read beside the texts of Epicurus, Lucretius seems to be going against the current of the Master's practice of de-individualizing and de-somatizing the process of dying. But Lucretius's goal remains the same as Epicurus's, even if the route is different. He not only prepares us for the actuality of the body's experience of death; he also reveals, far more vividly than Epicurus does, how much additional and unnecessary agony we inflict on ourselves through our anxiety about death. To this point an anti-Epicurean like Plutarch might object that the physical pain is not thereby lessened and therefore remains rightly terrifying. But the Epicurean could counter by pointing out that the philosopher's task is to deal with the fright; the pain of the body lies beyond his control and is self-limiting anyway. The fear belongs in the same category as troubling dreams and chimerical fantasies and is amenable to the same therapy. The art of healing, baffled, may "murmur in silent terror" (6.1179); but, thanks to the philosopher, the *dolor* of the mind can be soothed.

The mind's pain, then, is a major concern of Lucretius's finale, and in powerful terms. The analysis is no less effective for using the celebrated Athenian plague of Thucydides's history as his test case. The very remoteness of the example provides both objectivity and universality. The technique is similar to that used in Lucretius's attack on modern greed and aggression through the account of remote, primitive man in book 5.[23]

The plague, Lucretius suggests, is a situation in which each one of us—*unus quisque*—might find himself or herself suddenly "entangled," as if caught in a trap and "condemned" by unexpected circumstances to death. The repeated assonantal association of "death" and "disease," *mors* and *morbus*, subliminally suggests that illness, which can befall anyone anytime, can suddenly bring us face-to face with death (cf. 6.1138, 1144, 1221–22, 1232).

This concern with the direct experience of the body is one of the areas where Lucretius's emphasis differs most sharply from Epicurus's. This difference is due, perhaps, to the Roman love of the particular and the concrete: we may think of the importance of physical, corporeal detail in writers like Catullus, Ovid (especially in the *Metamorphoses*), Petronius, Seneca (in the *Tragedies*), Juvenal, Apuleius. It is also due to the poetic tradition in which Lucretius is working, with the sympathy for human suffering that is so marked in Greek epic and tragedy. But there is also an important difference in perspective. Epicurus, writing in the tradition of Greek philosophy, has his eye on the life of the gods as the ideal existence, and we may think of Plato's injunction that we become "like to the god insofar as is possible" (*Theaetetus* 176B). Roman philosophy, as Cicero and Seneca illustrate, is more mundanely practical. More than lack of time or space may have kept Lucretius from fulfilling his promise to write about the gods *largo sermone* ("with abundant discourse," 5.155; cf. 1.54).

Lucretius, to be sure, follows Epicurus in the ideal of the divine pleasure of serenity and wisdom and, in his most optimistic moments, in the belief that Epicureanism can lead us to "a life worthy of the gods" (3.321–22). But even where he articulates this ideal, he recognizes, however lightly, the gap between the gods' "distant removal" and "our affairs," from which, as mortals, we cannot be removed (1.44–49, 2.644–51).[24] And of the "affairs" from which we have the least abil-

---

[23] See Chapter Nine, below.

[24] For an optimistic reading of Lucretius's hope for godlike serenity, see

ity to remove ourselves, the body is the most intimate, and the most immediate. This concern with the body, and with the body's role in the anxieties surrounding death, as we shall see, surfaces most strongly in the first half of book 3. Viewed in this light, the plague at the end of the poem is the logical and emotional sequel to book 3 in exploring the psycho-physiological aspect of death in the process of dying.

Although apparently deviating from the style and practice of his teacher, Lucretius is nevertheless making an important contribution to Epicurean θεραπεία as the "cure of the soul." He has reserved the description of the plague to the end of the work not only because it forms the fullest test of Epicurean therapeutics, but also because it embodies the worst-case scenario of fear and anxiety in human life. Such fear takes over our whole being. The physical presence of death begins its work in our body and soon oppresses our spirit. A cold chill moves up little by little from the feet, makes us tremble all over, stifles our breathing, and leaves us, finally, paralyzed before a force that is emotionally as well as physically numbing. We lose our power to be "ourselves," in thought or action.

I am not inventing these details, but only paraphrasing Lucretius's own words as he continues with the symptoms of the plague (1190–96, with omissions):

> in manibus vero nervi trahere et tremere artus
> a pedibusque minutatim succedere frigus
> non dubitabat. item ad supremum denique tempus
> compressae nares [. . .]
> nec nimio rigida post artus morte iacebant.

The progression to the "stiff death" that finally spreads over all the limbs is, of course, a physical process, observed with clinical precision. But the attention to the spreading of these symptoms into the mind, with the resultant clouding of the senses and perceptions by perturbation, anxiety, mad terror at

---

Andrew Galloway, "Lucretius's Materialist Poetics: Epicurus and the 'Flawed Consolatio' of Book 3," *Ramus* 15 (1986): 54ff. Not interested in the tensions between Epicurean theory and Lucretius's poetry, Galloway pays no attention to the indirectness of and qualifications for "leading a life worthy of the gods" in 3.319–22 (p. 55).

the beginning of the *mortis signa* (1183–85), also suggests that this is a progressive paralysis of the soul's faculties as well.[25]

The plague can be read almost as an allegory of the bad death. Pain and fear are unrelieved by knowledge; depression is unaided by Epicurean science and the *voluptas* of being liberated from anxiety about the body. The ravaging of Athens seems to fulfil literally Epicurus's metaphor of death and "the unwalled city" (frag. 339, *supra*). We may recall the plague's journey from Egypt to the fields and streets of Athens as it invades "the city" (*vastavitque vias, exhausit civibus urbem*, "it ravaged the streets and drained the city of its citizens," 6.1140). As if to confirm this movement and to balance the opening description, Lucretius moves toward his conclusion with the grim arrival of the suffering "from the country into the city" (*nec minimam partem ex agris is maeror in urbem / confluxit*, "nor to any small degree did that grief flood from the fields into the city," 6.1259–60). Finally, as the suffering and pain win out, there remain "in the city" only the fear and violence that drive out the ancient custom of burial (*praesens dolor exsuperabat. / nec mos ille sepulturae remanebat in urbe*, 6.1277–78). But whereas Epicurus's fragment refers to the individual life, Lucretius (here following Thucydides) describes a whole society overwhelmed by dread and death.

Lucretius's virtuoso performance in evoking this horror at the very end of the work looks like rhetorical overkill. Hence distinguished interpreters like Cyril Bailey and Ettore Bignone have suspected that the poem is unfinished.[26] If this is the in-

---

[25] On the emotive quality of Lucretius's description of the plague, particularly in contrast to Thucydides, see Bright, "Plague," 619: "Each stage of the physical suffering is characterized by a mental state, so that the movement in Lucretius is emotional rather than clinical." Thus "the real struggle, the real decay and death, are in the spirit." D.E.W. Wormell, "Lucretius: The Personality of the Poet," *Greece & Rome* 7 (1960): 57, also observes that this account of the symptoms reflects Lucretius's "design to build the picture of the plague into a symbol of humanity's sufferings, and these at their worst are both physical and psychological."

[26] For views of the meaning of the plague, see Bailey *T. Lucreti Cari*, 3:1723–25 and 1759; Bright, "Plague," 620–32; Clay, *Lucretius and Epicurus*, 257–66, with recent bibliography in the notes (p. 343). See also below, Chapter Ten.

tended ending (as I believe it is), did Lucretius underestimate the effect of leaving the reader with these bleak impressions?[27] Or did he expect the reader to be sufficiently fortified by the previous arguments? Or is the plague the final test of the reader's understanding, as Diskin Clay suggests?[28] Or is it the culminating demonstration of the reader's need for the "true reason" and solace of Epicureanism?[29] Or is the power of death here, standing in such sharp contrast to the praise of Venus and her life energies at the poem's beginning, the triumph of Lucretius's underlying pessimism, his conviction, after all, of mankind's ignorance and folly?[30] Does it, rather, express his tragic sense of the eternal, unresolvable conflict (for mortals, at least) between creation and destruction? Or is it the final manifestation of the tension between the poet and the philosopher, between the Roman writer's recognition of irrationality and violence in life and the sweet reasonableness of Epicurus's teachings?

Interpreters have answered, and will continue to answer, these questions in different ways, and not all the solutions are mutually exclusive. Lucretius is not a simple poet, nor is his presentation of our struggle with death so simple as proving the non-survival of the soul. When we read book 3 in the light of the plague in book 6, we see that Lucretius does do justice to the root terrors concerning pain and the body that are not allayed by Epicurus's logic about being and non-being or by exhortations to serene memories of happiness in one's past. His engagement with this part of the terror of dying, as I suggested above, culminates in the closing scenes of the poem. It is, however, spread subtly over the entire work, but it is found in its most concentrated form in the first half of book 3, and it is to this that we must now turn.

---

[27] See Bailey, *T. Lucreti Cari*, 3:1724: "Others maintain that the artist here has got the better of the philosopher and that in his desire for a great dramatic conclusion Lucretius forgot the effect which it would have on his readers."

[28] See Clay, *Lucretius and Epicurus*, 225, 259, 262, 266.

[29] See ibid., 259.

[30] So Bright, "Plague," 628–32.

Chapter Three

THE WIND-SCATTERED SOUL

For LUCRETIUS, life is inherently fragile because it consists of an airy life-substance, the soul (*anima*), enclosed in the vessel of the body. Life, then, is no more secure than the vessel that protects it. Epicureans do not hesitate to remind us how fragile this envelope is. Philodemus, for example, observes that trying to preserve the body in death is like expecting glass and ceramic vessels, thrown together with steel, to survive unbroken for many years (*De Morte* 39.1–6). Lucretius himself compares our bodies to leaky or flawed vessels that can never be filled to our satisfaction (3.936ff., 1009–10, 6.19ff.).

Viewed from the perspective of the shell of body surrounding the life-soul, death is an invasion of our physical boundaries. Lucretius adumbrates this view of death at the end of book 1 and touches on it a number of times later.[1] Viewed from the perspective of the soul, death is a dissolution into air, a gentle dispersion into the winds. Epicurus often describes death as "dissolution," διάλυσις, but Lucretius adds the details of smoke or air, thereby placing himself into a poetic tradition as old as Homer. Because his poetry is imbedded in this tradition, he cannot entirely avoid (if he wants to) the note of pathos that resonates from it.

One result of such resonances is a continual shifting between the objective, distancing, third-person analysis of death in the framework of Epicurean physics, and a warmer, more affect-laden first-person or second-person discussion rooted in the literary tradition. This alternation gives a personal stamp to what might otherwise be a cold, impersonal discussion. The interplay between the two voices often takes the grammatical form of a change of persons, from the third person to the first

---

[1] On the boundaries of the body, see below, Chapter Five.

or second. We shall try to listen to the dialogue, sometimes the polyphony, among these voices as we follow the arguments for the mortality of the soul.

Early in his account of the soul, Lucretius takes pains to refute the notion that it consists in an intangible "harmony." The soul is corporeal, and its corporeality is proven by the two-pronged argument that life can continue even in a badly mangled body as long as a sufficient number of the vaporous soul-atoms exist, and conversely that death comes even if the body is intact provided that all of the soul-atoms have gone. As this is the first time that Lucretius describes the airy, wind-like nature of the corporeal soul, the passage is of some importance, and it is necessary to quote it at length (3.119–29):

> principio fit uti detracto corpore multo
> saepe tamen nobis in membris vita moretur;
> atque eadem rursum, cum corpora pauca caloris
> diffugere forasque per os est editus aer,
> deserit extemplo venas atque ossa relinquit;
> noscere ut hinc possis non aequas omnia partis
> corpora habere neque ex aequo fulcire salutem,
> sed magis haec, venti quae sunt calidique vaporis
> semina, curare in membris ut vita moretur.
> est igitur calor ac ventus vitalis in ipso
> corpore qui nobis moribundos deserit artus.

(First of all, it happens that when much of our body has been taken away, even so life often lingers in our limbs, and that same life in turn, when only few bodies [atoms] of heat have fled forth and the air is sent outward through the mouth, at once abandons the veins and leaves the bones behind, so that you can know from this that not all the atoms have equal roles nor equally prop up our safety, but rather these which are the seeds of wind and warm vapor take care that life linger in the limbs. There is, therefore, a warmth and a vital wind in the body itself that abandons our limbs when they are near death.)

Even in this purely "scientific," objective description, Lucretius conveys a sense of the preciousness of life and of the destructive power of death. The little phrase in 119, *detracto corpore multo*, "when much of our body has been taken away," introduces the motif of bodily injury that (as we shall see) develops steadily and more specifically as the book continues. The repeated line-end, *in membris vita moretur* (120 and 127), emphasizes the importance of life's presence in our body, while it is still able thus to "linger" or "wait." The dissolution of the airy soul into the winds is a natural process, but the small detail of "the few bodies [atoms] of heat" in 121 again presents life as a precious but threatened substance fighting a losing battle, as it were, against forces that vastly outnumber it.

Throughout the passage the dying body seems to be struggling to sustain life while its vital forces are abandoning it. The pathetic effort of that struggle is conveyed by the contrast between the repeated lingering of life (*vita moretur*, 120, 127) on the one hand and the repeated verbs of abandoning in 123 and 129 (*deserit . . . relinquit . . . deserit*) on the other. The metaphor of "propping up" the "health" of the body as if it were a tottering building (*fulcire salutem*, 125) reinforces this contrast between the ethereality of the fleeing soul-atoms and the material shell of the corpse that will soon be left behind.

A similar effect results from the rapidly accumulating detail about the specific bodily parts as the passage moves, with a kind of cool inevitability, toward death. There is a general reference to the injured body in 119 (*detracto corpore multo*) and then a continuing flickering of life lingering "in the limbs" (*in membris vita moretur*, 120). At this point Lucretius progresses to more vivid and individualized moments in the slipping away of life's slender essence. "Air is given out through the mouth" (*per os*, 122); the soul "abandons the veins" and "leaves the bones" (*deserit venas, ossa relinquit*, 123). The final stage comes when the "warmth and wind of life" now "abandons the *dying limbs*" (*calor ac ventus vitalis . . . qui nobis moribundos deserit artus*, 128–29). The lines set up an implicit contrast between the vulnerable airiness of the life-substance in 128 and the concreteness of the "limbs" whose physicality and subjection to suffering are implied in the adjective *moribundos*.

The addition of such details and the increasing specificity about the body itself in the reference to "veins," "bones," and "dying limbs" (*venas, ossa, moribundos artus*) transform the process of dying from abstraction to physical reality. The phrase (*ut*) *in membris vita moretur* in 120 ("so that life should linger in the limbs") is repeated in 127, just after dying has been more precisely visualized as a dynamic physical process, affecting not just "limbs" but also "veins" and "bones." The "dying limbs" become increasingly unable to retain the ethereal stuff that brings a body life. This elusive "wind of life" makes itself visible, as it were, only to "abandon our dying limbs" (*est igitur calor ac ventus vitalis in ipso / corpore qui nobis moribundos deserit artus*, 128–29).

Death may be "nothing to us," but at both the beginning and the end of this passage the personal "we" makes a prominent appearance: *nobis in membris vita moretur* (120); *nobis moribundos deserit artus* (129). Amid the impersonality of wind-atoms and separate organs the first person has a powerful effect. It virtually addresses the reader through his own mortality and unites author and reader in a common subjection to "our" bodies' fragility. This community of mortality implied by the generalizing *nobis* becomes more striking when we compare the generalizing second-person singular *possis* in 124, which describes the more removed reader who is involved mentally rather than physically and only makes an intellectual observation: *noscere ut hinc possis* ("so that you can know from this").

There is no emotionality or sentimentality in such effects, and Lucretius goes on at once with the stern, contemptuous command to abandon the notion of the soul as a "harmony" rather than as a physical substance, an idea stigmatized as worthier of poets than of philosophers (*redde harmoniai / nomen, ad organicos alto delatum Heliconi*, "Give up that name of harmony, brought down from lofty Helicon to musicians," 131–32). Yet his language conveys an awareness of death as something more than a remote atomic process. Specifically, the framing effect of *nobis* in 120 and 129, combined with the lingering of life conveyed in the repetition of this idea (120, 127, 129), does after all bring before us the meaning of death as an abrupt end to the conscious, feeling subject denoted by the personal pronoun "us."

This acknowledgment of the universality of death from a subjective as well as an objective perspective is an inseparable part of the poetic texture of the work. Lucretius presents the struggle between life and death as a fact of the world order; but he does not forget the human subject, like the old farmer at the end of book 2, who suffers when the balance swings toward death. The traditions of the long hexameter poem, reaching back to Homer and Hesiod, allow for this combination of distance and compassion, wisdom and sympathy.

As the book continues, Lucretius uses a series of similes or metaphors, drawn from Homer and the epic tradition, to describe death as the soul's floating off into the winds, like smoke or perfume. Visualized in this way, death is a peaceful "retreat" (*recessus*) and a "calm" that is free of anxious thoughts (*secura quies*, 3.210–11). The latter expression is suggestive of the gods' *sedes quietae* (3.18) and thus recalls the Epicurean goal of ἀταραξία, serenity of spirit.

These expressions occur early in book 3, where Lucretius is describing the fineness of the soul-atoms and the relative ease with which something of so subtle a weave (*tenui constet textura*, 3.209) departs from the body (3.211–15):

> quod simul atque hominem leti secura quies est
> indepta atque animi natura animaeque recessit,
> nil ibi libatum de toto corpore cernas
> ad speciem, nil ad pondus: mors omnia praestat
> vitalem praeter sensum calidumque vaporem.

(As soon as the care-free calm of doom has seized a man and the nature of mind and soul has departed, you would perceive nothing taken away from the entire body as far as appearance is concerned, nothing with respect to weight: death sets forth everything, except for the sensation of life and the warm breath.)

Here Lucretius de-emphasizes the quality of weight (*pondus*) in the body's materiality in favor of the "warm breath" of life (*calidum vaporem*, 215). In the following lines he compares the soul's "departure" (*recessit*) to the way in which the "bouquet of wine" vanishes (*Bacchi flos*) or the "sweet scent of perfume flees apart into the winds" (*spiritus unguenti suavis diffugit in auras*, 3.222). The verbs, all intransitive, present death as a gradual, painless process of departure: *recessit, cessit, evanuit, diffugit*. They provide the model, at the physical level—that is, in the terms of Epicurean atomic processes—for the right way of dying. Later Natura herself, personified and using direct second-person address, will enjoin this form of tranquil withdrawal upon the foolish mortal afraid of death: "Why do you not depart (*recedis*) like a guest, sated with life, and with mind at ease take anxiety-free rest (*securam quietem*, 3.938–39; cf. 3.211)?"

Yet the tranquillity of the scientifically detached description in 211–22 modulates to another tone, and here the pressure of death as a painful physical process is more urgent. In the next section, as Lucretius restates the vapor-like nature of the soul, he describes how its "fragile wind abandons those who are dying" (3.232–33):

> tenvis enim quaedam moribundos deserit aura
> mixta vapore, vapor porro trahit aera secum.

(For a certain thin air leaves the limbs, mingled with warmth, and then the warmth draws the air with itself.)

The verb *deserit* in 232 now deepens the sense of loss already implicit in the images of wine and perfume's flower in 221–22. The repetition of *vapore vapor* and the echoes in both sound and sense between *aura* and *aera* stress the airy lightness, and hence the fragility, of this principle of life. The contrast between these semantically related singular nouns, *aura, vapor,* and *aer,* and the weighty plural *moribundos,* with its spondees filling the fourth foot of the verse, reminds us that we are contemplating, after all, not an impersonal vaporous substance but "dying men."

Shortly before, in 217, Lucretius mentioned "veins, flesh, and muscles" in a more or less static account of how the soul is "woven" through the solid parts of our bodies (*nexam per venas viscera nervos*). He now recalls these parts of the body to describe how sensation spreads along our physical frame (248–51):

> inde omnia mobilitantur,
> concutitur sanguis, tum viscera persentiscunt
> omnia, postremis datur ossibus atque medullis
> sive voluptas est sive est contrarius ardor.

(Thence all things are set into motion, the blood is shaken, then all the flesh feels [it] through and through and finally it is given to the bones and the marrow, whether it is pleasure or the opposite kind of heat.)

The spreading of sensation is, of course, a physical process, involving movement through blood, vital organs, and finally marrow and bones. Yet this is also the process through which death enters our life, or, in Lucretius's terms, through which the vital substance departs from our bodies: compare 121–29 cited above. The paths of sensation that give us consciousness are also those traversed by its inevitable departure.

The phrase *concutitur sanguis* in 249 is especially important in conveying the fragility of our mortal body. Our blood is "stirred" or "shaken" as the blessed abode of the gods described in the proem never is: *sedes quietae, quas neque concutiunt venti* . . . (3.18–19). These lines on the gods seem to remain in Lucretius's memory in this portion of the book, for shortly before he uses the phrase *leti secura quies*, "the carefree calm of doom," to describe the power of death that lays hold of a man (*hominem leti secura quies est / indepta*, 211–12). The echo of the *sedes quietae* of the blessed gods here evokes the ultimate goal of the freedom from fear to which the death-threatened mortal may aspire. But at the same time, the echo of *neque concutiunt* in *concutitur sanguis* (19 and 249) also contrasts the mortal soul's fragility with the gods' untroubled permanence. Unlike them, our substance is blood, flesh, and bone (249–50).

This contrast, again, draws on the age-old definition of mortality by the opposition to the gods, "ageless and immortal forever." The adaptation of the Homeric Olympus to the peace of the Epicurean gods in the proem provides the traditional poetic reference point for the mortal condition (3.18–22; Odyssey 6.42–46). The juxtaposition of the gods' eternity and mortal fragility is strengthened by the fact that Lucretius's verb in 249, concutitur, is in fact a closer translation of the Homeric τινάσσεται of Odyssey 6.43 than is concutiunt in the proem (οὔτ᾽ ἀνέμοισι τινάσσεται, of Olympus, Od. 6.43; quas neque concutiunt venti, 3.19). Lucretius makes Homer's verb positive rather than negative and transfers it from the serenity of Olympus to the turbulent area of our struggle with mortality, "blood."

In 248–51, cited above, sensation gradually moves inward, from blood and entrails to bones and marrow. Contrarius ardor, "heat of the opposite kind" (251), is almost a euphemism, and its less pleasant implications are given in the following lines (252–57):

> nec temere huc dolor usque potest penetrare neque acre
> permanare malum, quin omnia perturbentur
> usque adeo ut vitae desit locus atque animai
> diffugiant partes per caulas corporis omnis.
> sed plerumque fit in summo quasi corporis finis
> motibus: hanc ob rem vitam retinere valemus.

(Yet not vainly is pain able to penetrate as far as here and the sharp suffering to flow through, but in fact they bring about the thorough disturbance of everything, to such a degree that a place for life is lacking and the parts of the soul scatter through all the pores of the body. But generally there is a limit to these movements in the topmost part, as it were, of the body: for this reason we are able to keep a hold on life.)

The scientific language of "pores" (caulas) and "movements" objectifies but does not remove the physical sensation of a pain that "penetrates" the body or a "sharp suffering" that "flows through" our entire physical being until the soul is fragmented into "parts" that are now dispersed outward "through all the pores of the body" (254–55). *Ut vitae desit locus*, "so that a place for life is lacking," is as neutral a way as possible to describe death. But it gains a deepened physical significance from the last line of the passage, where Lucretius suddenly shifts from third-person, scientific description to a first-person verb that itself implies the physical "strength" that "we" need in order to "hold on to life," to "hold back" the airy soul within the limits of the body (*vitam retinere valemus*). Otherwise those violent movements that "shake the blood" and disturb our "inward flesh" (*tum viscera persentiscunt*, 249) may not stop short of our body's surface but may in fact "penetrate" more deeply (253). Now it is not just the impersonal "flesh" or "vitals" that "feel," but "we" who "have the strength" to "hold on to life"—or not.

This passage illustrates how subtly, by delicate modulations of language, Lucretius can shift from a value-neutral description of death as a physical process to a more emotionally colored presentation of death within the value-laden context of mortality. This more affective presentation of death is implicit also in the personal form of the verb, *valemus*, in 257, with which we may compare the first-person pronouns in the physical descriptions of 120 and 129, discussed above. The same objective but sympathetic attitude also informs the images of the bouquet of wine and the scent of perfume in 221–22. Life is as fragile as those scents, and those scents are among the pleasures of being alive. The more general metaphors of "pain" that "penetrates" us or of the "bitter woe" that "flows through us" (*dolor . . . potest penetrare neque acre / permanare malum*, 252–53) also remind us that the mortal body is not just a value-neutral physical barrier, but a living tissue full of sense and feeling. The addition of the otherwise gratuitous adjective *acre*, "bitter," in particular seems to acknowledge the subjective dimension of the process of dying. It is the adjective that Lucretius chooses for his own passionate desire for poetic glory (*acri percussit thyrso*, 1.922–23).

The emotional significance of such metaphors surfaces later, in other connections. Thus the liquid metaphor of illness as a "bitter woe" that flows through or over us (*acre permanare malum*, 3.252) returns with far greater vividness and particularity in the description of epilepsy as a "bitter humor" that, after the attack, returns to its "hiding places" in the afflicted body (*reditque / in latebras acer corrupti corporis umor*, 502–3). In this passage too, Lucretius's focus is not so much the atomic nature of human physiology as the individual sufferer. The grammatical subject and the subject of his discourse is the sick man who totters as he tries to stand up when he gradually returns to consciousness (504–5):

> tum quasi vaccillans primum consurgit et omnis
> paulatim redit in sensus animamque receptat.

(Then tottering as it were, he first rises up and little by little returns to his senses and takes back his life.)

Here too Lucretius is drawing, if only indirectly, upon the ancient traditions of Greek poetry, with its deep emotional awareness of the discrepancy between intellectual consciousness and the fragility of our physical being. Conceivably he could have known descriptions like Sophocles' account of Philoctetes as he returns to consciousness after the spasms of agony in his poisoned foot.[2]

Lucretius's discussion of fatal disease in a different context shows the same alternation between the objective, scientific view and an emotional involvement characterized by compassion and indignation. It is illuminating to compare the following two reactions:

> praeterea genus horriferum natura ferarum
> humanae genti infestum terraque marique
> cur alit atque auget? cur anni tempora morbos
> apportant? quare mors immatura vagatur?
> tum porro puer, ut saevis proiectus ab undis

---

[2] Sophocles, *Philoctetes* 730–826. This passage may reflect knowledge of the medical tradition too: see my "Lucretius, Epilepsy, and *On Breaths*."

> navita, nudus humi iacet, infans, indigus omni
> vitali auxilio, cum primum in luminis oras
> nixibus ex alvo matris natura profudit,
> vagituque locum lugubri complet, ut aequumst
> cui tantum in vita restet transire malorum.

(In addition, why does nature nourish and increase the fearful race of wild beasts hostile to mankind on land and sea? Why do the seasons of the year bring diseases? Why does premature death prowl around? And then the child, like a sailor cast up from savage waves, lies naked on the ground, without speech, in need of every aid for life, as soon as nature has poured him forth amid travail from his mother's womb, and he fills the place with his wailing, as is right for one to whom there remain so many evils to pass through in life.) (5.218–27)

> nam cum res tantis morbis tantisque periclis
> temptarentur, ibi si tristior incubuisset
> causa, darent late cladem magnasque ruinas.
> nec ratione alia mortales esse videmur,
> inter nos nisi quod morbis aegrescimus isdem
> atque illi quos a vita natura removit.

(For when things should be tried by so many diseases and so many dangers, if there a grimmer cause had come to rest upon them, they would give forth destruction and great collapsing far and wide. For we seem to be mortal in no other way than this, that we grow sick among one another with the same diseases as those whom nature has taken out of life.) (5.345–50)

The second passage assumes the distanced, objective viewpoint of the scientific observer, scanning the totality of the universe with full acceptance of its alternation and balance of creative and destructive processes. Lucretius is here arguing that everything has an origin and therefore also an end. The subjection of men and things to "diseases and dangers" (345) implies their subjection also to death "if a grimmer cause should have come to lie upon them" (346). From this general point Lucretius moves in an a fortiori fashion to our mortality specifically: we know our personal end in death through the fact

that others have died before us from the same diseases with
which we are afflicted (349–50).

The affective quality of the phrase *si tristior incubuisset /
causa* in 346–47 marks some sympathetic identification with
the "we" of the next lines (*nos . . . quod morbis aegrescimus
isdem*, 349); and the sequence *mortales . . . aegrescimus* sug-
gests Lucretius's generalizing compassion for men as *aegris
mortalibus*, with its echoes of the Homeric δειλοῖσι βροτοῖσι.
Yet he goes beyond the Homeric formula in suggesting a
physiological basis of human misery in the association of the
mortal condition with subjection to disease through the play
on *mortales* and *morbis*. His perspective is that of the univer-
sal and eternal processes of creation and destruction, origins
and cataclysmic endings, and we may compare the objective,
entirely third-person account of the same phenomena in terms
of the "movement" and "blows" of the atoms in 1.954–59.
The account of death here, therefore, quickly retreats to the
objective language of the last line, from *nos* to *illi* and from
"dying" to "removal from life" (350). In this perspective,
death is merely Nature's endless process of clearing away
those whose time is over in order to make way for her new
creations. The juxtaposition of *vita* and *natura* here (*illi quos
a vita natura removit*) suggests that the root meaning of *na-
tura* as "birth" may be operative, so that those thus "removed
from life" will be the source of the new "births" to come (cf.
2.576–80; also 1.225–64, 540–50, and 2.875–82).

How different is 5.218–27, the first of the two passages
quoted above. Here Lucretius argues against the teleological
or providential conception of the world order. So disadvanta-
geous is our world to mankind that gods concerned with our
well-being could not have created it. *Natura* has left the ani-
mals better endowed than us humans. Lucretius now situates
himself fully within the world of men rather than in the im-
personal realm of Nature, and he sympathetically voices
man's indignation against the harshness of a world in which
both birth and death are so cruel. "Nurture," "increase," and
generous "birth" are for the beasts, not for man (*alit atque
auget*, 220; cf. *large parit*, 233–34). For mankind even the ra-

diance of birth (224) is heralded by a wailing that is equally appropriate to death (*vagituque . . . lugubri*, 226; cf. 2.576–80).

The forces of destruction become virtually personified in their hostile purposiveness: the year's seasons "bring on" diseases, and premature death "wanders" over the earth (220–21). Whereas animals enjoy the exuberance of earth and nature, man is cast up "from savage waves" (222; cf. 233–34), "poured forth" heedlessly by the pushing and straining of travail that an indifferent Nature requires of the mother (note the collocation of *matris* and *natura* in 225). The contrast between the metaphorical "shores of light" in 224 and the realism of the act of parturition in 225 stresses the pain that attends man's origins. *Natura* is far from being to men the "mother" that she is to animals (cf. 225; also *parit*, 234). The rhetorical questions of 218–21 form a breathlessly enjambed and increasingly pointed sequence, culminating in the sharp brevity of 221, *quare mors immatura vagatur*, "Why does premature death wander abroad?"

"Premature death" is the last item in the series. Seen in this highly rhetorical context, death is far from being the accepted physical process of nature's necessary "removal" from life in 350. It is, rather, the bitterly resented insult inflicted on man by an indifferent world order. Like the waning of life perceived by the old farmer at the end of book 2, it is viewed through the eyes of an intensely feeling subject, a compassionate sufferer-observer who protests on behalf of his fellow sufferers. Nevertheless, Lucretius's presentation of death in this passage remains on a more general level than in most of book 3. There are no first- or second-person pronouns. He speaks of the "human race" (219) or "the child" (222), but not of "us" or "you."

This contrast between impersonal process at the atomic level and the feelings of a personal subject at the level of consciousness corresponds to what Phillip DeLacy, in a celebrated essay, called the tension between process and value. Physical dissolution as an atomic process does not always remain wholly impersonal and neutral when referred to the feelings and perceptions of the intelligent beings who describe those processes and are aware of what they signify for their own existence.[3] This tension, as DeLacy showed, is not merely an indication of the "anti-Lucretius in Lucretius" or of the poet conflicting with the philosopher, but is something inherent in Epicurean doctrine itself. Hence it surfaces here, in ordinary, non-purple description, as a fundamental property of Lucretius's "scientific" style.[4]

This personal recognition of death takes the form of the slight stylistic shifts noted above, the intrusion of words like *moribundus* or *acer*, and the inevitable evocation of our fragile corporeal being in the enumeration of vital organs and fluids, as in 3.249–50 (*sanguis, viscera, ossibus, medullis*). These vital carriers of physical life (here and elsewhere in the book) are mentioned precisely when their fragility, susceptibility to disturbance, and potential for pain are in question (e.g., *concutitur sanguis*, 249–51):

> concutitur sanguis, tum viscera persentiscunt
> omnia, postremis datur ossibus atque medullis
> sive voluptas est sive est contrarius ardor.

(The blood is shaken, then all the flesh feels [it] through and through, and finally it is given to the bones and the marrow, whether it is pleasure or the opposite kind of heat.)

Although pleasure is an equally possible result of these physical movements, as 251 states, *concutitur sanguis* is threatening rather than inviting. The combination of "pain," "penetrating," and "bitter woe" in the next two lines (252–53) deepens this threat and suggests that the strong feeling in the vitals (conveyed by the repeated prefix in *persentiscunt, permanare, perturbentur*) will indeed be the *contrarius ardor* rather than the *voluptas*. *Ardor* itself is neutral, but in the context, and especially in combination with *contrarius*, it suggests another form of pain.[5]

---

[3] DeLacy, "Process and Value," passim.

[4] For other aspects of this tension, see Amory, "Science and Poetry," passim.

[5] For these reasons I doubt that *ardor* is as "neutral" here as Bailey, *T. Lucreti Cari*, ad 3.251, suggests. Elsewhere in book 3 it is associated with

There is an increasingly harsh note even in the seemingly neutral description of the soul as wind or heat that dissolves into the air as Lucretius enters more fully into his subject. The image of the soul as slipping away like the bouquet of wine or the scent of perfume in 221–22 becomes something more violent and potentially painful in view of the close bonding of soul and body in 327–28:

> quod genus e thuris glaebis *evellere* odorem
> haud facile est quin intereat natura quoque eius.

(Just as from pieces of myrrh it is not easy to *tear away* the scent without its physical substance also perishing.)

Death is no longer a "fainting away" (*evanuit*, 221) but rather a hard "tearing apart" (*evellere*), as the previous lines imply (325–26):

> nam communibus inter se radicibus haerent
> nec sine pernicie *divelli* posse videntur.

(For they cling together with common roots, nor do they seem capable of being *torn apart* without destruction.)

The verb *divelli* in 326 anticipates *evellere* in 327; *pernicies* presents death as a violent destruction. Death here is a forcible rending apart of intertwined elements that "cling to one another with their roots in common."[6] At a later point in the book those "roots" become a focal point for bodily violence: the eye, "torn away from its roots" (*avulsus radicibus*, 563), serves as an example of the mortality of the soul, since the organ severed from the body loses its power of sensation (558–65).

In 396ff. Lucretius is trying to prove that the *animus* (the principle of consciousness, will, and intelligence) is more essential to life than the *anima* (the diffused vital force). But, as

---

the "warmth" of passions (anger in 3.289) and the warming effects of wine (477).

[6] Bailey, *T. Lucreti Cari*, ad 325, excellently paraphrases, "The atoms of soul and body so interpenetrate each other (cf. 262) that they have, as it were, a tangle of common roots."

a side effect, he allows the soul's departure into the winds (*discedit in auras*, 400) to include more specific and visible effects of death. As the *animus* departs it "leaves behind the cold limbs in the chill of doom" (*et gelidos artus in leti frigore linquit*, 401). *Gelidos artus linquit* here, like *moribundos deserit* in 232, treats death as loss or abandonment; and the "abandoned" object, whether the limbs or the whole person, is viewed as either "cold" or "dying." There follows an image of mutilation (403–4); and the emphatically enjambed *vivit* in 405 presents the taking in of the life-giving air as part of the instinctive determination to struggle against death and to survive. Though the body is badly mangled, the man "lives and takes in the life-giving winds of the aether" (*vivit et aetherias vitalis suscipit auras*, 405). The repeated, almost formulaic *in auras* (400) now receives an elaboration in the two adjectives (*aetherias* and *vitalis*). In the context, these words express both the joy of the vital processes and the body's struggle to keep them going.[7]

The struggle for life in fact here takes the form of trying to receive and hold in the "winds" of air and life. Behind the dry, objective language is a recognition of the critical movement between the soul's enclosing of life energy in the first line (396), the too-easy departure *in auras* in 400, and the will to survive by continually receiving the air and winds that bring life in 405: *et magis est animus vitai claustra coercens* (the mind contains the enclosures of life to a greater degree, 396); *sed comes insequitur facile et discedit in auras* (but the soul follows easily as its companion and departs into the air, 400); *vivit et aetherias vitalis suscipit auras* (he lives and takes in the vital winds of the upper air, 405). The verb in 405, *suscipit*, may even express the rising and falling motion in the gentle effort of respiration. Breathing is itself a "lifting up" as well

---

[7] This passage contains in microcosm the struggle between life and death that pervades the *De Rerum Natura*. See especially the eternal conflict between the *motus exitiales* and the *motus genitales auctificique* in 2.569–80, on which see Perelli, *Lucrezio*, 41. See in general Anderson, "Discontinuity," 13ff.; DeLacy, "Process and Value," 123–24; Elder, "Lucretius 1.1–49," 115ff.

as a taking in of the delicate source of life brought on the winds.

Upon this movement of the airy soul follow the cumulative verbs of delaying death as the mutilated man clings to life (406–7):

> si non omnimodis, at magna parte animai
> privatus, tamen in vita cunctatur et haeret.

(If he is deprived not entirely but of a great part of the soul, nevertheless he delays in life and clings to it.)

Cunctatur et haeret in 407 repeats the idea of *at manet in vita* in 402 but adds the important subjective element of will, effort, and determined obstinacy in the face of death. The oscillation between life and death and the qualifications made by the conjunctions add to the effect of this struggle: *at manet* (402); *quamvis* (403); *si non omnimodis . . . at* (406); *tamen* (407); *dummodo ne* (410). In this passage too, as in 248–57 discussed above, there is a noteworthy, if almost imperceptible, change from non-personal subjects (*animus*, 396; *pars animai*, 399) to the personal subject of 402–7. The sentence begins at line 402 with a potentially generalizing relative construction (*at manet in vita cui mens animusque remansit*, "but he remains in life whose mind and understanding have remained"), but then gradually personalizes and individualizes this worst case, perhaps even with a grudging touch of admiration. This terribly mangled man, even so, "remains in life," "lives," "takes in the vital winds of sky," "delays in life and clings [to it]."[8] The personalizing metaphor of *anima* as the "companion" of the *animus* in 400 perhaps helps prepare for this shift (*sed comes insequitur*).

In 434ff. Lucretius continues his comparison of the soul to wind, cloud, or smoke: *et nebula ac fumus quoniam discedit in auras / crede animam quoque diffundi multoque perire / ocius . . .* ("And because cloud and smoke depart into the air, believe that the soul too is poured forth and perishes even more rapidly," 436–38). But shortly afterwards, proving that

---

[8] Compare the emphatic use of *vivere* in 3.50 and 6.1209.

the soul is born with the body and must therefore die with it, he shows death as a more vivid and violent process: "The body is shaken by the powerful force of age; the limbs collapse as their strength is blunted; the intellect is lamed; the tongue wanders; the mind totters," until all at once "everything fails" (451–54). At this point "the soul's whole nature is dissolved, like smoke into the high winds of air" (455–56):

> ergo dissolui quoque convenit omnem animai
> naturam, ceu fumus in altas aeris auras.

The periphrasis, *omnem animai naturam*, suggests the fragility of the soul's coming-to-be or "birth," as well as its end. The more elaborate phrasing of the airy dissolution in 456 adds pathos to an otherwise objective and concise vignette of death in old age[9]—a pathos that is logically unnecessary and even, from an Epicurean point of view, counterproductive.

Lucretius's next argument for the mortality of the soul is the equal subjection of both body and soul to illness and therefore to death. "Illness" and "pain" both have strong epithets. Diseases are "vast" (the epithet of Tityos's huge extent at the end of the book, 987), and pain is "hard" or "cruel" (*immanis morbos durumque dolorem*, 460). There follows a graphic account of a man in a coma, with its pathetic details of the grief of those who stand around him (468–70). Strictly speaking, these details are irrelevant to the argument.

Disease here works both by "touch" and by violent "penetration": *penetrant in eum contagia morbi* (471). The words "pain" and "disease" are now echoed from 460 (cf. *dolor ac morbus*, 472; *immanis morbos durumque dolorem*, "vast diseases and harsh pain," 460). Lucretius, however, inverts the order and now makes "disease" a quasi-personified force, "artificer of death" (*dolor ac morbus leti fabricator uterquest*, "for pain and disease are each an artificer of doom," 472). He again shifts the subject from *animus* (464) to the man himself (466ff.). Correspondingly, he moves death (*letum*) from a pas-

---

[9] For the concentrated brilliance of the description, see Kenney, *Lucretius III*, ad 453.

sive to an active role (*participem leti,* "sharing in death," 462; *leti fabricator,* "deviser of death," 472).[10]

Death is common, and Lucretius resumes his more objective, distanced tone in the next verse, *multorum exitio perdocti quod sumus ante* ("what we are taught by the destruction of many," 473). As Epicureans, we should be "instructed," *perdocti,* by these observations on the dying, so that we are untroubled by the concerns about the soul after death. Yet the austere *dolor ac morbus* (472) that teach the lessons of "process" (in DeLacy's sense) are also bearers of powerful and painful "value," as the descriptive terms like *immanis . . . durum* or *leti fabricator* indicate. The lines that introduce this passage (and are echoed in 472 in almost ring-composition), in fact, heap up all the woes of the human condition, of men as *mortalibus aegris* or the Homeric δειλοῖσι βροτοῖσι, in an accumulation of heavy nouns, alliterations, assonances, and polysyndeta (460–61): *immanis morbos durumque dolorem / . . . curas acris luctumque metumque* ("vast diseases and harsh pain, . . . sharp anxieties and grief and fear").

Alongside the scientific didacticism, Lucretius sounds again the voice of the poetic tradition, with its listing of mortal woes and its compassionate generalizations on the sufferings of mortality, as it is heard from Homer to Virgil.[11] With this listing of the mortal soul's woes we may compare the verses of Euripides quoted by Chrysippus and translated into Latin by Lucretius's contemporary, Cicero, in *Tusculan Disputations* 3.25.59:

[10] On *letum,* see Michels, "Death," 161–63, who, however, seems to me to give insufficient weight to the vividness of the metaphors in which it occurs. Waszink, "Letum," passim, esp. 250 n. 2 and pp. 253–56, points out that *letum* was originally a personified power of death, and something of that demonic significance may survive still for Lucretius, e.g., 1.852.

[11] On the poetry of mortality in the Greek hexameter tradition, see, for example, Jenny S. Clay, *The Wrath of Athena* (Princeton, 1983), 141ff.; William G. Thalmann, *Conventions of Form and Thought in Early Greek Epic Poetry* (Baltimore, 1984), 78ff. For tragedy, see Carlo Diano, "La catarsi tragica," in his *Sagezza e poetiche degli antichi* (Vicenza, 1968), 235ff., esp. 258–59.

mortalis nemo est quem non attingat dolor
morbusque; multis sunt humandi liberi,
rursum creandi, morsque est finita omnibus,
quae generi humano angorem nequiquam adferunt.
reddenda terrae est terra, tum vita omnibus
metenda, ut fruges. sic iubet Necessitas.

(There is no mortal whom pain and sickness do not reach. Many
must bury children and beget them in turn. Death is set as the
limit to everything that brings its anguish, all to no avail, to the
human race. Earth must be given back to earth; all must harvest
life, like the crops. So Necessity commands.)

Or, slightly after Lucretius, but drawing on earlier traditions,
there is Virgil's list of the personified evils at the entrance to
the Underworld, including "Grief, Anxiety, pale Diseases,
grim Old Age, Hunger, Poverty, Sleep kinsman of Doom, and
the mind's Evil Joys and deadly War" (*Aeneid* 6.274–79). Fur-
ther in the background lie passages like Odysseus's speech to
Amphinomus on the feebleness of mortal men (*Odyssey*
18.130–37) or this celebrated fragment of Simonides:

Small is the strength of men, and without effect their efforts; and
in a little lifetime [stands] toil upon toil. Over all equally hangs
death unavoidable. Of that the good men win an equal portion
with the man who is base. (frag. 520 in Page, *Poetae Melici
Graeci*)

Or, again from tragedy, there is this well-known text from
Sophocles, also using the cumulative effect of an enumeration:

Not to be born wins every accounting; but, when one has come
into the light, second best is to go there whence one has come as
swiftly as he may. For when youth is lost, bearing its airy follies,
what suffering wanders far outside his life? What woe does he
not have within? Envy, factions, strife, battles, killings. And at
the last, old age falls as his lot, unmingled, uncompanioned, un-
friended, where all of evil's evils share his house. (*Oedipus Co-
loneus* 1224–35)

After his discussion of the soul's susceptibility to disease,
Lucretius attempts to prove its mortality by showing that it is

divisible. This section of the book, as the argument demands, dwells on mutilation, which we shall discuss in Chapter Six. The image of the soul's dissolution into air returns, but it too is pervaded by the violence that marks this portion of the argument.

Although the soul "flows away like smoke" (*emanarit uti fumus diffusa*, 583) or "slips forth outside" to "swim off into the winds of air" (*prolapsa foras enaret in aeris auras*, 591), it first undergoes a violent partition and rending, conveyed by the verbs *dispertitam* and *distractam* ("divided," "pulled apart," 589–90), in a body that itself suffers terrible violence, decay, and putrefactive odors (581–87). Lucretius is proving the mortality of the soul through its dispersion and alteration in the body in the process of dying (cf. also *animai diffugiant partes*, "the parts of the soul scatter through all the pores of the body," 254–55). The description of this process, however, does nothing to alleviate the horror of the physical sufferings that death may bring in its train. The soul suffers a "cutting" or "splitting apart" (*discidium*, 581), and the body is afflicted with the foul odors of decay (*in taetro tabescat odore*, 581) and a putrefactive alteration that brings with it total collapse (*tanta mutatum putre ruina / concideret corpus*, "the body changed with so great ruin falls crumbling," 584–85). The notion of "cutting" (*discidium*) recurs some eighty lines later in a more vivid verbal form, the deliberate chopping up of a snake (*discidere ferro*, 659)—perhaps the first instance of animal vivisection in Latin literature.

The emphasis on the mortal decay in this passage (580–88) builds up from the preceding description of the gradualness of the soul's departure from the body (526ff.). Here too the soul goes off gently, like smoke, "scattered through the winds" (*dispersa per auras*, 544). Yet that mild quietus has a far harsher counterpart in the images of the fragmented body in 527–30, the "splitting" of the soul in 531 (*scinditur*; cf. *discidium*, 581), and its torn or mangled state as it is "scattered outside" (*dilaniata foras dispergitur*, 539).

In this part of Lucretius's argument, the gradualness with which "chill death" spreads throughout the body is the evidence for the mortality of the soul, for what is thus changeable and divisible must be mortal (528–30):

> in pedibus primum digitos livescere et unguis,
> inde pedes et crura mori, post inde per artus
> ire alios tractim gelidi vestigia leti.

(First the toes and nail on the feet grow purple, then the feet and legs die, and then through the other limbs go gradually the tracks of cold doom.)

In the discoloration of the extremities and the actual "dying" of the "legs and feet," the victim dies synecdochically, limb by limb. The limbs die, but death itself marches on, leaving its "tracks" over the defeated body: *gelidi vestigia leti. Letum,* far from being the *secura quies* of natural physical "process" (211), is here a quasi-animate being whose "steps" are impressed on the immobilized, moribund limbs of the dying man, from the toes up, as it "gradually" (*tractim*) tramples him down.[12] Death's gradual progression along the limbs is a graphic feature of the process of dying that Lucretius repeats in his account of the plague (6.1190–92):

> in manibus vero nervi trahere et tremere artus
> a pedibusque minutatim succedere frigus
> non dubitabat.

(The sinews in the hands did not cease to pull, nor the limbs to tremble, nor the cold to advance bit by bit up from the feet.)

For all of Lucretius's avowed concern with dispelling the fears about death, this passsage (528–30) is one of the most vivid descriptions in Latin literature of its relentless progression.

Here too Lucretius's poetry of science manages to assimilate the affective qualities of the literary tradition. The deathbed

---

[12] *Tractim,* from *tractus,* "a drawing" or "pulling," means literally "in a long drawn-out manner" (*Oxford Latin Dictionary*). Lucretius uses this adverb one other time, to describe how clouds scrape against one another to produce thunder (6.118–20). We may compare Plautus, *Amphitruo* 313: *ego illum tractim tangam, ut dormiat.* We may perhaps wonder if the connotation of prolonged tactile contact is relevant to the *tractim* of 3.530.

scene is a recurrent motif in the literary representation of death (a fact that only demonstrates its continuing power to affect readers and hearers). Again, Lucretius probably draws on what must have been common experience among his readers, who, in a time before hospitals or nursing homes, would have watched over a dying person and discussed among themselves his or her last moments. Homer's Andromache regrets that Hector did not "dying reach forth his hands from the bed nor speak some firm word that I would remember in my nights and days as I pour forth my tears" (*Iliad* 24.743–45). Nearly a thousand years later, Tacitus, describing the end of his father-in-law, regrets that he could not "be present in the illness, embrace the failing man, be sated with his face and look," for, he goes on, "we would surely have received injunctions and words to fix deep within our mind" (*Agricola* 45.4). We may also recall scenes from Greek drama, like Admetus's farewell to his wife in *Alcestis* or the finale of the *Hippolytus*. Even if we allow for literary stylization, such scenes must have been an important part of the experience of death and must have been deeply imprinted on the survivors' memories.[13]

Later in the book, Lucretius describes *letum* as part of the atomic process of dissolution. Death is a disturbance of the soul-atoms only somewhat greater than that which occurs in sleep (928–30):

> maior enim turba et disiectus materiai
> consequitur leto nec quisquam expergitus exstat,
> frigida quem semel est vitai pausa secuta.

(For a greater disturbance and scattering of our matter follows with death, nor does anyone awaken and rise up whom once the cold cessation of life has pursued.)[14]

As we have noted earlier, the end of this passage shifts back from the impersonal account of the atomic *materia* to a per-

[13] For the importance of the final words of the dying person in Greek views of death, see Garland, *Greek Experience*, 20.

[14] With Kenney, *Lucretius III*, ad 3.928, I prefer Goebel's emendation, *turba et disiectus*, to the more difficult reading of O and Q, *turbae disiectus*, retained by Bailey, *T. Lucreti Cari*, ad loc.

sonal subject: *ne quisquam expergitus exstat* (929). The consolation of the ease of death once more is informed by a realistic sense of its finality; and the adjective *frigida* in the next line, recalling *gelidus*, epithet of *letum* in 530, does nothing to soften the mood. Indeed, even this attempt to present death at its gentlest recalls more (literally) chilling lines like 401: *et gelidos artus in leti frigore linquit* ("leaves the frozen limbs in the cold of doom").[15]

When Lucretius creates a personal dialogue with the individual who fears death, he reverses his earlier procedure and goes from the second-person singular of *iam iam non domus accipiet te laeta* ("now, now the joyful home will not receive you," 894) to the third-person plural, *non addunt* (901; also 902), and then to his moralizing psychology: men, if possessed of the proper vision, would "free themselves from great anxiety and fear of mind" (*dissoluant animi magno se angore metuque*, 903). The foolish man's misguided involvement with the deceased is expressed through the interplay of "you" and "we" as he (illogically) contrasts his eternal grief with the insensibility of the departed (3.904–8):

> "tu quidem ut es leto sopitus, sic eris aevi
> quod superest cunctis privatu' doloribus aegris.
> at nos horrifico cinefactum te prope busto
> insatiabiliter deflevimus, aeternumque
> nulla dies nobis maerorem e pectore demet."

("But you, just as you are asleep in death, so for whatever time remains will you be removed from all woeful pain. But we, near you burned to ashes on your fearful tomb, have wept over you insatiably, and no day will ever remove from our breast the mourning eternal.")

The deluded speaker groups victim and survivor together in a single tableau, unified by the personal pronouns, "we" and

---

[15] The relative paucity of epithets for *letum*, stressed by Michels, "Death," 161–62, is counterbalanced by their intensity. The evidence does not support her contention that Lucretius's phraseology "does not betray . . . any suppressed fear of death for himself" (p. 163). Arguments about what Lucretius "himself" may or may not have feared, however, are notoriously slippery.

"you," and by the common spatial relationship implicit in the preposition "near" (*prope*). By the juxtaposition of "made ashes" and "you" (*cinefactum te*) and the double concentric envelopment of *cinefactum te* by *horrifico . . . busto* and in turn by *nos . . . deflevimus*, he interjects himself into the imagined "horrors" of death and burial. The imagined scene creates a spatial, and thus an emotional, relationship with the dead; but this very excess of closeness is false to the reality of death.

Lucretius answers this cloying overpersonalization of death with dry logic (*igitur*), an impersonal gerundive construction, a series of neuter pronouns (*illud, hoc,* and *quid*), and the generalizing *res* (909–11):

> illud ab hoc igitur quaerendum est, quid sit amari
> tanto opere, ad somnum si res redit atque quietem,
> cur quisquam aeterno possit tabescere luctu.

(But from this man one must then ask this question: what is so bitter if the matter returns to sleep and rest, as a reason for why anyone should waste away in grief eternal.)

The "eternal" weeping and grief for the first- and second-person subjects in 906–8 is now answered by a general, non-personal, philosophical inquiry that calls such "eternal lamentation" deeply into question (*cur . . . possit*, 911). The intensely personal fact of grieving in 907, *insatiabiliter deflevimus* ("we wept insatiably"), has now become the modal form, *possit tabescere* ("why anyone should waste away"), in an indirect question; and the "we/you" construction of these lines has changed emphatically to *quisquam*, "anyone." In these shifts between the personal and the general Lucretius simultaneously recognizes the intensity of such emotions and treats them, therapeutically, with a healing distance.

The foolish man of 904, like the reader throughout the poem, is addressed here in the second-person singular, as *tu*. Like the personalized reader, he is being shown, indirectly, that he holds the remedy to his fear within his hands, for *leto sopitus*, "asleep in death," is in fact the key to the tranquillity

that the wise man experiences in the face of death. Even
Homer became quiet with the "same sleep" as all other mor-
tals (*eadem aliis sopitu' quietest*, 1038). The "sleep of death"
for the fool (*leto sopitus*, 904) is the "sleep of peace" for the
wise (1038). Just this failure to grasp *quies* gives the fool his
proper epithet: *cur non* ... / *aequo animo capis, securam,
stulte, quietem* ("Fool, why with calm spirit do you not take
up a rest that is free of care," 938–39).

  As Epicureans, we should be just as calm in the face of
death's *secura quies* as were the founders of the philosophy
(1041–42): Democritus "of his own accord placed his head in
the way of death; Epicurus himself met death when he had
traversed the course of his life's light" (*sponte sua leto caput
obvius obtulit ipse. / ipse Epicurus obit decurso lumine vitae*).
As mortals subject to dread and anxiety, however, we cannot
hide the terror that death provokes in us, even in the midst of
the poet's exhortations not to be afraid (1076–79):

> denique tanto opere in dubiis trepidare periclis
> quae mala nos subigit vitai tanta cupido?
> certa quidem finis vitae mortalibus adstat
> nec devitari letum pote quin obeamus.

(Finally, what evil desire for life drives us on so to tremble
amidst these uncertain dangers? A fixed limit of life stands over
mortals, nor is it possible to avoid the doom that we must meet.)

Our desire for continued life may be folly, but the "end" still
"stands over" us with vivid power. *Adstat* here in 1078 takes
up the even more vivid description of death standing by our
very head in 959 (*nec opinanti mors ad caput adstitit*) and the
dead man imagining that he stands beside his own body in 883
(*adstans*). Again the language shifts from the generic *mortali-
bus* in 1078 to the personal *obeamus* in 1079. For all the in-
tellectually accepted inevitability of death, the "we" of this
verse cannot help but view it in negative terms (*nec quin*). In
the double negatives of this verse (1079), Lucretius acknowl-
edges the reluctance that "we" feel in the face of what we can-
not avoid—a reluctance that separates "us" ordinary mortals

from the sages who willingly "go to meet" what "we" shun (compare *quin ob-eamus* with *ob-vius ob-tulit ipse*, 1079 and 1041).

Lucretius's account of the mortal soul has taken us from the objective "facts" of Epicurean physics through the mythical Hades of the poets. The scientific arguments that constitute the hard core of proof threaten, at times, to overwhelm the reader with their abstraction, detail, and complexity. But a thread, slender at times, of personal concern offers encouragement and even a kind of consolation. Nature's voice is demanding and remote; but it is at least a personal voice addressing us the readers as individuals and persons, not just agglomerations of atoms. And even Nature has an occasional light touch. She is a scold, but her voice of reason, good sense, and limit becomes introjected as our own, at least "sometimes" (1024).

The last word in the book belongs to "eternal death," whose outlook over the infinite centuries of non-being ahead might seem to offer cold comfort (1090–94). Yet the lines immediately preceding are another address to "us," in the first person, opposing the torment of infinite desire of life to the infinity of time after our death: "Nor by stretching out life can we take away a jot of death's time, nor can we take away anything from being less long dead" (1087–89). The Epicurean notion of limits sounds the voice of reason and sensible resignation, if not of hope, amid these infinite spaces.

The message is not only a personal one; it is also reduced to the manageable compass of our tangible physical needs (3.1083–84):

> post aliud, cum contigit illud, avemus
> et sitis aequa tenet vitai semper hiantis.

(And when [that desire] is obtained, we want something else afterwards, and the same thirst for life always holds us open-mouthed.)

We recognize that, in our foolish desire for ever more life, we are indeed like Tantalus or the Danaids (980–81). Rebuked, we return gratefully to the limits of our mortal being and, as Nature suggests, surrender that infinite progression of "months" and "years" that belongs neither to mortal time nor to us but to "the time of death" and to "Death eternal" (1088, 1091).

Chapter Four

NOTHINGNESS AND ETERNITY: THE FEAR
OF THE INFINITE

FEAR AND THE SUBLIME

For Plutarch, as we observed in Chapter One, the fear of death is closely associated with the fear of the infinite. Epicurus, he argues, does not really dispel our fear of death as the limitless abyss, a fall into a bottomless "ocean of non-being." For modern man, as for ancient man, the infinite is potentially a source of terror. Lucretius, however, does not seem to share modern man's fear of nothingness, the sensation of anxiety in contemplating the void of limitless space.[1] "Je vois ces effroyables espaces de l'univers qui m'enferment," wrote Pascal in a famous passage. "Le silence éternel de ces espaces infinis m'effraie."[2]

Epicurean science, like Copernican astronomy, displaces man from the center of the universe where Plato and Aristotle had placed him. But Epicurean rationalism uses this displacement in a way very different from Pascal and in a far more optimistic spirit. In another famous passage, for example, Pascal draws from the theory of an infinite universe the conclusion that man is helpless and lost before a secret that he can never penetrate, engulfed by the unknown: "The end of things and their beginnings are for [man] invisibly hidden in an impenetrable secret." Man is equally incapable of seeing "the nothingness from which he is drawn and the infinite where he is swallowed (*englouti*)."[3]

---

[1] On this point, see Lortie, "Crainte anxieuse," 60, who cites the passages from Pascal's *Pensées*.

[2] Pascal, *Pensées*, no. 201.

[3] Ibid., no. 199.

Epicurus's (and Lucretius's) view of infinity, however, is intended to counter just this sense of helplessness. For Lucretius, man's terrors lie not in nothingness and meaninglessness—the nightmares of modern man—but in the coercive power of an external force, in this case control by arbitrary, anthropomorphic gods. Indeed, Lucretius can make good therapeutic use of the majestic vistas into the infinite reaches of the universe that Epicurean science has achieved. Here, with Homer behind him, he can draw upon the epic grandeur of the high style, the poetry of the sublime;[4] and his use of the infinite tends toward the sublime rather than the sentimental. He has little in common with, say, Leopardi's infinite, the sweet lostness and submersion of self in nature:

> Così tra questa
> immensità s'annega il pensier mio:
> e il naufragar m'è dolce in questo mare.[5]

When Lucretius contemplates the vastness of the night sky, it is not so much its infinity that arouses anxiety as the ignorance of the celestial movements. That ignorance, to be sure, includes not knowing the sky's limits (*ecquae sit finis*, 5.1213) or its power to survive in "the eternal stretch of measureless time" (*perpetuo tractu . . . immensi aevi*, 5.1216–17).[6] But these anxieties relate more to the fear of the gods than to the fear of infinity *per se*: the grandeur of infinite space can make our mind contract in fear (*cui non animus formidine divum / contrahitur*, 5.1218–19).[7] In contrast to the terrors that the ignorant man feels about the unlimited in space and time, however, stands the Master's mental exploration of the "mea-

---

[4] For the sublime style in Lucretius, see Conte, "*Hypsos*," esp. 361–62, 365–67. *Sublimis* is Ovid's epithet for Lucretius in *Amores* 1.15.23.

[5] Leopardi, "L'infinito," conclusion ("Thus in the midst of this immensity my thought drowns, and in this sea to be shipwrecked is sweet to me").

[6] The notion of an infinite time of punishments or sufferings after death, however, is a source of anxiety that the philosopher must strive to remove (5.1020ff.).

[7] See in general 5.1204–21, esp. *deum immensa potestas*, 1209; *divinitus aeterna donata salute*, 1215. It is interesting that 1.1004, in the context of infinite space, is repeated in 5.1216, on the fear of the gods.

sureless universe" (1.72–74: *atque omne immensum pera-
gravit mente animoque*, 1.74).[8] Epicurus's own intellectual
quest offers the proper model for overcoming our anxiety
when we contemplate the infinity of space.

Infinite space, combined with an infinite supply of matter, is
basic to Epicurean physics, and Lucretius closely follows the
outline of the Master's thought in presenting these principles
at the end of book 1 (958ff.; cf. Epicurus, *To Herodotus*, D.L.
10.41–42). Infinity nevertheless is a tempting subject for a
poet, and Lucretius responds to it with an expansiveness of
style very different from the compact dryness of his teacher.

He introduces the subject immediately after the intense, per-
sonal statement of his own vocation and achievement as a
poet, the so-called Second Proem (1.921–50). The bridge pas-
sage to the discussion of infinity begins with an assertion of
the "invincible flight" of the indestructible atoms eternally
through time (*solidissima corpora / perpetuo volitare invicta
per aevum*, 1.951–52) and ends with a tribute to the power of
this measureless expanse and vast depth of infinite void (*im-
mensum pateat vasteque profundum*, 1.957). Lucretius con-
veys his feeling for the majesty of infinite space through a
grandiose negative comparison (1.1002–5):

> est igitur natura loci spatiumque profundi,
> quod neque clara suo percurrere fulmina cursu
> perpetuo possint aevi labentia tractu
> nec prorsum facere ut restet minus ire meando.

(The nature of space and the space of the deep is something that
the bright lightnings could not traverse in their course as they
glide through the eternal reaches of time, nor could they bring it
about that [in their movements] there remains less [space] for
traversing.)

The swift movement of celestial fires across vast distances be-
longs to the sublime style, and this continues as Lucretius ex-

[8] On the stylistic elevation of the passage, see Conte, "*Hypsos*," 355–57.
Cf. also 2.1046ff. On the vastness of Epicurus's vision and the importance of
infinity in the poem as a stimulus to thought and inspiration, see Michels, 165.

plores the alternative possibilities of either infinite space and limited matter or finite space and infinite matter (1.1014ff.). Neither combination can sustain the continuing life of an infinite universe. The argument for the infinity of both space and matter, therefore, is drawn into the poem's recurrent dynamic of life battling death. The infinite multiplicity of atomic combinations elicits again the sublime style (1.1031–34):

> efficit ut largis avidum mare fluminis undis
> integrent amnes et solis terra vapore
> fota novet fetus summissaque gens animantum
> floreat et vivant labentes aetheris ignes.

([The universe] brings it about that the streams renew the greedy sea with river's broad waves and the earth warmed by the sun's heat makes new its offspring, and the race of living beings, sent forth from below, flourishes, and the gliding fires of the heavens have life.)

The effect approximates what Kant termed the "mathematical sublime," the overpowering impression of magnitude, that Lucretius conveys through the alliteration of "many modes and mutations" in 1024 (*multa modis multis mutata per omne*) as well as through the enumeration here of the manifestations of creative energy in sea, earth, and sky.

Infinite space, like infinite time, has a more menacing face, however, and we encounter this at the end of the book, as Lucretius combats the view that air and fire move continually upward and outward. In that case, he argues, the entire universe would collapse "through the empty void" so that nothing would be left of our world "except empty space" and disjoined atoms (1.1102–10). Despite some problems of text and interpretation, it is clear that this vision of infinity is one of fearful chaos, closely associated with death, for "in whatever part [of things] you establish the lack of matter, this part will be the gate of death for the world, and here all the crowd of matter will issue forth" (1.1111–13). One could perhaps gloss this passage by Longinus's comment on the battle among the gods in the *Iliad* (*On the Sublime* 9.6): "Do you not see, my

friend, how, when the earth is torn asunder from its founda-
tions and Tartarus itself is laid bare and the entire cosmos is
overturned and cracks apart, how then everything all to-
gether—the heavens, Hades, things mortal and immortal—
fight with one another in that battle and join in the danger?"
Indeed, Lucretius's lines, like those of Homer here, exemplify
that quality of "the terrible" τὸ φοβερόν, τὸ δεινόν that Lon-
ginus regards as essential to the sublime, or what Kant called
"the terrifying sublime."[9]

Infinity is sublime, and for that reason terrifying; we need
Epicurus's guidance to remain free of fear. Lucretius's aim—
in contrast to the aims of the sublime style—is ultimately to
allay, not arouse, fear; and to counter the bleak picture he has
painted, he ends with the illumination of knowledge, to which
his own modest work (*parva opella*) leads, bringing light to
these dark places, "so that blinding night cannot snatch away
your journey [and prevent you] from seeing through to the
limits of nature: thus one thing kindles light for other things"
(1.1114–17):

> haec sic pernosces parva perductus opella;
> namque alid ex alio clarescet nec tibi caeca
> nox iter eripiet quin ultima naturai
> pervideas: ita res accendent lumina rebus.

This journey to enlightenment recalls Epicurus's journey to
the flaming limits of the world at the beginning of the book
(1.72ff.) and reminds us that we too are making an analogous
journey, but with the benefit of a great predecessor.

Lucretius returns to this point at the beginning of book 3.
This opens with Epicurus raising life up from darkness, and
continues with him dispelling the "mind's terrors" as the
"walls of the world yield" and the poet sees the endless swirl
of atoms in the void (3.16–17). This vision, however, is not of
infinite night, chaos, and universal destruction but of the

---

[9] Immanuel Kant, *Observations on the Feeling of the Beautiful and the Sub-
lime*, trans. J. T. Goldthwait (Berkeley and Los Angeles, 1960), sec. 1. Kant
describes this sublime as "accompanied with a certain dread or melancholy"
(pp. 47–48).

peaceful abode of the gods, bathed in liquid radiance, serenity, and creativity. In this free, expansive view into infinite space Lucretius shares something of what Epicurus might have felt on mankind's momentous first journey to the world's fiery walls. The combination of a "certain divine pleasure and shuddering fear" that "seizes" the poet as he beholds what has been laid bare by the "force" of Epicurus (*quaedam divina voluptas percipit / atque horror*, 3.28–29) is the fear that we mortals experience in the presence of the numinous; it is also a reasonable account of the sublime style, as described by Longinus.

This vision gives no ordinary human pleasure. It is not circumscribed by the aesthetic. It is "divine pleasure," accompanied by a "shudder" as much of fear as of joy. Its power lies not only in the positive "uncovering" of nature "in every part" (3.28) but also in the negative vision, as it were, the absence of obstruction, so that the poet's feet seem suspended over the vast nothingness of void thus opened beneath him (3.26–27):

> nec tellus obstat quin omnia dispiciantur,
> sub pedibus quaecumque infra per inane geruntur.

(Nor does the earth stand as an obstacle against everything being discerned, whatever goes on below through the void, beneath my feet.)

Epicurus's "force," to which Lucretius here owes the vision (*tua vi*, 29), could reach the flaming edges of the world and leave superstition crushed beneath his feet (1.72–79; *pedibus subiecta*, 1.79). Lucretius describes that journey of Epicurus from the outside, as it were, in terms of its achievement and results. The only subjective feature is the active will to succeed, when he "dared to raise his eyes and take his stand" against superstition and desired to break through nature's barriers (1.64–71). Speaking of himself, however, Lucretius dwells on his subjective responses, in the first person. He is a passive recipient, "seized" by the emotional force of the "pleasure" and the "shudder."

Infinite space and matter evoke grandeur and inexhaustible creative energy, whose awesome or fearful side is held under control by knowledge and serene pleasure (3.26–27). Infinite time is more frightening. Epicurus, we recall, specifically addressed this area of anxiety in his *Letter to Menoeceus*, urging us to think in terms of the time we have in this life and not the limitless time beyond us. The acceptance of the limit on desire, essential to happiness in Epicurean ethics, depends on relinquishing infinite time. Lucretius deals straightforwardly enough with the time before our birth and extends the point by analogy to the time after our death: neither can be a concern to us once our consciousness has departed with the soul's separation from the body (3.830–46).[10] At the end of the book, however, though he is making the same point, he shifts his perspective from the human subject to the power of death itself (3.1087–94):

> By extending our life we take not a jot away from the time of death (*tempore de mortis*) to prevent us from being any less long dead. Go on storing up as many ages as you like: eternal death will remain waiting nonetheless. Nor will he who has made an end of his life from today's light of day (*ex hodierno lumine*) be any less long dead than he who died many months and years ago.

The admonitory tone here, as elsewhere, may draw on the shock effect of the diatribe: death is in command, forever.[11] The departure "from today's light" is dwarfed, intentionally, by the vast shadow of death stretching infinitely before us. We know, of course, that this is the darkness from which Epicurus has lifted us, in the book's opening: "O you who were able to lift so bright a light forth from the shadows, illuminating the goods of life" (3.1–2, reading *e tenebris*).[12] But the stark clo-

---

[10] For a discussion of this passage and its implications, see Furley, "Nothing to Us?" and Nussbaum, "Mortal Immortals."

[11] See Wallach, *Lucretius and the Diatribe*, 102ff.

[12] The mss. evidence for the reading of 3.1 is ambiguous: Oblongus reads *o*, kept by Kenney, *Lucretius III*, ad loc.; Quadratus omits the word, which Bailey, *T. Lucreti Cari*, ad loc., takes to be evidence for a rubric initial, to be added later, which, with the Italian mss., he takes to *e*, the reading also fa-

sure seems to recognize the terrors inherent in the prospect of a hereafter without a clear "boundary of sufferings" or "limit of punishments" (*terminus malorum, poenarum finis*).

The antidote to such fear, for Lucretius as for Epicurus, is limit. We can thereby turn away from the irrational hopes or fears held out by the unlimited, whether this is the empty abyss of time (3.1086ff.) or the torment of "eternal pain" (3.990) or eternal desire (3.1003ff.). The ordinary mortal fears the unlimited that can "disrupt all the fortunes of his life" if he sees no "certain end to woes" (*certam finem . . . aerumnarum*, 1.104–9). Lucretius gives this warning to Memmius, but he has already provided the antidote in Epicurus's victorious vision of the "flaming walls of the world" and his reassuring knowledge of the "deep-set boundary stone" (*alte terminus haerens*, 1.77; cf. 2.1087), the fruit of Epicurus's heroic journey in 1.74–77. One who has been "defeated" (*victus*, 1.102) by the false myths of the poet, as Epicurus *victor* was not (1.75, 79), is unable to stand up against the fears inspired by religious superstition and the poets who perpetuate them (1.106–7).

The anxieties aroused by contemplating eternal time in connection with death appear first in an indirect or "displaced" form, namely in the eternal grief of the mourning survivor. The quality of eternity here belongs to the emotions of the living rather than to the suffering or nullity of the deceased himself. Using the vivid technique of dialogue form, Lucretius lets the mourner address the deceased (3.904–11):

> "tu quidem ut es leto sopitus, sic eris aevi
> quod superest cunctis privatu' doloribus aegris.
> at nos horrifico cinefactum te prope busto
> insatiabiliter deflevimus aeternumque
> nulla dies nobis maerorem e pectore demet."
> illud ab hoc igitur quaerendum est, quid sit amari
> tanto opere, ad somnum si res redit atque quietem,
> cur quisquam aeterno possit tabescere luctu.

---

vored by the majority of editors. The reading *e* seems to me preferable for the sense and more in accordance with Lucretian usage but is not crucial to my point.

("Just as you are put to sleep in death, so will you be for all of
time that remains freed of grievous pains. But we have wept over
you insatiably nearby when you were cremated at the fearful
tomb, and no day will take the eternal sadness from our breast."
But from this man we must ask this too, what so great bitterness
is it, if things return to sleep and peace, [as a reason] why any
one should waste away in eternal mourning.)

The mourner experiences the dead man's eternity as a kind of
sleep in which he will be free of life's pains "for all of time that
remains" (904–5). His own "eternity," in contrast, is only of
tears and grief (*aeternumque . . . maerorem*, 907–8). The poet
replies by returning to the image of "sleep," but now as a
source of the "calm" (*quies*) that cancels out the "eternity" of
wasting grief (*somnum . . . atque quietem . . . aeterno . . . ta-
bescere luctu*, 910–11).[13] He again harks back to the motif of
quies that he had introduced in the proem of book 3 as a sign
of the eternal blessedness of the gods (*sedesque quietae*, 18).
The verbal echo helps us to recall this *quies* as the foil to the
eternal misery of the benighted speaker and as the proper
model for a happier attitude toward life and death (cf. 211,
939, 977).

Within the present context, the mourner's own words hold
the secret of his release from needless suffering. If he properly
understood what it means to be "laid to sleep in death," *leto
sopitus*, he would cast off his anxiety about the hereafter and
recognize that in fact death offers a "greater freedom from
anxiety" than does sleep (cf. *leto sopitus* in 904 with *somno
securius* in 977). The irrational anxiety of the eternal "sleep of
death" is thus transformed into the philosophical truth of the
freedom from suffering and care that death, properly seen,
may offer us (977). Lucretius reinforces this point with a rhe-

---

[13] *Tabescere* here, though conventional (cf. Greek τήκειν, "to melt," often
used in the same sense), sounds a grim note. In other contexts also, sleep is
not necessarily so reassuring: describing the scattering of the soul atoms in
sleep in 4.916–24, Lucretius warns us that only a part of the soul can be so
disturbed and scattered; otherwise "the body would lie there drenched with
the eternal cold of doom" (*namque iaceret / aeterno corpus perfusum frigore
leti*, 4.923–24).

torical question about the time before our birth: *numquid ibi horribile apparet, num triste videtur / quicquam*? ("Does anything fearful appear there, anything grim?" 976–77).[14] As a "mirror" of the time to come, our oblivion before birth should banish any residual "shudders" or "grimness" when we contemplate infinite time. Near the end of the book, Lucretius cites Homer as a specific instance of one who "was put to sleep in calm rest" (*sopitu' quietest*, 1038; cf. *secura quies* in 211 and 939).

THE LOSS OF CONSCIOUSNESS

The threatening vacuity and immensity of death in the paean to the power of *mors aeterna* at the end of book 3 appear in another, more specifically physical form in the book's recurrent descriptions of the loss of consciousness because of age or illness. Each of these moments of weakness is a form of death, either directly, as part of the process of the soul's separation from the body, or indirectly, in accordance with Epicurean psychology. As Lucretius tells us repeatedly, a slightly greater disturbance of the soul-atoms will in fact bring death (3.252–55 and 485–86; cf. 5.345–47). Sleep, he reminds us, is only a stage removed from chill death (4.916–24); and, as we have noted earlier, sleep is a comforting model for death in its serene, untroubling aspect in book 3 (910–11, 977).

The several descriptions of fainting and related phenomena within book 3 have the explicit function of proving the soul's susceptibility to disease and to dissolution into its component atoms; therefore these are among the most important proofs of the soul's mortality. The bodily changes accompanying the loss of consciousness, however, give indirect expression to some of the fears of death as a massive attack on our physical being. In particular, by associating death with the sensation of drowning or sinking into a sea of darkness, Lucretius depicts some of the anxieties that Plutarch singled out in his criticisms

[14] For this argument in a contemporary philosophical context, see Furley, "Nothing to Us?"

of Epicurus, and he presents them vividly: the loss of control, the dissolution of identity, the entrance into a mysterious zone or substance that is ominously black or engulfing.

Fear belongs to the illnesses of the soul. When the mind has been disturbed by a violent fright, powerful symptoms occur (3.152–58): sweating, pallor, ringing in the ears, the darkening of the eyes, and finally total collapse: *denique concidere ex animi terrore videmus / saepe homines* ("we often see men fall as a result of the terror in their mind," 3.157–58). Here too the description progresses from the almost clinical account of the separate parts of the body to the spectacle (*videmus*) of watching men drop in terror. With the addition of a few details and adjectives of color, like *rubentis* and *atrae* ("reddening," "black"), and a slight increase of verbal over nominal constructions, we would not be far from the first symptoms of the plague of Athens in book 6. We may compare 3.152–56 and 6.1145–50:

> verum ubi vementi magis est commota metu mens,
> consentire animam totam per membra videmus
> sudoresque ita palloremque exsistere toto
> corpore et infringi linguam vocemque aboriri,
> caligare oculos, sonere auris, succidere artus.

(But when the mind is more disturbed by a violent fear, we see the entire soul share in this sensation throughout the limbs and thus [see] sweating and paleness come over the entire body; [we see] the tongue broken and the eyes become darkened, the ears ring, the limbs collapse.) (3.152–56)

> principio caput incensum fervore gerebant
> et duplices oculos suffusa luce rubentis.
> sudabant etiam fauces intrinsecus atrae
> sanguine et ulceribus vocis via saepta coibat
> atque animi interpres manabat lingua cruore
> debilitata malis, motu gravis, aspera tactu.

(At first they bore their head heated with fever and both eyes reddened, with a glazed light poured over them. Their throat too sweated inside dark with blood, and the path of their voice was constricted, closed off by sores, and the tongue, speaker for the mind, flowed with blood, weakened by suffering, heavy in movement, rough to the touch.)   (6.1145–50)

The description of the collapse in 3.152–58, however, points in a direction quite different from the clinical symptoms of book 6. These lines are surely a conscious reminiscence of Sappho's famous poem on the power of love (31 Lobel-Page), imitated also by Lucretius's contemporary, Catullus (poem 51).[15] Why does Lucretius here refer to a lyric poem famous for its intensity in conveying the devastating physical effects of passion? I would suggest that Lucretius is making a deliberate attempt to evoke the atmosphere of vehement personal emotion, transferred from love to death. He thereby reminds us, indirectly, of the overpowering feelings that death, like love, excites in most men and women—only to check this (for him) misplaced intensity with the knowledge of the impersonal atomic processes and the calm and reason attendant on such knowledge. The excited style of lyric poetry calls attention to individual feelings, through the sounds as well as the sense of the opening verse, with its strong alliteration: *verum ubi vementi magis est commota metu mens* ("but when the mind is more disturbed by violent fear," 3.152). Lucretius continues this style more directly in the Sapphic asyndeta and polysyndeta of 153–56. But the impersonal, objective style of

[15] Bailey, *T. Lucreti Cari*, ad 3.152–58, in contrast to Heinze, regards Lucretius's echo of Sappho as "most likely," but offers no suggestions about the reasons for such imitation. Sapphic influence is also maintained by Rudolf Stark, "Sapphoreminiszenzen," *Hermes* 85 (1957): 330. Kenney, *Lucretius III*, ad 154–56, is more hesitant. Lucretius has changed the order of the "symptoms" in Sappho (frag. 31 Lobel-Page), but the parallels are still impressive: *sudoresque palloremque existere toto / corpore* (154) and ἴδρως . . . τρόμος δὲ παῖσαν ἄγρει, χλωροτέρα δὲ ποίας (13–14), and cf. also *animam totam* and παῖσαν ἄγρει (14); *infringi linguam vocemque aboriri* (155) and γλῶσσα †ἔαγε† (9) along with φώναισ' οὐδ' ἐν ἔτ' εἴκει (7–8); *caligare oculos, sonere auris, succidere artus* (156) and ὀππάτεσσι δ' οὐδ' ἐν ὄρημμ', ἐπιρρόμ-/βεισι δ' ἄκουαι (11–12). The rapid accumulation of physical details in 154–56 may also be due to Sappho and is the quality for which "Longinus" quotes the poem (*De Sublimitate* 10.3). Catullus's imitation of the poem around the same time (poem 51) also makes Lucretius's use of it here all the more likely.

didactic hexameter poetry reclaims this phenomenon for reason in the shift back to the prosaic statement of intellectual recognition in 158, *facile ut quivis hic noscere possit* ("so that anyone at all can recognize this").

The clash of styles and genres in this passage—lyric and didactic, emotional intensity and philosophical argumentation—creates another field upon which Lucretius can project his struggle against the powerful anxieties that death carries with it. Through the intertextual echo, he carries the battle against the fear of death into its own ground, the ground of intense, overpowering emotion. He may be also reminding us of the related and equally harmful irrationality of erotic passion. The evocation of Sappho is a sophisticated, indeed Alexandrian, mode of recognizing the emotional energy that those anxieties mobilize in us.[16]

After 152ff., there is a steady increase in the seriousness of the injury and the presentation of bodily suffering (cf. 341ff., 396ff., 450ff.). The next description of fainting, in fact, involves a mortal wound, a cut deep within (*intus*) bone and muscle, with a consequent collapse to the ground (170–74):

> si minus offendit vitam vis horrida teli
> ossibus ac nervis disclusis intus adacta,
> at tamen insequitur languor terraeque petitus
> suavis et in terra mentis qui gignitur aestus,
> interdumque quasi exsurgendi incerta voluntas.

(If a less fearful blow of a weapon, driven within, strikes the life, laying bare the bones and sinews, even so there follows a weakness and a sweet seeking of the earth and a dizziness of the mind that takes place on the ground and sometimes as it were an unsure will to get up.)

The transitional clause, *si minus offendit vitam vis horrida teli* ("if a less fearful blow of a weapon strikes against life"), links

---

[16] For Alexandrian techniques in Lucretius's poetry, see Kenney, "Doctus Lucretius," *passim*; also Walter Wimmel, *Kallimachos in Rom*, Hermes Einzelschrift 16 (Wiesbaden, 1960), 106 and 226–37; Robert J. Brown, "Lucretius and Callimachus," *Illinois Classical Studies* 7 (1982): 77–97; and J. K. Newman, *The Classical Epic Tradition* (Madison, Wis., 1986), 110ff.

this fainting closely with death; and the expression is the converse of that in 252–55 and 485 (if a greater blow should occur, death would result). *Mentis aestus* in 173 belongs to the imagery of the turbulent sea that Lucretius associates with cosmic dissolution and death in the shipwreck passage of 2.552–68.[17] He will repeat the image later, in the description of an epileptic attack (3.493–94). It is related also to the images of drowning that will be discussed below.

The troublesome detail of the "sweetness" in the stricken man's "seeking of the earth" (*terrae petitus suavis*, 172–73) need not imply any suicidal longing for death and oblivion in Lucretius's personal psychology, as Logre has suggested.[18] Rather, it marks the shift from the objective to the subjective dimension of the event that we have noted in other instances and will see again later (cf. the discussion of line 467, below). The small touch effectively conveys the weakened man's sensation of extreme shock, when the sickly-sweet "languor" leaves only the desire to collapse on the ground. The "unstable desire to get up" in the next verse continues this subjective portrayal of the action. The motif continues later in the harsher and more specific scene of mutilation in 651–52.

Such interruptions of sensation or motor control are important proofs of the mortality of the soul, demonstrations of the imperfections that an immortal substance would not have. Lucretius returns to this point from a somewhat different direction in 459ff. Here he is more general about the cause of the collapse; but this very generality allows for stronger and more painful ills, for both body and soul: hence the "vast illnesses and harsh pain" of 460 (*immanis morbos durumque dolorem*). Now the intelligence has lost its way and wanders (*avius errat*, 463), speaks nonsense (464), and sinks into a heavy coma as if into the deep sea (464–69):

> dementit enim deliraque fatur
> interdumque gravi lethargo fertur in altum
> aeternumque soporem oculis nutuque cadenti,

<hr/>

[17] On this sea imagery and death, see Anderson, "Discontinuity," 21–22.
[18] Logre, *L'anxiété*, 196–97.

unde neque exaudit voces nec noscere vultus
illorum potis est, ad vitam qui revocantes
circumstant lacrimis rorantes ora genasque.

(The mind wanders and makes delirious utterances and some-
times is borne by heavy sluggishness into deep and eternal sleep
with eyes and nod falling, nor can it hear the voices or recognize
the faces of those who stand around calling it back to life, be-
dewing their faces and cheeks with tears.)

The passive construction of *fertur in altum* . . . *soporem* asso-
ciates the loss of consciousness with drowning. *Cadenti* at the
end of the verse reinforces the sensation of a physical falling.
The details, quite superfluous to the argument, of the "nod
that falls," of "eternal sleep," and of the tear-stained cheeks of
those who stand around (and presumably above) the victim
add to the scene a pathos that the philosophical argument *per
se* does not require, nor is there any equivalent to this affective
depiction in the extant writings of Epicurus.[19] Catullus's "sin-
gle perpetual night of sleep" (*nox est perpetua una dormienda*,
5.6) may serve to remind us of the chilling note of "deep and
eternal sleep" here.

In 155–56 the voice was interrupted and the ears were ring-
ing. In 467–69 the focus shifts from the physical symptoms to
the subjective state of the injured person: he (or his mind)
"does not hear the voices and *is not able to know* the faces"
(*nec noscere vultus / illorum potis est*). The verb *noscere* helps
underline this concern with consciousness. The change from
the indicative *exaudit* to the modal *noscere . . . potis est* con-
tributes to the same effect and could even suggest the vain ef-
fort of the sufferer to return to his senses. These small touches

[19] Note too the vividness of the quasi-metaphorical *penetrant* in 3.471
(*penetrant in eum contagia morbi*), and cf. *penetravit* in 476. It is true that
the "deep and eternal sleep" of 466 is the coma and not death, as editors
suggest (both Bailey, *T. Lucreti Cari*, and Kenney, *Lucretius III*, ad loc.). But
everything in the context points to the unlikeliness that this afflicted man will
survive or awaken: cf. 472–73. On the pathos of the scene, see Perelli, *Lucre-
zio*, 45–46. On possible medical sources, see my "Lucretius, Epilepsy, and *On
Breaths*."

enhance the contrast between the waning consciousness of the enfeebled patient and the intense emotions of the weeping by-standers.

Here too Lucretius had only to add a few details to convert such a scene into a powerful depiction of the horror of death, such as occurs in book 6. There, just after describing the sharp attacks of the fear of death (*mortis metus his incesserat acer*) that led men even to amputate their genitals in order to stay alive, Lucretius lists accompanying symptoms, including amnesia (6.1212–14):

> usque adeo mortis metus his incesserat acer.
> atque etiam quosdam cepere oblivia rerum
> cunctarum, neque se possent cognoscere ut ipsi.

> (To such a degree had the sharp fear of death come upon them. And forgetfulness of all things seized some, so that they could not recognize even themselves.)

In this more drastic situation, the afflicted are unable to recognize not others, but themselves; the number is now plural rather than singular; and the surroundings contain not sympathetic onlookers, but only wider fields of death (*nec tristia saecla ferarum / exibant silvis*, "nor did the saddened generations of wild beasts go out of the forests," 6.1220–21; *incomitata rapi certabant funera vasta*, "desolate funerals, unaccompanied, struggled to be rushed off," 6.1225).

To return to book 3, the scene of 463–69 does not sentimentalize, and Lucretius pulls back at once to the inevitable conclusion in the next verse: *quare animum quoque dissolvi fateare necesse est* (470). He is more concerned with bringing "you," the reader, to "affirm" the atomic principle than with involving "you" in the scene of suffering. In contrast to the unconscious state of the sufferer, who cannot "recognize faces," we the hearers or readers are to be "instructed" about the universality of death. Not just this single scene of probable death (cf. *aeternum soporem*, 466), but "the destruction of men," on more than one occasion (*ante*), is our teacher (*multorum exitio perdocti quod sumus ante*, "something that we

have been thoroughly taught previously by the death of
many," 473, with a possibly significant change from the pow-
erful *letum* of 462 and 472 to the more neutral *exitium*).

The shift of perspective within this passage transforms the
static deathbed scene into a dramatic encounter. By taking ac-
count of what the dying man is himself no longer able to per-
ceive (*neque exaudit voces nec noscere vultus / illorum potis
est*, "nor can he hear their voices or recognize their faces,"
467–68), Lucretius gives him a certain existence as a sentient
subject, even though that subjectivity is ebbing. Beside him
and emotionally involved in his condition are "those (*illorum*)
who stand around" this moribund figure and tearfully "call
him back to life" (*illorum . . . ad vitam qui revocantes / cir-
cumstant*, 468–69). The poet visually takes in the two sets of
actors, the dying and the surviving, and gives the different suf-
fering on each side its due. The enjambed possessive genitive,
illorum, skillfully joins the two parties and syntactically ex-
presses the bond between them. The dying man cannot "rec-
ognize their faces" on the one hand, and on the other those
"faces" that he cannot see are covered with the tears shed over
his condition (*vultus . . . ora genasque*).

Lucretius's eye catches both parties in the essential postures
of their situation, almost as if the features become the sym-
bolic expression of a theatrical mask. The "faces" reveal the
gulf that imminent death already sets between them. On the
one side is a failing perception of "faces" (*nec noscere vultus*);
on the other side are "countenances and cheeks" bedewed
with tears (*rorantes ora genasque*). That gulf between the dy-
ing and the surviving is also expressed syntactically and mor-
phologically in the contrast of the negative infinitive, *nec nos-
cere vultus*, of the dying man and the active, first-conjugation
verbs (two of them participles) that describe the survivors (*re-
vocantes, circumstant, rorantes*, 467–68). The repeated sound
pattern of the resonant *-am*, *-an-*, and *-or* characterizes the
more open realm of "life" that the survivors still possess:

> ad vit*am* qui revoc*an*tes
> circumst*an*t lacrimis *ror*antes *or*a gen*a*sque.

In 591 the departing soul of the dying man "steps forth and swims off into the winds of air" (*prolapsa foras enaret in aeris auras*). The lines just preceding the great diatribe against the fear of death sound the clarion call of confident triumph, *nil igitur mors est ad nos*, dwelling on the soul's ills (and therefore its mortality); but they use a more threatening image for the departure from life (828–29):

> adde furorem animi proprium atque oblivia rerum,
> adde quod in nigras lethargi mergitur undas.

(Add the mind's own madness and its forgetfulness of things, add the fact that it is drowned in the dark waves of sluggishness.)

By the end of this section of the book, the sensation of "being carried into a deep eternal sleep by a heavy coma" in 465 has fully emerged into the metaphor of "drowning" in "black waves"—waves whose color is the color of death (cf. *mortis nigrore*, 3.39; cf. also the sea imagery of 3.493–94, of an epileptic attack).

Oblivia rerum recurs in book 6, just after the sharp attack of the "fear of death," as a culminating horror of the plague (*usque adeo mortis metus his incesserat acer. / atque etiam quosdam cepere oblivia rerum*, "To such a degree had the keen fear of death advanced upon them. And forgetfulness of all their circumstances also seized certain ones," 6.1212–13). If we examine lines 828–30 in their relation to similar descriptions in the poem as a whole, then, it seems as if Lucretius, at one level, conquers and dismisses the fear of death with the Epicurean *tetrapharmakon* (cf. 830). But, just at this point, at another level, he invokes one of death's most powerful and anxiety-producing effects through his imagery of darkness and drowning and through the repeated theme of the loss of consciousness (829–30).

Reading retrospectively may help us to appreciate the special force in these descriptions of the soul's "drowning," for in book 6, near the end of the account of the plague, death by suffocation appears in its full horror. Many bodies lie near the foundations, Lucretius says, "their life choked off by the excessive sweetness of the water" (interclusa anima nimia ab dulcedine aquarum, 6.1266).[20] Close at hand is death as a crowded, crammed enclosure: omnia complebant loca tectaque; quo magis aestu / confertos ita acervatim mors accumulabat ("they kept on filling up all the places and buildings, so that death kept on heaping them up all the more in piles, packed together in that heat," 1262–63).[21] But even within book 3 this image of the coma's "black waves" gains impact from the descriptions of the process of dying and losing consciousness in the earlier part of the book.

Epicurean doctrine, as Lucretius uses it, has the power to open these dark, occluded scenes to the vast spaces of the universe and the light of reason. The infinite may hold fear of a sort, but it is accompanied by the intense pleasure of new and wide knowledge, as we see in the proem of book 3. The result is the tonic energy and confidence in facing the world that Epicurus brought back from his victorious quest (1.72ff.). Fear of this sort is followed not by constriction and agitation, but by expansion, calm, and joy, as if one were to behold the abode of the gods (3.16–24).

This combination of expansive vision, calm but intense joy, and awe corresponds, on the level of poetic style, to the sublime. Lucretius fortifies us first with the sublime vision and then shows us the oppressive, soul-contracting anxiety that we are now prepared to meet. Hence his technique is to begin with radiant and confident proems and to move to dark, threatening book-endings. On a broader scale, he places the heroic journey of Epicurus early in the poem. The grandeur of

[20] With the dulcedine here, contrast the imagery of "sweetness" as the traditional quality of the goodness of life (e.g., dulcis vita, 2.997, 3.66, etc.) and its continuation in children (dulces nati, 3.895). With the destructive dulcedo here in 6.1266, cf. the tacita dulcedo of 3.896. I do not, however, agree with Logre, L'anxiété, 196–97, that suavis in 3.173 indicates a suicidal longing for death on Lucretius's part. On 6.1264ff., Perelli, Lucrezio, 121, remarks, "Solo la fantasia lucreziana poteva giungere a una così terrificante visione della degradazione umana, che anticipa l'orrore dei campi di sterminio nazisti."

[21] On the imagery of constriction in connection with death, see below, Chapter Seven. Cf. also the threatening image of the leti portas in 3.67.

infinite space and matter at the end of book 1 and at the beginning of book 3 precedes the menacing infinity of time at the end of book 3. The serenity of the individual philosopher's death at the end of book 3 precedes the mass death and collective panic in the poem's last scene. Even within the proem of book 3, the calming effect of the gods' home precedes the thrill of awe at the void beneath the poet's feet as nature's secrets stand fully revealed (3.16–24, 25–30). In order to achieve the effect, both poetic and philosophical, of expansion and release, however, Lucretius must also make us feel the narrowing anxieties about the body. It is to these that we now turn.

Chapter Five

THE WORLD'S BODY AND THE HUMAN
BODY: WALLS, BOUNDARIES, AND
MORTALITY

AMONG MOST OF THE PEOPLES of the world, as anthropologists like Mary Douglas and Susan Postal point out, the boundaries of the body receive the greatest symbolic elaboration, in clothing, masks, markings, rituals, and other expressive forms.[1] All societies and all individuals use such "defensive barriers," both literal and figurative; and the nature of these defenses is an important clue to the conceptual framework within which an individual or society operates in the world.[2] "The body," Mary Douglas observes, "is a model which can stand for any bounded system. Its boundaries can represent any boundaries which are threatened or precarious."[3] Given the interchangeability of microcosm and macrocosm in Epicurean physics, however, the converse of this statement also holds true. In the Lucretian universe, the stress at the boundaries of the world magnifies to cosmic proportions the stress upon our individual bodies.[4] In both cases, the outer perimeter is the vulnerable area.

Epicurus had insisted on infinite worlds and their dissolu-

---

[1] See Douglas, *Purity and Danger*, 114–28; Susan Postal, "Body Image and Identity: A Comparison of Kwakiutl and Hopi," *American Anthropologist* 67 (1965): 455–60, passim.

[2] See Seymour Fisher and Sidney Cleveland, *Body Image and Personality* (Princeton, 1968), 206.

[3] Douglas, *Purity and Danger*, 115.

[4] The analogy between microcosm and macrocosm was probably used by Democritus and is well established in Greek scientific thinking, e.g., in the Hippocratic corpus and in Plato. See G.E.R. Lloyd, *Polarity and Analogy* (Cambridge, 1971), 252–67; D. Furley, *The Greek Cosmologists*, vol. 1 (Cambridge, 1987), 157–58. See now Schiesaro, *Simulacrum*, 74ff.

tion (*To Pythocles*, D.L. 10.88). In Lucretius the death of the world is a drama of its outer boundaries, enacted between the "walls of the world" (*moenia mundi*) and the atoms constantly battering them from outside.[5] The process reflects some of our most basic fears about the violation of bodily boundaries. Early in the poem he tells how age and time threaten to reach "inside" living matter and "devour it entirely" (*penitus peremit consumens materiem omnem*, 1.226). The doom of things threatens to destroy them "beneath its very teeth" (*leti sub dentibus ipsis*, 1.852), not unlike Catullus's "evil shades of Orcus" that "devour all that's lovely" (*malae tenebrae / Orci, quae omnia bella devorastis*, 3.13–14).

At the end of book 1, refuting the view that the ethereal fire will move to the edges of the universe, Lucretius gives a vivid image of "the world's walls flying apart, dissolved through the great void" and the "sky's thunderous regions collapsing from above" while the "earth is drawn away from beneath our feet," so that "in a point of time there is nothing left except desolate void and dark first-beginnings" (1.1102–10). The conclusion of the next book corrects this false cosmology, but the results are not very different: "The walls of the great world all around, overrun in the attack, will give forth their collapse and crumbling ruin" (*sic igitur magni quoque circum moenia mundi / expugnata dabunt labem putrisque ruinas*, 2.1144–45).[6]

The consistent analogy in this conclusion between the world's workings and the vital processes of a living being (cf. "food," "eating," "nurture," "veins," 2.1125, 1127, 1136, 1147) makes it clear how intimately our own bodies share in these experiences of the "body" of the macrocosm. Indeed, the same terms that describe the world's disintegration here recur for the end of an individual life in book 3. There the soul's departure leaves the body "changed by so great a collapse that

[5] For the image of the "walls of the world" in Lucretius's "dramatic conception" of the universe, see Klingner, "Philosophie und Dichtkunst," 146–47.

[6] On these two passages, see Müller, "Die Finalia," 199–200.

it falls crumbling" (*tanta mutatum putre ruina / conciderit corpus*, 3.584–85); here the world's walls crash "into crumbling ruins" (*putris ruinas*, 2.1145).

Staying alive, according to Epicurean physics, is quite literally a matter of defending your physical boundaries. It is at the outermost surface of the body, *in summo corpore*, that the issue of life and death is decided. In describing the soul in book 3, Lucretius explains that its movements and disturbances are generally limited to this outer zone (*plerumque fit in summo quasi corpore finis / motibus*), and in this way we can hold on to life (3.252–57). Death is most clearly visible at "the outermost perimeter of the limbs," *extima membrorum circumcaesura* (3.219), as Lucretius observes when he notes that this external surface can be intact even when the vital soul is gone and no life remains (3.216–20; cf. 4.647).

Every creature, as a compound of atoms, needs to keep on taking in matter (nourishment) in order to sustain its borders and thus resist the constant hammering of atoms from outside (2.1133–40). So it is with our world. When a world or a human being no longer has a sufficient supply of atoms to maintain its "walls," it disintegrates or dies. Lucretius describes this process a number of times, most fully at the end of book 1, on the creation and eventual destruction of our world (1.1021ff.). Given infinite numbers of atoms and an infinite space (void), our world came together through the chance blows and unions of atoms and will continue to exist as long as new atoms replenish those which are lost. In this way the rivers and seas are renewed and "the earth, warmed by the sun's heat, continues to renew its offspring; and the race of living beings, thus sent up, flourishes, and the fires of the heavens, gliding [through the sky], live" (1.1028–34).

A few lines later Lucretius compares this process in the universe with that in an individual human being (1.1038–43):

nam veluti privata cibo natura animantum
diffluit amittens corpus, sic omnia debent
dissolui simul ac defecit suppeditare
materies aliqua ratione aversa viai.

> nec plagae possunt extrinsecus undique summam
> conservare omnem quaecumque est conciliata.

(For just as the nature of living things, deprived of food, flows apart, losing its bodily substance, so all things have to be dissolved as soon as material fails to supply it, for some reason turned aside in its course. Nor can the blows from every direction outside preserve every world that has been brought together [in atomic formation].)

The analogy is, in a sense, scarcely necessary because the preceding lines have already brought the invisible movements of atom and void to bear on the large-scale processes of animal and plant life. The very casualness with which the processes themselves slip into analogy shows how easy is the passage between the macrocosmic movements of decay and renewal in the universe and those in our own bodies. The identification is helped by the fact that *corpus* means both "body," in the sense of our limbs and tissue, and "atom"; and we can see Lucretius exploiting this double meaning in the phrase *amittens corpus*, "losing substance," in line 1039.

In the argument for the mortality of the world in book 5, Lucretius describes its subjection to "diseases" (*morbis*) in exactly the same terms as he does the human body.[7] In both cases "some harsher cause" will bring not just sickness but total destruction (cf. 5.346–47, *ibi si tristior incubuisset / causa*, "if some grimmer cause had pressed upon things"; 3.485–86, *paulo si durior insinuarit / causa*, "if a somewhat harsher cause slipped within"). The "diseases" of the world, moreover, include natural disasters like conflagrations, torrential floods, and earthquakes, which themselves involve death for "generations of men" and cities and towns (5.339–42), so that here, too, there is both analogy and continuity between the death of the world and the deaths of men. The

---

[7] On the importance of "disease" as a link between human mortality and the mortality of the world, see Clay, *Lucretius and Epicurus*, 260. The relationship, however, as this chapter will try to show, is more than just a method "of reducing his reader's awe before what is extraordinary in nature," as Clay here suggests.

same applies to the subsequent a fortiori arguments from the disintegration of rocks and the collapse of mountains, which include the "monuments of men" (*monumenta virum*, 5.311) and other man-made structures like "lofty towers" and the "shrines and images of the gods" (5.306–7).

In expounding the physical basis for this inevitable destruction of our world and everything in it, Lucretius repeats verbatim the verses about the mixture of atoms and void that he had used for the mortality of the soul in book 3.[8] The arguments for the mortality of the world proceed a fortiori from the mortality of its separate parts, i.e., the physical phenomena among which we live, including our own bodies. In book 3, however, the argument moves in just the opposite direction: the totality of the universe (what Lucretius calls *summarum summa*) is eternal because there is nothing outside of it into which it could dissolve. Our souls, however, do not fulfil this necessary condition of immortality and are therefore mortal. Lucretius might seem to be guilty of circular reasoning, but this is only apparent. One of his points is that the examples of mortality are interchangeable, whether they are the microcosmic compounds (our souls) or the macrocosm (our world), because both are subject to the same atomic processes. Only the totality of things, the entire infinite universe, with its infinite number of worlds, is immortal.

Just as the macrocosm of the world's "body" and the microcosm of the invisible "bodies" of the atoms teach us about the inevitable destruction of our own bodies, so our bodies teach us about the death of the world. Hence the diseases of the world described in book 6 both cause the deaths of men and provide analogies to the frailty of human flesh. In like manner, the power of the disintegrative processes—what Lucretius briefly calls *letum*, "doom"—to engulf the entire universe has its human counterpart in the engulfment of the entire city of

---

[8] The passages are 5.351–63 and 3.806–18. For our argument it does not matter which passage was written first: see Bailey, *T. Lucreti Cari*, ad loc. (pp. 1125–26).

Athens by the plague at the end of the poem. This is the human, social equivalent to the chaos at the end of the world.

The death of the world, then, is not just a displacement or projection of anxieties about our bodies upon the natural world; it is also a magnificently terrible blow-up on the vast screen of the universe of the gradual, inevitable dissolution continually going on, visibly and invisibly, within our physical frame. Logically, Lucretius has little need for such a displacement, for in his materialist system microcosm and macrocosm are not just analogues of one another but parts of the same continuum. Psychologically, however, the analogies between the death of the world and the death of the person do help prepare the reader to confront the reality of his own individual death in book 3. For this reason, perhaps, Lucretius anticipates the arguments of book 5 and chooses to end each of his first two books with vivid accounts of cataclysm.[9]

The movement of the poem is thus a gradually intensifying experience of personal death, and the fear of death is intimately bound up with concerns about the integrity of the body's boundaries. World-death at the end of books 1 and 2 leads into the inexorable death of the individual in book 3 and the futility of hoping for the survival of our souls after the physical disintegration of our bodies. Books 5 and 6 show us our world's frailty and certain end. The imbedding of personal death in the death of the world at the conclusions of books 1 and 2 is balanced, finally, by the imbedding of personal death in the death of an entire society at the end of the poem.

The death of worlds is just as "natural" as the death of individual persons, and just as inevitable. Yet by keeping before us the physical processes of decay and dissolution in the world's body, Lucretius indirectly reminds us of the decay and dissolution going on, at every moment, in our own bodies, particularly after we have passed our prime and begun the

---

[9] Klingner, "Philosophie und Dichtkunst," 139–44, has excellent observations on the shifting of this topic in Lucretius's argument, but I do not agree with his analysis of the reasons (the poet's fascination with destruction, his pessimism, and the lack of complete integration of the poetry and the philosophy).

downward slide toward death (cf. 2.1120–32). By letting us envision and accept this process writ large in the natural world, Lucretius can overcome something of our own denial of death and thereby begin to free us from fearing it.

The first step is to overcome our denial of the world's mortality, which Lucretius recognizes as "something new and wondrous" and hence "difficult to persuade with words" (*res nova miraque menti*, 5.97; *quam difficile id mihi sit pervincere dictis*, 5.99). The proof of the world's mortality is largely the task of books 5 and 6, but Lucretius prepares the way by his preliminary accounts of cosmic destruction in books 1 and 2. Even we moderns, faced with global warming, the erosion of the ozone layer, and (more modestly) the disintegration of the pyramids (Horace's example of indestructible monumentality, *Odes* 3.30), are reluctant to admit the fragility of our world. How much more solid the world seemed to the ancients, lacking modern technology's power of radically transforming the face of nature. In both Greek and Roman poetry, in fact, it is a commonplace that the natural world endures though we humans die: *soles occidere et redire possunt* or *damna tamen celeres reparant caelestia lunae*.[10] Lucretius, then, has to emphasize repeatedly how flawed, faulty, and vulnerable it is.

In giving his detailed account of the end of the world, Lucretius may well be working out his own images. The extant writings of Epicurus show little of the detail and attention given to the subject in Lucretius. Epicurus's lost *Great Epitome* or *On Nature* may have supplied such details, but the one surviving text that does discuss the end of the world gives us a sense of how much personal coloring Lucretius has added (*To Pythocles*, D.L. 10.88):

> A world (κόσμος) is the enclosing circuit of the sky, including stars and earth and the phenomena; and when this is

---

[10] "Suns can set and rise again," Catullus 5; "Nevertheless the swift moons can repair the losses in the heavens," Horace, *Odes* 4.7; cf. pseudo-Moschus, *Epitaph for Bion* 99–107; in general Marco Fantuzzi, "Caducità dell' uomo e eternità della natura: variazioni di un motivo letterario," *Quaderni Urbinati di Cultura Classica*, n.s. 26 (1987): 101–10.

dissolved everything in it will receive its dissolution, since it is a fragment of the infinite and it has its end in a limit (πέρας) that is either rare or dense, either revolving or in a state of rest, and it is round or triangular, or has some such outline (περιγραφή).

We may contrast the much more vivid images of the boundaries of the world at the end of Lucretius's second book and the other passages discussed above.[11]

The same earth that is the mother of all things is also their common grave (5.259). The converse of this process is the Epicurean principle of ἰσονομία: life and creation are always counterbalancing death and decay, and vice versa. Early in the poem Lucretius briefly explains how organisms live only "until a force comes against them that beats them apart by its blows or else penetrates into them through their empty spaces and dissolves them" (*donec vis obiit quae res diverberet ictu / aut intus penetret per inania dissolvatque*, 1.222–23). The atomic substance into which they disintegrate, however, is not destroyed, for if time and decay should consume what it destroys, "from what source does Venus lead back the race of living creatures, each after its kind, into the light of life, or from what source does earth, in her variety and artifice, nurture and increase each [species] after its kind, when it has been led back [to life], providing its food? Whence do the native springs and far distant rivers keep supplying the sea? Whence does the aether nurture the stars?" (1.225–31):

> praeterea quaecumque vetustate amovet aetas,
> si penitus peremit consumens materiem omnem,
> unde animale genus generatim in lumina vitae
> redducit Venus, aut redductum daedala tellus
> unde alit atque auget generatim pabula praebens?
> unde mare ingenui fontes externaque longe
> flumina suppeditant? unde aether sidera pascit?

[11] See Green, "Dying World," passim, esp. 52ff.; also Klingner, "Philosophie und Dichtkunst," 136–44, who takes up Bignone's suggestion that Epicurus's theory of the mortality of the world is part of his polemic against Aristotle.

Here, as in 1.1031–34, cited above, Lucretius mentions the renewal of the rivers in the earth and the fiery bodies in the heavens (1.230–31; cf. 5.281–305). Warming to the theme of nature's regenerative energy, Lucretius gives more emphasis to creation than to destruction at this point of the poem; and he goes on soon after in his celebrated verses on the new lambs that gambol over the grass on unsteady legs, drunk with the pure milk (1.259–61). The disintegrative processes, so far, have no such vivid language. He will, however, reverse this balance in the closing sections of the work.

Cosmic destruction comes home to us mortals simply and tangibly in the account of the earth's waning fertility at the end of book 2. The earth, worshipped earlier in the book in the wild corybantic rites as the Great Mother because of her boundless fertility (2.594ff.), is now like a woman past the age of childbearing, no longer capable of producing new life with the same abundance (2.1150–52). The extraordinary vision of the world's periphery at the beginning of the poem belongs to Epicurus, who "traversed the limitless all in his mind and spirit" and penetrated even beyond "the flaming walls of the world" (1.72–74). Here, however, the onlooker is only a humble farmer.[12] Lucretius thus puts the spectator of world decay very much inside the dying world, and also inside the poem. We as readers become spectators of an unphilosophical spectator who "does not grasp" (*nec tenet*, 1173) the truth of the death going on constantly around him.

This scene qualifies the misplaced, superstitious worship of earth as Great Mother in the middle of the book (cf. 2.645–60).[13] But it also balances the proem of the book, with its very different kind of spectator, one who is momentarily outside the struggles between life and death, growth and decay, because he has attained the privileged viewing-place of the gods, occupying the "lofty, tranquil regions fortified by the learning of the wise" (*munita tenere / edita doctrina sapientum templa*

---

[12] On the effect of this lowly personage here, see Klingner, "Philosophie und Dichtkunst," 147–48.

[13] On this relationship, see Müller, "Die Finalia," 205 and 226–27.

serena, 2.7–8). Such a metaphorical "fortification" is far more secure than the physical boundaries of a living being, "fortified by vital forces" that will eventually fail (cf. *vitalibus ab rebus munita tenetur*, of the mortal soul, 3.820). It is even stronger than our own world as a whole, whose walls, as we have seen, will be "stormed" by the battering of atoms from outside (*expugnata*, 2.1145).[14]

In the proem of the next book Lucretius will make himself into just such a philosophical spectator of the world processes as he experiences both "divine pleasure" and mortal "awe." He looks out over the mysteries of the infinite universe revealed by Epicurus (3.25–30):

> at contra nusquam apparent Acherusia templa
> nec tellus obstat quin omnia dispiciantur,
> sub pedibus quaecumque infra per inane geruntur.
> his ibi me rebus quaedam divina voluptas
> percipit atque horror, quod sic natura tua vi
> tam manifesta patens ex omni parte retecta est.

> (But nowhere appear the regions of Acheron, nor does the earth stand in the way to obstruct the view over all those things that go on throughout the void beneath my feet. At these things a certain divine pleasure seizes me and a shuddering awe, because nature has been revealed and opened up to clear view in every direction by your force.)

The farmer at the end of the previous book, however, stands in the full immanence of his involvement with the earth and its fruits. Aged himself, he both identifies and is identified with his aging fields. Unable to see the system in which he participates, he can only "weary the heavens" with misplaced com-

---

[14] On the possible Epicurean sources of the image of the philosopher as a fortified city, see Clay, *Lucretius and Epicurus*, 65 and 186–88; cf. Epicurus, frag. 339 Usener, and *Kyriai Doxai* 7, 13, 14. The image, however, seems far stronger in Lucretius. Clay's arguments for its importance in Epicurus's own writings are not strong. For further discussion, see Clay, "Epicurus' Last Will."

plaints, ignorant "that all things are gradually wasting in decay" (*nec tenet omnia paulatim tabescere*, 2.1173).[15]

The vision that Epicurus's *ratio* has brought to us is so far from this blind enclosure in process that it in fact opens upon a kind of anti-world. This is the lucid divine space whose untouched, inviolate condition only sets off more clearly the constantly attacked, ever-decaying world in which we (and everything else) exist. The parting of these "walls of the world" (*moenia mundi / discedunt*, 3.15–16) reveals the blessed peace of the gods that frees us from fear (3.17–24):

> apparet divum numen sedesque quietae
> quas neque concutiunt venti nec nubila nimbis
> aspergunt neque nix acri concreta pruina
> cana cadens violat semperque innubilus aether
> integit, et large diffuso lumine ridet.
> omnia suppeditat porro natura neque ulla
> res animi pacem delibat tempore in ullo.

(There appears the divine majesty of the gods and their peaceful abode, which no winds shake or clouds besprinkle with mists, nor does any white falling snow, congealed with sharp frost, violate it, but the cloudless ether covers it over always, and it smiles with broadly radiating light. Nature supplies all things, nor does anything at any time mar the peace of their spirits.)

In our world, however, the parting of the "walls of the world" is the ultimate stage of mortality (1.1094–95, 2.1144–45).

In the gods' world, nature "supplies everything," whereas for mortals there will inevitably come the time when not enough substance will be "supplied" to fend off disintegration (*suppeditare*, 2.1138; cf. 1.231). This sky is unshaken by wind

---

[15] Note the progression of the motif of old age and decay in this passage, from the rather neutral attribute of the farmer as "old," *grandis* (1164), to the farmer as "sower of the old and wrinkled vine" (*vetulae vitis sator atque vietae*, 1168, with Heinsius's emendation), to the closing image of "all things going to the tomb [?], worn out with the aged span of time" (*omnia . . . ire / ad capulum [?] spatio aetatis defessa vetusto*, 1173–74). For some interesting thematic links between the end of book 2 and the proem of book 3, see Müller, "Die Finalia," 200–204.

or cloud, in contrast to the skies of the mortal world, "struck," pierced, or traversed by lightning, rain, heat, and the other atmospheric disturbances. These prove its imperfections and signal its eventual collapse (cf. 6.281ff., 513ff., 591ff., etc.). In his account of thunder early in book 6, for example, Lucretius describes how "everything seems so shaken by thunder" (*tonitru concussa*) that even "the vast walls of the capacious world seem to be rent and to gape apart" (*divulsa repente / maxima dissiluisse capacis moenia mundi*, 6.121–23). The "cloudless aether" of the gods' realm is never "violated" by snow or ice, whereas in our world we must take care not to believe that heavenly bodies are "inviolable in their strength" (*inviolabilia haec ne credas forte vigere*, 5.305; *inviolabilis* occurs only here in Lucretius).

Although descriptions of growth, decay, and disintegration pervade nearly every part of the poem, there is a strong progression from the somatic terms describing the death of our world at the end of book 2 to the mortality of the soul in book 3. The brief glimpse of the inviolate abode of the gods in the proem of book 3 sets off the ineluctable mortality of our bodies and our world in the rest of the book. The old farmer at the end of book 2, then, helps form the transition between the impersonal, cosmic disintegration of worlds and the deaths of individuals in our world.

Having used the world's death in the first and second books to prepare us for the personal deaths of the third, Lucretius can draw on that personal knowledge of death to convince us in books 5 and 6 of the counter-intuitive truth that our entire world will perish. Each of us constitutes a miniature atomic world. The imperfect "vessel" of our bodies is the exact counterpart, in microcosm, of the *moenia mundi*, the vast walls of the world. Just as these latter will eventually fly apart and scatter to the void all the atoms that lie within (cf. 1.1103–13, 2.1143–44), so the vessels of our bodies will eventually be unable to protect the vital souls that they contain, and at their collapse will scatter the soul-atoms within to the winds (3.440–44; cf. also 554–57 and 936).

Given that boundaries are the zones where life is threatened, it is not surprising that images of walls, fortresses, armor, and the like describe the vulnerable areas both of worlds and of people. Such imagery is clearest in the accounts of cosmic destruction that we have already mentioned (cf. 1.1102ff., 2.1144ff., 5.1213–14, 6.121ff.). And, as we have observed, Epicurus's privileged knowledge and status as sage derive from his heroic journey to the boundaries of the world (1.73–74) and his vision out beyond them.

The philosopher experiences these boundaries without the fear of death, and Lucretius benefits from his Master's vision (3.16–17): *diffugiunt animi terrores, moenia mundi / discedunt, totum video per inane geri res* ("The mind's terrors scatter in flight; the walls of the world part, and I behold [all] things being carried on through the entire void"). In this vista the opening of the world's walls brings not panic but the "scattering of the mind's fears." The careful chiastic balance between *diffugiunt animi terrores* and *moenia mundi discedunt* enhances the philosophical response to this more tranquil dissolving of the world's boundaries. Immediately after comes the vision of the gods' invulnerability (*apparet divum numen*, 3.18ff.). This vision of an indestructible divine abode is hard to reconcile with Epicurean physics[16] and is therefore to be regarded as at least in part metaphorical. It forms a pendant to the dissolution or penetration of boundaries that is the inevitable fate of every organism in the universe, our bodies included.

Just as the collapse of a being's outer perimeter means its death, so the creation of boundaries is a first step toward making life. Human life results from the interior knitting together of soul and body at birth, set apart within "the limbs of the mother and the womb" (3.344–47): "From life's beginning, the reciprocal contacts of body and of soul, set back within the mother's limbs and womb (*maternis etiam membris alvoque reposta*), so learn their vital movements that separation cannot take place without illness and suffering." The cre-

---

[16] See A. A. Long and D. Sedley, eds., *The Hellenistic Philosophers*, vol. 1 (Cambridge, 1987), pp. 147–48.

ation of life, in other words, requires this removed space of shelter within the mother's body. The creation of our entire mortal world begins with the making of boundaries as aether, spreading out in all directions, "with greedy embrace closes in all the rest of things" (*avido complexu cetera saepsit*, 5.466–70). Lucretius draws a beautiful analogy with the morning mists rising from the newly formed earth "weaving" a kind of web of cloud beneath the sky (*subtexunt nubila caelum*, 5.466). This subtle fabric forms the world's necessary enclosure; but we are also reminded of the creative embrace of Venus in the proem of book 1 and her attempt to "surround" Mars with her sacred body (*circumfusa super*, 1.38–39), also in the service of life and creation.

In the existing world the boundaries that assure survival can be more solid. In describing the abundance of animal species, such as elephants, Lucretius gives the example of India, which these creatures fortified "as with a wall of ivory, so that it could not be penetrated within, so great is the force of these beasts" (2.537–40):

> India quorum
> milibus e multis vallo munitur eburno,
> ut penitus nequeat penetrari: tanta ferarum
> vis est.

Shortly afterwards he explains how men surrounded Earth, as Great Mother of the gods and of life, with her crown of cities "because fortified in her lofty places she maintains [literally, holds up] cities" (2.606–7):

> muralique caput summum cinxere corona,
> eximiis munita locis quia sustinet urbis.

Sicily, in its grandeur and power, is both rich in fertility and "fortified by a great force of men" (*rebus opima bonis, multa munita virum vi*, 1.728). Over against the wondrously "fortified" Sicily, however, stands the Sicily perforated by the volcano of Aetna in book 6, where fires "breathe forth" through the "jaws of the mountain" (*per fauces montis*), so that the "fiery storm, arising with no small destruction and establishing its power throughout the Sicilian fields, turns the eyes of the neighboring peoples to itself" (6.639–43). The result of this vision of earth's fiery caverns is just the opposite of the security of earth's fortified boundaries. Here the spectators "fill their breasts with fearful anxiety at what strange new things nature might be devising" (6.645–46):

> cernentes pavida complebant pectora cura,
> quid moliretur rerum natura novarum.

We may once more contrast the serenity of the philosopher at such borders in the proems of each of the first three books.[17]

One of the requirements for immortality is that an organism be "held strong, fortified from [by] its forces of life" (3.820)— a condition fulfilled figuratively at least by the "lofty and tranquil regions" of godlike peace, "fortified by the teachings of the wise" in the proem of book 2 (2.7–8). We mortal creatures, however, have souls that dissolve in air "like smoke" and bodies that "crumble in decay," like the worlds themselves (*putre ruina*, 3.583–84; *putris ruinas*, 2.1144). Our "walls" are the perishable boundaries of a "vessel" that is both fragile (3.440–45, 793) and internally flawed (6.17–23). Our corporeal boundaries are weak both from within and from without, just like the doomed world we inhabit. Within these mortal limits, we can try to "fortify our old age with children" (*gnatis munire senectam*, 4.1256); yet that very fact of old age is the mark of our mortality.

So far are we from immortality that the condition of our existence is penetrability. The mixture of void and solid atoms in all things makes possible the absorption of nourishment through our veins (cf. 6.946); and the same process holds both for our bodies and for the world-body (2.1122–49). Our vital processes, like perspiration or the growth of hair, depend on the porous condition of our physical being. In book 6 Lucretius draws the analogy with similar processes in the natural

---

[17] See Müller, "Die Finalia," 205, who contrasts the *horror* of the philosophical awe in 3.29–30 with the superstitious awe *horrifice* (2.609), in the processions honoring the Great Mother.

world, such as the penetrability of rock by water in a cave (6.921–48). We owe our sense perceptions to the same penetrability. Hearing, for instance, depends on voices that "fly between the barriers and enclosures of the house" (*inter saepta meant voces et clausa domorum / transvolitant*, 1.354–55).[18] That same *summum corpus* or outermost surface of the body that is involved in the loss or retention of the vital soul for life or death is also involved in the processes of perception (4.29ff., especially 31, 43, 59, 64; cf. 3.255–57).

The corollary of these life-sustaining penetrations of our corporeal boundaries is the eventual disintegration of the boundaries. The rupture of these defenses at any point creates the "gate of death" (*ianua leti*, 1.1112, 5.373) through which the delicate soul-atoms stream forth. In like manner, one who is close to death stands "at the threshold of doom," *in limine leti*, at a kind of boundary point (2.960, 6.1157, 1208). To be born, correspondingly, is to "enter the threshold of life" (*vitae cum limen inimus*, 3.681) or, in a broader spatial field, to come "into the shores of light" (*in luminis oras*).

It is the "enclosures of life," *claustra vitai*, that protect our vital essence and are "dissolved" or "totter" in collapse when we are old or suffer disease (1.414–15, 6.1153; cf. 3.396ff.). These *claustra vitai* are to the microcosm of the individual human body what the *moenia mundi* are to the world as a whole. Lucretius makes the connection explicit in his lengthy analogy between water in the cave, perspiration, nourishment, and the growth of hair to which I referred above (6.921–44). He goes on here to explain how cold pierces metals, how voices pass through the "stony barriers of houses" (*dissaepta domorum saxea*, 6.951), and how clouds or storms traverse the zones "where the breastplate of the sky closes in [the heavens] all around" (*denique qua circum caeli lorica coercet*, 6.954).

His next point is the way in which "the force of disease slips into [us] from outside" (*morbida visque simul, cum extrinsecus insinuatur*, 6.955); and he proceeds at once to storms in the sky and on earth (956–57). Despite the lacuna after 954, it is clear that the same conditions govern the human consti-

[18] Cf. Epicurus, *Letter to Herodotus*, D.L. 10.49.

tution and the remotest reaches of the heavens (*quandoqui-dem nil est nisi raro corpore nexum*, "since there is nothing that is not woven of rare body," 958). In fact, the "sky's breastplate" exactly corresponds, in macrocosm, to the "shield" (*tegmen*) of the body protecting the individual human soul from dispersion into air (3.576f., 604; cf. *tegmen*, of the warrior's shield literally, in 3.649).

The great plague at Athens, some two hundred lines later, arrives as a foreign invader, "arising deep within the borders of Egypt," crossing those boundaries on a long journey, and then coming at last to "rest heavily upon the whole people of Pandion" in Athens (6.1141–43):

> nam penitus veniens Aegypti finibus ortus,
> aera permensus multum camposque natantis,
> incubuit tandem populo Pandionis omni.

The effect of this "force of disease" (*morbida vis*, as in 6.955, above), is to move "through the throat," "fill the breast," and then "flow into the saddened heart of the sick," where "the enclosures of life totter" (6.1151–53):

> inde ubi per fauces pectus complerat, et ipsum
> morbida vis in cor maestum confluxerat aegris,
> omnia tum vero vitai claustra lababant.

As plague is the hostile invasion of a political territory, individual illness is the invasion of a body's interior territory. Harmful substances can "strike diseases" into us (*morbos incutere*, 6.772). "Many hostile atoms," the poet continues, "pass through the ears, many slip through our very nostrils, harmful and rough in their contact" (*multa meant inimica per auris, multa per ipsas / insinuant naris infesta atque aspera tactu*, 6.777–78). We may be reminded too of the way that the "contagions of disease penetrate" into our mind, as well as our body, as a sign of the soul's mortality in book 3 (*penetrant in eum contagia morbi*, 3.471). The verb of this hostile "entrance," *insinuare*, generally denotes the invasion of disease (6.777 and 955), but it also describes other assaults upon our physical being, deep injury (3.485) and fear (5.73). More benignly, it decribes sense perception, which, as we have noted, is the positive side (along with nourishment) of the penetrability of our bodily boundaries.[19] By the same token, the penetrability of our bodies is also responsible for pain (2.963–65, 3.252), drunkenness (3.475–76), and of course ultimately death (1.221ff., 3.485–86 and 807–8, 5.353–54).[20]

The psychological invasion of our boundaries can be no less deleterious, particularly as we receive fantasies or dreams as *simulacra*, that is, the outer shells of things that penetrate the surface of our body. Fear of the gods can "slip into our breasts" (5.73–74). Passionate love is a wound (4.1015ff.), and its poisonous sweetness "drips into our heart" (*in cor stillavit*, 4.1059–60). Such love also takes the form of a deluded and empty attempt to cross physical boundaries as the lovers "fasten their bodies [together] greedily and join their mouth's saliva" (4.1108–9), but it is "all in vain because they can tear nothing away nor can they penetrate and go with whole body into [the other's] body" (4.1110–11). Since lovers can take in no solid substance to sate their impossible desires, they can exchange only empty images and so remain in a state of tormented, ever-renewed frustration. Thus they are caught in a morbid situation of non-nurture and decay, a kind of living death as "they waste away with a hidden wound" inside their bodies (*tabescunt vulnere caeco*, 4.1120).

The analogies between worlds and persons have a middle term in the boundaries of cities. To take a small but telling instance, Lucretius draws an analogy between earthquakes and the trembling of our limbs when we are cold. Such catastrophes bring not just the collapse of specific cities like Sidon and the Peloponnesian Aegium, but more generally "many cities sank deep into the sea with their citizens" (*multae per mare pessum / subsedere suis pariter cum civibus urbes*, 6.589–90).

---

[19] So 2.436, 684; 4.331, 525; 6.802, etc. For sense perception as penetration generally, see 1.491, 534; 4.612, 699–700, 718–19, 728ff., etc.

[20] The language of 2.963–65 stresses the effect on the "interior abode" of the body when it is struck by force: *trepidant in sedibus intus*. Compare the similar description of a blow "driven within" laying bare bone and muscle in 3.170–71, esp. *intus adacta*.

So too, the great plague at Athens begins as a journey from one political "territory" to another.

Fortified cities and their destruction, as we have seen, bulk large in Lucretius's depictions of death and destruction.[21] Human civilization reaches its apogee with the building of "strong towers" and the dividing up of the earth (5.1440–41):

> iam validis saepti degebant turribus aevum
> et divisa colebatur discretaque tellus.

(And now they passed their lives hedged in with strong towers, and the earth, divided and partitioned, was being tilled.)

The rapid enumeration of civilization's triumphs soon follows, including walls (1448), sailing, agriculture, laws, and so on.

This material fortification of boundaries as the acme of human evolution, however, is ironically undercut by the fragility of all the walls and enclosures of life, whether of the world or of the individual. The only truly "pure security," Epicurus writes, comes from the spiritual "tranquillity" (ἡσυχία) of his philosophy and from "withdrawal from the many" (*Kyriai Doxai* 14). The irony in Lucretius's verses becomes even stronger in the light of another celebrated saying of the Master: "Against everything else it is possible to provide security; but as far as death is concerned all of us mortals inhabit an unwalled city" (frag. 339 Usener = *Sententiae Vaticanae* 31). Elsewhere Epicurus compares the turbulence in the soul caused by sexual activity to "a house moved from its foundations" (frag. 17 Usener, p. 118.1–2). Lucretius's use of a similar image is both more detailed and more threatening: he compares a body from which the life has departed to a house collapsing into crumbling ruin (*putre ruina conciderit corpus*) when "its foundations have been moved from their place deep down" (*penitus quia mota loco sunt / fundamenta*), and the

---

[21] To the examples mentioned earlier we may add 6.239–42, the power of lightning bolts to "lay open towers" (*turris discludere*), destroy homes, tear wooden timbers away, and move the "monuments of men."

soul pours forth through all the limbs and pores as if through cracks and apertures (*foramina*, 3.583–88).

Although the extant fragments of Epicurus show little of Lucretius's acute sensitivity to somatic boundaries, his admonitions against sexual intercourse (frag. 62 Usener, D.L. 10.118) suggest that such boundary anxiety is not entirely Lucretius's invention.[22] Nevertheless, Epicurus's terms for the "boundaries" of the world are rather neutral and abstract, words like "limit" or "enclosure" (πέρας, περιοχή, περιέχειν, ἐμπεριλαμβάνειν).[23] When Philodemus quotes Epicurus's remark about death and the unwalled city (frag. 339 Usener, above), his context is the general ephemerality and uncertainty of life (*De Morte* 37.18ff.). This is an important theme in Epicurus, to be sure,[24] and the image does bring together walls and the motif of death; but it does not receive the elaboration that Lucretius's poem gives it.

Lucretius doubtless owes to Epicurean physics the continuities and analogies between the death of the world and the death of the self. But his rich poetic elaboration of somatic imagery gives physical death a concreteness and immediacy not to be found in the Master's extant works. Epicurus's own rather dry account of disturbances in nature like lightning, earthquakes, waterspouts, comets, and the like shows little disposition to developing analogies between world-body and human body (see *Letter to Pythocles*, D.L. 10.99–116). Lucre-

[22] On sexual intercourse and fears of "boundary pollution," see Douglas, *Purity and Danger*, 125–26. We may compare the scenes in Stanley Kubrik's film, *Dr. Strangelove*, where the mad general fiercely protects the perimeters of his base on the one hand and is obsessed with the idea of conserving bodily fluids on the other. Epicurus too is interested in boundaries and, judging from his negative view of sexual intercourse ("It never did one good, and one is lucky if it did not do harm," frag. 62 Usener), may have been dubious about the loss of bodily fluids. His setting for philosophy, the Garden, is also a safely bounded world.

[23] See Epicurus, *Letter to Herodotus* (D.L. 10.73–74) and *Letter to Pythocles* (D.L. 10.88–90); also frag. 303 Usener.

[24] See *Kyriai Doxai* 7, 13, 14. In the last of these (14) Epicurus derives the "purest security" not from material goods but "from peace of mind and withdrawal from the many."

tius conceives of Epicurean philosophy as a fortified city, as the proem to book 2 shows; but whether Epicurus did so is far from certain. Diskin Clay suggests that Epicurus himself used such metaphors for his thought, but the evidence is not strong. Aside from the negative formulation of fragment 339 (death and the unwalled city), no word for walled city or fortification actually occurs, only the verb περιοδεύειν and its noun derivative, περιοδεία, which means "to make the rounds of the circuit" (D.L. 10.36 and 85).[25] There is certainly nothing comparable to Lucretius's vivid language of walls, gates, thresholds, and breastplates.

In order to grasp the totality of the universe, Lucretius had to accompany Epicurus, vicariously, to the flaming edges of the universe (proem to book 3). The vision includes the principle of the eventual destruction of our world. But the poet gives these images of cosmic weakening and collapse a new direction and a new power as this world-death becomes a magnified version of our individual deaths.[26]

The plague at Athens is the culmination of the vulnerability of boundaries. It is, as we have seen, an invasion of Athenian territory. In following its manifestations, Lucretius traces in excruciating, step-by-step detail how the deadly "force of disease" enters and destroys a living human organism. And in its larger role in the book, the plague is the ultimate example of that porous, permeable state that is the condition of both life and death for all physical organisms, whether these are all the worlds in the *summa summarum* of the universe or all the human bodies in a great city.

[25] On these terms, see Clay, *Lucretius and Epicurus*, 187–88, and his "Epicurus's Last Will," p. 263 with n. 25. See above, note 14.

[26] See, for example, 6.936–58, esp. 954–55, discussed above.

Chapter Six

THE VIOLATION OF CORPOREAL BOUNDARIES, 1

Introduction

One of Lucretius's most pervasive poetic techniques is his use of figurative language to describe the incessant separation and reunion of atoms in the physical processes underlying the rhythms of life and death. His imagery for the destructive movements in these processes is particularly vivid. Thus in the celebrated *magnum mare* passage of 2.551ff. he compares the *disiectus materiai* of death and dissolution to the effects of a shipwreck.[1] Later in book 2, anticipating the argument of book 3, he describes the force of a blow that nearly "dissolves the vital knots of the soul from the body and sends it forth through all the pores" (2.949–50). Should the hurt be less severe, the "vital movements" may "conquer" and, as it were, "quell the massive disturbance from the blow" (*vincere et ingentis plagae sedare tumultus*), calling them back "now from the very threshold of doom" (*leti iam limine ab ipso*, 2.955–61). The struggle for life here takes the figurative form of riot and disorder in the commonwealth. In a slight mixing of metaphors, when the riot is quelled, the injured person is brought back from the verge of an exile that would send him into the chaotic realm of *letum*.

Book 3 continues this theme of dispersion or dissolution of constituent atoms in the movement toward death. The subjection of the soul to just this process is one of the major proofs of its mortality. The images that convey this dispersive process

---

[1] The interaction between compounds of *con-* and *dis-* is noteworthy throughout this passage (2.560–64). For further discussion see the references cited in Chapter Three, note 7.

continue the frequency of compounds in *dis-*, but also involve more direct physical violence than those of book 2. Specifically, they involve mutilation or other severe bodily injury. These, we have seen, reflect an underlying concern with the violation of physical boundaries as one of the principal areas into which Lucretius displaces the otherwise suppressed anxiety about the process of dying and the dissolution of the individual consciousness into nothingness.

This displacement of anxiety appears in descriptions of several closely related phenomena: (1) mutilation; a heightened awareness of the separate parts of the body—limbs, organs, physical functions—as detached, quasi-autonomous items; (2) absorption of the body into another foreign substance by swallowing or other forms of engulfment; (3) reduction of the body to a degraded state by putrefaction; (4) external pressure, of a painful or deleterious nature, on the surface of the body by constriction or compression, including the internal constriction of anxiety (*angor*); and (5) a feeling of oppressive mass or weight exerting such pressure.

Many of these violations of corporeal boundaries occur in the list of the false fears about the body after death, especially in 3.870–93. Lines 888–93 powerfully describe the sensations of a body "suffocating in honey" or "stiffening with cold" or "crushed from above by the weight of earth." Even the first part of the book, however, shows a preponderance of descriptions of bodily suffering, utilized as parts of the various proofs of the mortality of the soul. These concerns, I suggest, are relevant also to the fears about the living body's dissolution into death. In fact, this anxiety about corporeal suffering establishes a firmer connection between the two parts of the book than is generally acknowledged.

The closing section of the book, in other words, displaces anxiety about dying from the living body to the corpse and from the feelings of the conscious individual to the atomically constituted *anima*. To take one instance, Lucretius chides the fearful man for not separating himself from the corpse that he will be after death (3.885–87):

> nec videt in vera nullum fore morte alium se
> qui possit vivus sibi se lugere peremptum
> stansque iacentem se lacerari urive dolere.

(Nor does he see that in true death there will be no other "himself" who, living and standing there, could lament that "he" is taken away from "himself" and grieve that he is lying there being torn or burned.)

But before this point of clarification is attained (cf. *nec videt*, 885), just this confusion of the living and dead body is part of that anxiety about boundary violation which Lucretius arouses and dwells on in the language and imagery of the first half of the book.

This confusion between the living and the dead body works both ways. Philosophically, it enables Lucretius the Epicurean to demonstrate the folly of the fear of death by revealing that we wrongly displace anxieties from the body to the soul. Poetically, the intellectual recognition of improper displacement too easily becomes the shocked recognition that "we" are that dead body (cf. 3.881–87). The repeated reflexive pronouns throughout this passage encourage the reader to identify his or her self with the "laid-out body" in a way that may not necessarily allay anxiety. Philosophically, we may accept the absolute division between our living and dead selves, as Epicureanism urges us to do. Poetically, the lines also convey that sense of a created, perceiving, and feeling self whose loss is precisely what we dread. The very repetition of the participles "standing" and "lying" (*adstans*, 883; *stansque iacentem*, 887) evoke those familiar perspectives of our physical being that we are asked to give up.

Not infrequently, Lucretius combines different kinds of boundary violation. In proving that the soul's violent "tearing away" from the body must destroy it, for example, he presents the separation as a harsh rending (*nec sine pernicie divelli*, 325). Returning to the process some fifteen lines later, he adds "cutting" (*discidium*), violent "shaking" (*convulsi*), and "rotting" (*putrescunt*); and he shifts the focus from the generalized "body" (*corpus* in 323–24) to the separate, vulnerable "limbs," abandoned and defenseless before their inevitable destruction (341–43):

> non, inquam, sic animai
> discidium possunt artus perferre relicti,
> sed penitus pereunt convulsi conque putrescunt.

(Not thus, I say, can the limbs, left behind, endure the splitting off of the soul, but torn away they perish deep within and they putrify.)

The alliterations of *pen-* . . . *per-* and *con-* . . . *con-*, the tmesis, and the personal intervention (*inquam*) all add emphasis to the violence.[2] In 347 Lucretius repeats *discidium*, now restating that it cannot occur *sine peste maloque*. *Malum* is among the most general words that Lucretius could choose for physical suffering, but *pestis* suggests the painful process of physical deterioration that Lucretius will describe in the closing section of his poem (cf. *pestilitas*, 6.1098, 1125, 1132). The neutral atomic language of impingement and motion (*contagia motus*, 3.345) here also stands next to a verse about the fetus "hidden away in the *limbs and womb* of the mother" (*maternis etiam membris alvoque reposta*, 346). *Discidium*, the very next word (347), has a chilling effect after this reminder of the vulnerability of life in its most biologically dependent form: *discidium ut nequeat fieri sine peste maloque* (347).

MUTILATION

The proofs of the soul's mortality are remarkable for the accumulation of images of bodily mutilation. These accounts of mortal injuries or deep lacerations of the living body, as I suggested above, counterbalance the mutilations of the dead body in the last part of the book (3.870–93). Concern with the latter can be dismissed as vain and foolish fear, and Lucretius's

---

[2] Note too the interplay between *dis-cidium* here (342 and 347) and the compounds in *con-* in 348–49.

skillful rhetoric enables him to make short work of these anxieties about the corpse after death. But the first half of the book has given us gripping and involving descriptions of the mangled living body. In these accounts the pain, the crippling, and the prolonged agony of death at its most horrible appear in disturbingly violent form. Into such images Lucretius the poetic thinker displaces the fears about death that are not overtly confronted as part of his Epicurean philosophical theory.

The most striking instance of this displacement is the fear of being torn apart by creatures of the wild. Three times the foolish man, fearing death because of the inhumation or cremation of his corpse, expresses anxiety about the rending of his body by birds or animals: *flammis interfiat malisve ferarum* ("perishes by flames or by the jaws of wild beasts," 3.872); *corpus uti volucres lacerent in morte feraeque* ("how birds and wild beasts will tear his body in death," 880; cf. *lacerari*, 887); *nam si in morte malumst malis morsuque ferarum / tractari* ("for if in death it is an evil to be mangled by the jaws and biting of wild beasts," 888–89). There seems to be a progression toward more specific, vivid, and fuller expression, especially in the last passage (888–89), with its heavy alliteration and wordplay on *malum*, "evil," and *malis*, "jaws."[3] The exaggerated style is an intentional mockery of the complainer's folly. Yet just these images of being devoured by the "jaws" of animals, here softened by the general verbs (*interfiat, lacerent, tractari*), recur in what is doubtless the poem's single most violent image of painful death, early man falling prey to wild beasts (5.990–93):

> unus enim tum quisque magis deprensus eorum
> pabula viva feris praebebat, dentibus haustus,
> et nemora ac montis gemitu silvasque replebat
> viva videns vivo sepeliri viscera busto.

---

[3] See Wallach, *Lucretius and the Diatribe*, 44–45, who remarks on the rhetorical amplification in these lines. Lines 879–81, with the description of a body torn by birds, may be influenced by Pacuvius's *Iliona*: see Ernout and Robin, *Lucrèce*, ad loc., and Wallach, *Lucretius and the Diatribe*, 34–35.

(For then each one of them, caught, was providing living food to
wild beasts, gulped down by the teeth, and [each] would fill the
groves and mountains and forests with his groaning, seeing his
living flesh being buried in a living tomb.)

The gratuitous detail of the mangled person's "seeing" (*vi-
dens*) his "living entrails" disappear into his killer's maw adds
psychological horror to the scene.[4] Burial "alive" here takes
on the most extreme and excruciating form of primary bound-
ary anxiety, the absorption of one's life-substance, violently
and painfully, into the engulfing life of a cruel and powerful
creature. The interlocking repetitions of the same sound for
"life," "seeing," and "flesh" (*viva . . . viva . . . vivo // vi-dens
. . . vi-scera*) tie together the different parts of this anxiety:
concern for basic life-process and survival; the horror of being
conscious of the event; and the exposure of one's interior or-
gans to ghastly destruction and to engulfment in the vitals of
another being. The addition of *viscera* in 5.993 in particular
makes clear the extent of the mutilation and carries the threat
to life into the deep cavities of the body. Less detailed but also
illuminating is the dream of those who "as if they are being
eaten by the biting of a panther or savage lion, fill everything
with great shouting" (*et quasi pantherae morsu saevive leonis
/ mandantur magnis clamoribus omnia complent*, 4.1016–17)
This scene is literally a nightmare.

Both in the theme of conscious awareness and in the sound
pattern, these scenes invite comparison with the foolish man's
concern about the laceration of his body after death in 3.885–
87 (translated above):

> nec *vi*det in *ve*ra nullum fore morte alium se
> qui possit *viv*us sibi se lugere peremptum
> stansque iacentem se lacerari uri*ve* dolere.

---

[4] On the verbal power and pathos of 5.990ff., see Bonelli, *I motivi pro-
fondi*, 237–38. The passage intensifies the similar effect of *per viscera viva per
artus*, of pain, in 2.964. It would be interesting to view this passage as a ma-
cabre, destructive inversion, characteristically Lucretian, of Epicurus's con-
cern with the belly as the seat of pleasures (which Pigeaud, *Maladie de l'âme*,
226, following Logre, calls "la situation menacée de ce corps épicurien tel qu'
il est conçu originellement, corps poreux . . .").

The pre-civilized man in book 5 is "alive" to "see" (*vivus, videre*, 5.993) his body's terrible suffering. The foolish man of 3.885, though belonging to the civilized and indeed urban present, "does not see" the non-existence of that self which, "alive," can mourn that "he" is being torn apart (*nec videt . . . vivus . . . se lacerari*). The terrors of primitive man belong to the actual, physical dangers of this life; those of Lucretius's contemporaries belong to the imagination and pertain to a self and to a "life" (cf. *vivus*, 3.886) that does not exist. In book 5 the "seeing" is a literal vision, and the object seen is not a corpse but the viewer's own separated and still living flesh. The scene has a surreal, nightmarish quality (cf. the actual nightmare of 4.1016–17), and one may be reminded of the tortures depicted by Bosch or the ogre-like cannibalism of Goya's "Saturn." Though couched in negative form (*nec videt*), these lines of book 3 offer an antidote of reason to this horrible tableau of a man's physical destruction in a setting of primordial savagery.

Lucretius's picture in book 5 has still more graphic horror in store. The hapless victim is not killed outright, but dies a lingering death, because of the devoured state of his body (*corpore adeso*). He holds his "trembling hands" over the "ghastly wounds," utters the "awful cries," and feels the "savage writhing pains" (*vermina saeva*, 5.994–98). In sound and metrical position these *vermina saeva* echo the *viscera* of 5.993, and these "agonies" become virtually personified as a life-destroying force (*donec eos vita privarant vermina saeva*, "until the writhing pains have deprived them of life," 5.998).[5] In both scenes the special horror of the bodily violation lies in the visual experience: looking upon the mangling of one's own body.

Alongside the nightmarish scene of 5.990–98 we may set the other great nightmare scene of primitive violence of book

---

[5] The association of these *vermina* with death is particularly strong because popular etymology connected the word with *vermes*, "worms" (see Paulus-Festus 515 Lindsay, quoted by Bailey, *T. Lucreti Cari*, ad loc.), despite the actual etymology from the root of *vertere*.

5, the use of wild beasts in war (5.1308–40).[6] Here too terrible mangling by biting occurs (*validis morsibus*, 5.1322; *validis . . . caedebant dentibus apri*, 1326; *dentis adactus*, 1330). Though entrails are not specified, this passage does describe the gored "sides and bellies, underneath," of horses (*latera ac ventris . . . subter*, 1324). This passage stands in a close thematic relation to 3.642–56, to be discussed in greater detail later. The hamstrung horses, like the man with his foot cut off in book 3, make a futile effort to get up (cf. 5.1331–33 and 3.651–53). Scythe-armed chariots occur in both passages (3.642, 650; 5.1300). In fact, the wild beasts that "grow hot with gore" in 5.1313 verbally recall the scythe-armed chariots that "grow hot with gore" in 3.642–43.

> nequiquam, quoniam *permixta caede calentes*
> turbabant saevi nullo discrimine turmas.

> (All in vain, because [the beasts], *growing hot with mingled gore*, ravaged their own squadrons, making no distinctions.)
> (5.1313–14)

> falciferos memorant currus abscidere membra
> saepe ita de subito *permixta caede calentis*

> (They say that scythe-bearing chariots, *growing hot with the mingled gore*, often suddenly sheared off limbs.)[7] (3.642–43)

The phrase *caede calentis* in book 3, however, describes not the living animals (the stricken horses) but rather the instrument of the mutilation, the *falciferos currus* themselves. The difference between the two passages is significant. The language of book 3 stresses the body's alienation from itself in the violation of physical boundaries. Thus its hot vital fluid, now spilled into the exterior scene of the fighting, "warms" the otherwise cold blades of the murderous chariot.

Lucretius's sensitivity to death by mutilation is so keen that

---

[6] For further discussion of this problematical passage, see below, Chapter Nine.

[7] On the association between these two passages, see Bonelli, *I motivi profondi*, 240.

he represents even the dissolution of the impersonal elements of our world as metaphorical rending by teeth. Commenting on the untenable view that water and fire are the basic elements, he remarks (1.851–52):

> nam quid in oppressu valido durabit eorum
> ut mortem effugiat, leti sub dentibus ipsis?

(For which of them in the strong press will endure so as to flee death, beneath the very teeth of doom?)

Death, even in so remote and non-personal a form, is still the rending of the vulnerable tissue of a living and sensate creature. In this case, even the atomic compounds are "crushed" and "devoured" as if by the "teeth" of a ravening monster. The passages from book 5 cited above suggest that metaphors like those of the crushing weight or of the "teeth of death" should be allowed their full visual force.[8]

The plague at the end of book 6 completes the dossier of nightmarish outbreaks of massive corporeal injury in the poem. The numerous connections with book 3 need not be repeated here. The three passages—the devoured flesh, the beasts in battle, and the plague—are interrelated by verbal similarities and common imagery. Any one of these passages alone would be enough to suggest that the physical pain of death and the horror of fatal injuries reflect serious anxieties about the vulnerability of the body. The surface argument of book 3, that death is a painless process of the airy soul's floating off into the winds like smoke, is a highly sublimated form of these concerns.[9] In fact, as we have seen, bodily injury as a

---

[8] On the vivid force of *letum*, see Waszink, "Letum," passim; also above, Chapter Three, notes 10 and 14. The suggestion of animal violence in *dentibus* here is perhaps reinforced by *refrenat* just before (1.850). For the importance generally of the literal sense of words in Lucretian imagery, see West, *Imagery and Poetry*, ch. 1.

[9] On this passage in its context, see Regenbogen, "Lucrez," 349–50, who notes the irrational violence behind the philosophical argumentation: "Immer stehen hintergründliche Schrecken bereit, zum Angriff gegen die Tröstungen der Philosophie vorzuschreiten" (p. 350).

prelude to a painful and ugly death inspires some of Lucretius's most powerful poetry.

These vivid accounts of physical injury in books 5 and 6 have two other features in common that are important for their subsurface psychological implications: (1) they belong to a remote stage, definitely bracketed as "not of the present moment," whether that stage be the primordial past of pre-civilized life or the historical past of Thucydides's Athens; (2) they intrude into the flow of the argument with a thrust of poetic and emotional energy that is surprising. These features stamp the above passages with an intensity that sets them off from their immediate contexts; they are marked as belonging to a special order of reality. An unexpected, unpredicted energy seems to be pushing up to the surface something alien, remote, and possibly repressed.

Interpreters like Logre and Perelli view this phenomenon as an expression of Lucretius's own unconscious anxieties. But it is worth making the effort, as this study attempts to do, to see it as part of the total fabric of the poem—a fabric that is sometimes rough or uneven, to be sure, but one that also contains the knowledge of the painful experiences that the poem is ultimately seeking to overcome in leading us on the path to Epicurean serenity of mind. By making his reader experience the physical horror of dying, even in the displaced forms of book 3, Lucretius convinces him or her of the need for a *ratio*, a philosophy able to accept death in all its reality without dread, depression, or despair. For this reason, as Diskin Clay suggests, the plague is a kind of final test of the reader (see Chapter Two, above). But it is also the ultimate proof of our need for the *vera ratio* of Epicureanism, as well as the ultimate incentive, to both poet and reader, for mastering its difficult concepts and foreign terminology.

The reality of death's power intrudes in this way not because Lucretius the poet and Lucretius the philosopher are at odds, but because Lucretius, as *both* poet and philosopher, knows and can reveal the dark secrets of the human heart, the *caecum stimulum* that lies hidden beneath. This darkness is, after all, the other side of his great theme, the illumination of cosmic space by bright, victorious, philosophical radiance, the light of Epicurus's science and wisdom. And that light is never stronger than at the point when Lucretius is about to embark on the darkest part of his subject and the greatest of the fears that afflict mankind (3.1–30). It shines strongly again, for a moment—but an important moment—near the end of the book, in Epicurus's celestial radiance (3.1042–44), just before the unrelenting affirmation of "death eternal" dwarfs into endless nothingness the "daily light" in terms of which man measures his little life (*nec minus ille diu iam non erit, ex hodierno / lumine qui finem vitai fecit . . .* , "nor will he who has made an end to his life with today's light cease to exist for any less long a time . . . ," 3.1092–93).

Within book 3, the motif of mutilation makes an early appearance in the argument for the mortality of the soul. In noting the close conjunction of body and soul, and therefore their common mortality, Lucretius moves quickly from fainting in terror (3.151–60, discussed above) to the collapse that results from a deep wound. In describing the injury that causes the loss of consciousness, he gives detailed attention to the violence done to the body (3.170–74):

> si minus offendit vitam vis horrida teli
> ossibus ac nervis disclusis intus adacta,
> at tamen insequitur languor terraeque petitus
> suavis et in terra mentis qui gignitur aestus,
> interdumque quasi exsurgendi incerta voluntas.

(If a less fearful blow of a weapon, driven within, strikes the life, laying bare the bones and sinews, even so there follow a weakness and a sweet seeking of the earth and a dizziness of the mind that takes place on the ground and sometimes as it were an unsure will to get up.)

Although *minus* marks this injury as less than fatal, the power of the thrust, conveyed by the phrase "the shuddering force of the weapon . . . driven within" (*vis horrida teli . . . intus adacta*), works in the opposite direction and dramatizes the extent of the hurt. The two halves of this phrase, in fact, frame the devastating effects of the blow on the body, the laying bare of bone and sinew (*ossibus ac nervis disclusis*). *Intus* is so placed as to modify both *disclusis* and *adacta*: the bones and sinews are "uncovered within" their enveloping flesh, and the weapon is "driven within" that protective layer to reach what should be covered.

As in the account of the wild beast devouring his human victim in book 5, Lucretius gives a visual presentation of this laying bare of the inner tissues of the body (*disclusis*). Here too, as in two of the afflictions described later in book 3 and also in the description of the hamstrung horse in book 5, the injured person tries to stand up (*quasi exsurgendi incerta voluntas*, 3.174). The very "unsteadiness" of that effort (*incerta*) and the word *voluntas* add pathos by calling attention to the subjective state of the wounded man. There is an implicit contrast between the "will," ineffectual as it is, and the external force of the weapon (*vis horrida teli*) that has "struck his life" (*offendit vitam*). On the other hand, Lucretius presents the symptoms of the fainting as almost tangible items that "follow," as if in a familiar, expected sequence (*et tamen insequitur . . .*).

The interplay between the almost clinical austerity of the list of symptoms in 3.172–73 and the sensitivity to the physical suffering in the preceding lines (*vis horrida, disclusis, intus adacta*) keeps the pathos under strong intellectual control. Lucretius thus maintains a careful balance between a sympathetic response to a fellow creature's grievous injury, implicit in a detail like the "unstable will to get up," and the philosophical generality of the whole argument. Important for this restraint too is the logical structure implied by the adversative *at tamen* in 172 and the deductive force of *ergo* in 175, as Lucretius turns away from the specific organs (*ossibus ac nervis*, 171) and from the preciousness of *vitam* (170) to the more general "corporeal nature of the mind" and the "corporeal" force of "weapons" (*corpoream natura animi* and *corporeis telis*) in his concluding point (175–76):

> ergo corpoream naturam animi esse necessest,
> corporeis quoniam telis ictuque laborat.

(Therefore the nature of the mind must be corporeal, since it suffers from corporeal weapons and blows.)

The repeated *corporeus* picks up the logical flow of the argument that the soul must be material because it is vulnerable to material force (cf. *nonne fatendumst / corporea natura animum constare animamque*, 167). Thus Lucretius moves us back from sympathy with the injured person (implicit also in the emphatically enjambed *suavis* of 173) to atomic principles.

It is instructive to compare 3.170–76 with an earlier account of a hard blow that disrupts consciousness and nearly causes death (2.944–62):

> Praeterea quamvis animantem grandior ictus,
> quam patitur natura, repente adfligit et omnis
> corporis atque animi pergit confundere sensus.
> dissoluuntur enim positurae principiorum
> et penitus motus vitales impediuntur,
> donec materies, omnis concussa per artus,
> vitalis animae nodos a corpore solvit
> dispersamque foras per caulas eiecit omnis.
> nam quid praeterea facere ictum posse reamur
> oblatum, nisi discutere ac dissolvere quaeque?
> fit quoque uti soleant minus oblato acriter ictu
> relicui motus vitales vincere saepe,
> vincere, et ingentis plagae sedare tumultus
> inque suos quicquid rursus revocare meatus
> et quasi iam leti dominantem in corpore motum
> discutere ac paene amissos accendere sensus.
> nam qua re potius leti iam limine ab ipso
> ad vitam possint collecta mente reverti,
> quam quo decursum prope iam siet ire et abire?

(Besides, a harsher blow than its nature endures suddenly strikes some living creature, and goes on to disturb all the senses of its mind and body. For the positions of the first-beginnings [atoms] are dissolved and the vital movements are hindered deep within until the matter, shaken through all the limbs, loosens the vital knots of the soul from the body and drives the soul scattered out through all the pores. For what power should we suppose that such a blow would have, if not to shake up and dissolve each thing? It also happens that, if a blow has been less sharply struck, the rest of the vital movements are often accustomed to win, to win and to put down the great disturbances of the blow and to call everything back again into its own paths and to shake off the movement of doom that is, as it were, now ruling in the body and to rekindle the senses that have almost been lost. For by what means can things return again to life with mind once more gathered together other than by going to the place where their course is nearly run through, and then turning back?)

Lucretius is here equally aware of the threat to life and the struggle to maintain the "vital movements" and to "shake off the movement of death that, as it were, now rules in the body" (955, 958–59). The threat to life here remains at the atomic level, as the book's concern with atom and void requires. Even so, there is something approaching a drama of life and death in the effort to keep the soul-atoms together in the shaken body. Yet Lucretius carefully subordinates the violence of the injury to the invisible atomic processes of placement, entwinement, and separation. There are no vivid details of a weapon laying bare bone and muscle, as in 3.171. Indeed, the passage in book 2 deflects the suggestion of individual suffering or pain by the de-individualizing metaphor of calming a political disturbance (*ingentis plagae sedare tumultus*, 956) and by the undeveloped figure in the last lines of death as a journey to a remote, mysterious place (962). The passage is a tour de force in describing the recovery from severe hurt without mentioning a personal subject at all. The sufferer is the vague and general *quamvis animantem* in the first line (944), "any sentient creature," or the undefined plural subject (possibly the "vital movements" themselves) in the last two lines.

The description in 3.170–74, to be sure, is not much more explicit about a personal subject, although *languor* and *voluntas* come closer. But the body's suffering in that passage is much more specific. At the same time, the passage in book 2 helps prepare for the more explicit physicality of death in book 3, especially as it goes on to describe pain as occurring "when the atoms of matter, disturbed by some force throughout the living flesh, throughout the limbs, tremble in the seat within" (963–65):

> dolor est ubi materiai
> corpora vi quadam per viscera viva per artus
> sollicitata suis trepidant in sedibus intus.

Though Lucretius here acknowledges the power of pain over the "living flesh" in the inner reaches of the body (*in sedibus intus*), he still avoids mentioning a personal subject, as is perhaps appropriate for his present argument, that atoms themselves have no sensation. In this same objective, de-personalized spirit, then, he goes on in the next verses to the complementary sensation of pleasure (*blanda voluptas*).

Elsewhere in the first half of book 3, the mortal soul's separation from the body, though sometimes depicted as a gentle drifting away, as of smoke into air, also takes more violent forms.[10] These are the "penetration" of a hostile "force" into the body (*penetrare*, 252, 471); a "splitting apart" (*discidium, discidere*, 342, 347, 581, 639, 669; cf. 659; also *scinditur*, 530); "rending apart" (*dilaniata*, 539); "tearing away" (*divelli*, 326; cf. *evellere*, 310 and 327; *avulsus*, 563); and various modes of division and partition (*dispertitam*, 589 and 638; *distractam*, 590; *divisa*, 667).

On two occasions Lucretius draws his illustrations from what is perhaps the most anxiety-provoking of physical mutilations, injury to the eyes. In the first case, the eye around the pupil is mangled (*lacerato oculo*, 408) or "cut around" (*circum caedas aciem*, 411). In the second passage the eye is "torn out from its roots" (*avulsus radicibus*, 563). In describing a decapitated head, Lucretius also gives the detail of the wide staring eyes (*oculosque patentes*, 655).[11] It is hard to gauge the possible impact of such a description on Lucretius's audience,

---

[10] On the soul's departure as smoke, see above, Chapter Three. See also Bailey, *T. Lucreti Cari*, and Kenney, *Lucretius III*, ad 656ff.

[11] For the echo of Ennius in *oculos patentes* in 655 (*Annales* 472–73 Vahlen), see below p. 142, n. 21.

but we may recall the special horror attaching to the mutilation of the eyes in Sophocles's Oedipus plays and its aftermath in Seneca; and we may note too the close association of eyes and life in Lucretius's contemporary, Catullus,[12] as well as Lucretius's own favorite images of light and vision for moral and scientific knowledge. The phrase *splendidus orbis* in 415 conveys the poet's appreciation of the healthy eye. The fiery, flashing eye is the sign of animal fierceness, as in the case of the lion in all his "violent force" (3.289–98, especially 289, *cum fervescit et ex oculis micat acrius ardor*, "when he seethes in anger and the warmth flashes more sharply from his eyes"), whereas the eyes "swim" in fluid confusion for the drunken man whose mind is besotted with wine (*madet mens, nant oculi*, 3.479–80).

The simile of eye and pupil in 408ff. is an effective way to set forth the relation of *anima* and *animus*. Like the pupil, the *animus* is the more essential to life; and the familiar association of light and life from Homer on may have contributed to this analogy ("to see the light" = "to be alive"; cf. Lucretius's *in luminis oras* for birth).[13] Nevertheless, the violence of the image, reinforced by the repetition of the physical damage (*lacerato oculo*, 408; *circum caedas aciem*, 411), is somewhat surprising. In the second passage, this violence is almost gratuitous: Lucretius could have spoken of the eye as merely "removed" rather than "torn from its roots" (563).

The vulnerability of the body conveyed by the pupil-eye simile of 408–15 stands in a part-whole relation to the physical vulnerability of the body as a whole: pupil is to eye as consciousness (*animus*) is to the vital principle of life (*anima*). Lucretius is arguing that the *animus* is more important to life than the *anima*, and that if the *animus* departs the *anima* "follows easily as its companion and departs into the winds" (400). The ease of the departure of the vital air of life, however, stands in sharp contrast to the "limbs cold in death's

---

[12] Seneca, *Oedipus* 958–79 and *Phoenissae* 179–81; Catullus 3.5, 44.1, 82, 104.2.

[13] For the importance and positive value of light imagery in Lucretius, see West, *Imagery and Poetry*, ch. 7.

chill" in the following line (401), and especially to the tenacity for life conveyed by the verbs *manet . . . remansit* in 402 and *cunctatur et haeret* in 407. Framed by this instinctive determination to stay alive is the vivid contrast between the process of taking in the "life-giving winds of the aether" and the mutilated state of a body doomed to death (403–5):

> quamvis est circum caesis lacer undique membris
> truncus, adempta anima circum membrisque remota
> vivit et aetherias vitalis suscipit auras.

> (However much his trunk is mutilated with the limbs cut all around, nevertheless, with the soul taken away and removed from the limbs, he lives and takes in the vital winds of the upper air.)

The phrase *circum caesis lacer undique membris / truncus* is one of the poem's most powerfully condensed expressions of massive physical injury.[14] Its position here provides an effective foil to the beauty of the life process in the following line. The context also heightens the emotional impact of the injury. The separation of *caesis . . . membris* by *lacer undique*, the repetition of *circum . . . membris* in 403–4, and the emphatically enjambed *truncus* and *vivit* all reinforce the contrast between death and life, the critical injury to the body in desperate, life-threatening circumstances and the regularity of the process of breathing. The beauty of taking in the vital air and the tenacity of life (especially 402, 405, 407) give a special poignancy to an injury that means certain death.

Further verbal repetitions within this passage emphasize the analogy between the soul and the eye. Lucretius uses the phrase *circum caedas aciem* of the entire body in 403, but he echoes it in two later descriptions of the eye alone: *laceratus circum* in 408 and *circum caedas aciem* in 411. Within this

---

[14] On the syntax of these lines, see Bailey, *T. Lucreti Cari*, ad 403–4 and ad 405. I follow Bailey and Kenney, *Lucretius III*, in taking *truncus* as a noun ("the trunk"), rather than as an adjective ("mutilated," with Heinze). The shift of subject from *animus* to the man himself, to his mutilated "trunk," and back to the man himself (*vivit, suscipit*, 405), is expressive of the part-whole contrast that makes the sense of mutilation in this passage so powerful.

analogy between the soul and the eye in 413–15 a double contrast conveys the vulnerability of our physical being to loss through injury. First, the "healthy" eye, with its "bright circle," contrasts with the "devoured" state of the injured pupil. Second, the "light" of vision (implicit also in the "brightness" of the healthy eye) contrasts with the "shadows" of the blindness that follows this injury (413–15):

> at si tantula pars oculi media illa *peresa* est,
> occidit extemplo *lumen tenebraeque sequuntur*,
> *incolumis* quamvis alioquist *splendidus orbis*.

(But if only a tiny part of the middle of the eye is *eaten away*, at once the *light* dies and *dark shadows follow*, however much the *bright circle* is otherwise *unharmed*.)

Here too Lucretius's small, qualifying words, *tantula* and *alioqui*, add pathos to the organ's vulnerability. Repetition of the key words for light and health from 408–10 reinforces the point (408–10):

> ut, lacerato oculo circum si pupula mansit
> *incolumis*, stat cernundi vivata potestas,
> dummodo ne totum corrumpas *luminis orbem*.

(So that if the pupil has remained *unharmed* while the eye is torn all around, the power of perceiving stands firm, endowed with full life, provided that you do not ruin *the light's circle*.)

The phrase *vivata potestas* in 409 forges another link between the preciousness (and fragility) of life and that of the eye's vision (cf. *at manet in vita*, 402; *aetherias vitalis suscipit auras*, 405; *tamen in vita cunctatur et haeret*, 407).

Here, as elsewhere, Lucretius does not let us dwell too long on the physical pain and incapacitating suffering, but concludes with a sharp restatement of his philosophical thesis and the objective language of the "treaty" that governs *animus* and *anima* in the "eternity" of atom and void (416): *hoc anima atque animus vincti sunt foedere semper* ("by this treaty soul and mind are forever bound"). The eternity of the *foedus* maintains a perspective beyond the fragility of the precious, easily injured organ. Returning to his scientific discourse, the poet reaffirms his largest horizons and the constants that his philosophy discovers in our mortal, vulnerable world.

From this passage on (402ff.), however, there is a steady insistence on mutilation and the loss of consciousness: the injured eye of 402–16, the scenes of coma and epilepsy in 465–505, the gradual spread of "death's cold tracks" over the limbs in 529ff. (and cf. *dilaniata*, "torn apart," 539). These images culminate in the unexpected violence of the scene that we have already mentioned, the scythe-armed chariot, whose blades, "hot" with the victims' blood, cut off limbs (*abscidere membra*, 642; cf. 645). Lucretius does not spare us the gory details of the severed limbs that are still trying to do their work (649–56). There is nothing in the logic of the argument *per se* that prepares us for such details. But the passage is less of an illogical intrusion if, as I have argued, it contains another kind of "logic," namely an underlying insistence on the physical pain that accompanies death and on the death-dealing power of bodily injury, always ready to deprive us of the light and winds of the upper air (cf. 405–15).

This passage (634–56) resumes and concentrates the previous images of the soul's being "cut apart" or split off. There is a heavy accumulation throughout of verbs of mutilation: *dispertita* (638); *discissa* (639); *disicietur* (639); *abscidere* (642); *abscisum* (645, 654). This extraordinary passage has a no less extraordinary sequel, the bloody cutting up of a snake "into many parts," which "you may see twisting with the wound and spattering the earth with gore" as it bites its severed hinder part to suppress the pain of the "heavy wound" (657–63).

Within both of these passages Lucretius gradually shifts his emphasis from objective, external detail to the feeling of pain or the subject's impression of continuing effort and action just at the point of the limb-severing blow. Thus the snake in the second passage, "smitten by the pain" (*icta dolore*), makes the effort (*petere*) of biting its hinder parts with the purpose (*ut*) of checking the pain by the biting (662–63): *ipsam seque retro*

*partem petere ore priorem / vulneris ardenti, ut morsu premat,
icta dolore.* The second line, with its interlocking word order
and suggestively placed *ardenti* (keeping the reading of the
manuscripts against Brieger's *ardentem*), is remarkable for its
implication of the active, "burning" pain of the wound (*vul-
neris ardenti . . . dolore*) and the helpless savagery of the crea-
ture that has only its "biting" (*morsus*) to help itself. The wild
creature's "bite" is now turned from possible use against man
(cf. *minanti*, 657) to use against itself. Instead, man has be-
come the aggressor and the mutilator. The "burning pain of
the wound" in 663 gives a sympathetic, feeling interpretation
to the matter-of-fact reference to a "fresh wound" three lines
before (660–61): *omnia iam sorsum cernes ancisa recenti /
vulnere tortari* ("you will observe all the parts, cloven apart,
twisting about with the fresh wound"). *Vulnus* occupies the
same metrical position in both verses. The shift of pronouns
from the generalized second person (*cernes*) in 660 to the
third-person reflexives (*ipsam seque*) in 662 also helps to
move us subtly from objectivity to identification with the feel-
ings of the wounded serpent.

In a similar way the description of the scythe-armed chariot
begins with the physical objects (chariot, limbs, earth, 642–
45) and then proceeds to the "feeling of pain" (here in the
negative, *mobilitate mali non quit sentire dolorem*, "because
of the swiftness of the injury he cannot feel the pain," 646).
There follow the warrior's "eagerness" in his total involve-
ment in the battle as he "seeks after" the fighting (*petessit*,
648) and his failure to "grasp" the loss of an arm or a leg
when he "tries" to get up (649–53):

> nec tenet amissam laevam cum tegmine saepe
> inter equos abstraxe rotas falcesque rapaces,
> nec cecidisse alius dextram, cum scandit et instat.
> inde alius conatur adempto surgere crure,
> cum digitos agitat propter moribundus humi pes.

(Nor does he grasp that the wheels and rushing scythes have torn
off among the horses the left hand that has been lost with its

shield, nor does another grasp that his right hand has fallen when he climbs and presses forward. There another tries to get up with a leg that has been taken away, while the dying foot nearby on the ground moves the toes.)

Coming just at the point where the violence escalates to a new level of specific detail, *tenet* is brilliantly placed in its context, for it suggests both the physical act of "holding" and the subjective, intellectual recognition of "understanding" or "grasping." It thus serves as a pivot between objective event and identification with the sufferer's mental processes. The detail of the other man who "attempts" to get up (*conatur*) thematically connects this passage to the earlier injury by the "force of weapon" in 170–74 and the epileptic attack of 499–505 (cf. *quasi exsurgendi incerta voluntas*, 174, and *primum consurgit*, 504). The physical mutilation in warfare also looks ahead to the horses injured in battle in 5.1330–33.[15] These echoes within book 3 mark the steady mounting of the physical violence of the injury, climaxing in 649–63.

It is an aspect of Lucretius's pervasive ethical concern that the almost surrealistic horror of these dismemberments belongs to war, one of the poem's great manifestations of the irrational violence that most needs the cure of Epicurean reason.[16] At the level of personal sensation and individual feeling, however, these passages also acknowledge the pain of severing a limb. Thus they associate that pain with the book's suppressed anxiety about death as a terrifying rending of one's bodily substance. We have already noted the frequent recurrence of images of splitting apart or separation (often marked by compounds in *dis-*) in the account of the soul's dissolution throughout the book (e.g., 326–27, 342–47, 531–39). The vivid descriptions of amputated limbs or severed bodies in these illustrative passages may be regarded as projections of anxieties about primary boundary violation that belong to the

[15] On these connections, see Perelli, *Lucrezio*, 46–47.

[16] On this recalcitrant irrationality of violence and war in Lucretius, see most recently Bonelli, *I motivi profondi*, 243–44; also below, Chapter Nine.

fear of dying. In these passages death is far harsher and more frightening than the dissolution of an airy vapor into the winds elsewhere in the book.

ORAL ENGULFMENT

As the vivid metaphor of destruction "beneath the very teeth of doom" implies (1.852, discussed above), death appears under the image of a devouring beast. In describing the life of early man in the latter part of book 5, Lucretius notes that grief over leaving the sweet light of life was not greater then than it is now (5.988–89): *nec nimio tum plus quam nunc mortalia saecla / dulcia linquebant lamentis lumina vitae.* But he follows this generalizing, resonant verse on the sorrows of mortality with a nightmarish oral fantasy of being eaten alive (5.990–98). Previously in book 5, in proving the mortality of the world, Lucretius uses another image of devouring to describe the general doom that awaits our world (5.373–75):

> haud igitur leti praeclusa est ianua caelo
> nec soli terraeque neque altis aequoris undis,
> sed patet immani et vasto respectat hiatu.

(In no way, then, is the gate of doom foreclosed for the heavens nor the earth nor the deep waves of the sea, but it lies open and looks upon them with its vast gaping.)

The gate of death becomes virtually a living mouth, a huge gaping maw (*vasto hiatu*), endowed even with a kind of vision (*respectat*). The vastness of the aperture is vividly portrayed by the expressive hyperbaton and elision (*immani et vasto respectat hiatu*). Cosmic destruction here, personal destruction in the remote past (5.990–98): both take the same form, actual or anticipated, of engulfment by fierce jaws.[17]

---

[17] On the image of the jaws or the gates of death, see Michels, "Death," 161–63. Cf. also the "devouring" power of anxiety in the allegorical interpretation of Tityos's punishment at the end of book 3, *quem volucres lacerant atque exest anxius angor* ("whom the birds tear and constricting anxiety devours," 3.993). Philodemus, by contrast, refers in a very general, unadorned

As a follower of Epicurus, and also as a contemporary or near-contemporary of Catullus, Virgil, and the elegists, Lucretius is acutely aware that the sufferings of mankind are not all physical. Indeed, the keenest sufferings may be of the heart. Lucretius recognizes the concrete reality of these emotional sufferings by giving them the metaphorical form of a physical injury: they are "wounds of life," *vulnera vitae* (3.63; cf. 5.1197).[18] Human life, in its pursuit of false happiness, "consumes its time amid empty anxieties" (*in curis consumit inanibus aevum*, 5.1431). So too the frustration of passionate love derives from the "bites" and "teeth" that take in no real nourishment, only empty images (*simulacra*, 4.1079–96; cf. *dentis*, 1080; *morsus*, 1085). The tearing of Tityos's liver is only a mythical allegory for the real anxiety that "devours" our spirit (*exest anxius angor*, 3.993). Finally, the mutilation of the eye in 3.408ff. appears as a vivid metaphor of eating: that organ is "gnawed about" or "eaten through" (*si tantula pars oculi media illa peresa est*, 413).

SEPARATED PARTS

In his various references to dismemberment, Lucretius insists on the discreteness of the severed limbs or organs. From the point of view of Epicurean psychology, this emphasis corresponds to the divisibility of the soul into its constituent atoms. Thus Lucretius can effect a smooth, logical return from the bloody details of the chopped snake in 657–63 (cited above, in part) to the cool analysis of the material processes (664–69):

> omnibus esse igitur totas dicemus in illis
> particulis animas? at ea ratione sequetur
> unam animantem animas habuisse in corpore multas.

---

way to "our being devoured by fish" in his point about the unimportance of the fate of our body after death (*De Morte* 32.36–37, τὸ ὑπ' ἰχθύων καταβρωθῆναι).

[18] On this metaphor see Elder, "Lucretius 1.1–49," 92.

ergo divisast ea quae fuit una simul cum
corpore; quapropter mortale utrumque putandumst,
in multas quoniam partis disciditur aeque.

(Shall we then say that there are entire souls in all of those small
parts? But by that reasoning it follows that one living creature
has many souls in its body. Therefore that [soul] which was one
has been divided up along with the body; wherefore both must
be considered mortal because each is divided up equally into
many parts.)

The descriptions of the amputations, however, are far less ab-
stract; and a line like 662, *ipsam seque retro partem petere ore
priorem*, gives a brilliant syntactic imitation of the very pro-
cess of partition, as the snake's body virtually falls into a
"back" and "front" part, separated by the mouth's "seeking."
The repetition of the syllable *re-* (*re-tro, pete-re, o-re, prio-
rem*) and the other sound patterns of the verse enhance this
word-painting of reversed movement.

The preceding passage, on the amputated limbs of warriors,
also gives special attention to the severed limb: hand, leg, foot,
toes (649–53). The severed head is the culminating horror,
and the word order again enacts its removal from its trunk
(*caput abscisum . . . trunco*, 654). The next line mentions the
face but also singles out one particular part, the "staring eyes"
(655). These details are not isolated instances but hark back
to previous descriptions, especially the spread of cold death
up from the toes and feet in 527–30 (compare 653) and the
mutilated or torn-out eyes of 403ff. and 563–64.

In the other places where Lucretius indicates extreme bodily
laceration, dismemberment, or other injury, he strongly con-
veys the separateness of the individual organs or limbs. In
3.551–52, for example, just before mentioning the decay of
limbs, Lucretius stresses their separation from the body, re-
peating the disjunctive prefix, *se-*: *seorsum / secreta ab nobis*.
The following passages are typical:

verum ubi vementi est commota metu mens,
consentire animam totam per membra videmus

sudoresque ita palloremque exsistere toto
corpore et infringi linguam vocemque aboriri,
caligare oculos, sonere auris, succidere artus.

(But when the mind is disturbed by violent fear, we see the entire
soul join in that feeling throughout the limbs, and thus sweating
and paleness comes over the whole body and the tongue is bro-
ken and the voice fails, the eyes are misted over, the ears ring,
the limbs collapse.)[19]   (3.152–56)

inde omnia mobilitantur,
concutitur sanguis, tum viscera persentiscunt
omnia, postremis datur ossibus atque medullis.

(From there everything is set into motion, the blood is shaken,
then the flesh feels it, and it is given to the furthest bones and
marrow.)   (3.248–50)

denique saepe hominem paulatim cernimus ire
et membratim vitalem deperdere sensum;
in pedibus primum digitos livescere et unguis,
inde pedes et crura mori, post inde per artus
ire alios tractim gelidi vestigia leti.

(Often we observe a man pass away little by little and limb by
limb lose vital sensation; first the toes on his feet grow livid, and
the nails, then the feet and legs die, then after that the tracks of
cold death advance by degrees through the other limbs.)
                                                           (3.526–30)

Such enumerations also characterize the clinical objectivity of
the symptoms of the plague, as in 6.1185–89:

sollicitae porro plenaeque sonoribus aures,
creber spiritus aut ingens raroque coortus,
sudorisque madens per collum splendidus umor,
tenvia sputa minuta, croci contacta colore
salsaque, per fauces rauca vix edita tussi.

---

[19] Bollack, *Raison*, 461, points out that Lucretius here shows mortality un-
der the three aspects of *anima*, *animus*, and *corpus*.

(The ears troubled and full of sounds, the breathing thick and heavy and coming infrequently, the shining dew of sweat dripping along the neck, thin and small spittle, touched by the color of crocus [yellow] and salty, brought up with difficulty through the throat with hoarse coughing.)

In addition to the clinical observations of the medical tradition behind this description, such passages reveal the poet's preoccupation with the vulnerability of our physical frame. He recognized that we are all ultimately the sum of our discrete, exposed parts.[20]

In the passages cited above, we may observe how terms for the organic wholeness of the body, generally at the beginning, like *omnia* (248) *hominem* (476), and *hominem . . . vitalem sensum* (526–27), contrast with the enumerated limbs, organs, or faculties that follow. Lines 548–57 perform this operation twice, first in the protasis and then in the apodosis:

> et quoniam *mens* est *hominis* pars una, loco quae
> fixa manet certo, velut aures atque oculi sunt
> atque alii sensus qui vitam cumque gubernant,
> et veluti manus atque oculus naresve *seorsum*
> *secreta ab nobis* nequeunt sentire neque esse,
> sed tamen in parvo liquuntur tempore tabe,
> sic animus per se non quit sine corpore et *ipso*
> esse *homine*, illius quasi quod vas esse videtur
> sive aliud quid vis potius coniunctius ei
> fingere, quandoquidem conexu corpus adhaeret.

(And because the *mind* is one part *of a man*, which remains fixed in a definite place, just as are the ears and eyes and other senses that govern life, and just as the hands and eye or nostrils *sepa-*

---

[20] See my remarks in "Ovid," 58. Cf. A. R. Ammons's poem, "Hibernaculum," on death as the "mechanical" failure of individual organs:

> a brain lobe squdging /
> against the skull, a soggy kidney, a little vessel / smartly plugged . . . /
> . . . so much more mechanical, physical than / spiritual seeming grief.

rated off from us cannot have sensation or exist but still are melted with decay in a short time, so the mind cannot exist without the body and *the man himself,* because he seems to be, as it were, the vessel of the mind, or something even more closely joined if you care to imagine it, since the body clings to it in close intertwining.)

In the protasis, the fixity of the *mens* in its established place corresponds to the unified identity of the man (*hominis*) as a sentient being. But after the enumeration of the separate organs of perception in 549–51, Lucretius introduces the notion of the separation from the body (*seorsum, secreta,* 551–52); and directly upon this point he adds their physical decay (*sed tamen in parvo liquuntur tempore tabe,* 553). Conversely, in the apodosis, the *animus* appears in its relation to "the man himself" (*ipso homine,* 554–55), but the sentence moves away from this seat of unified intelligence to the corporeality of the "vessel" that encloses it and to the physical gesture of its tight "clinging" to the *animus* (*coniunctius . . . adhaeret,* 556–57). Lucretius's point is the dependence of the soul on its physical container or "vessel," the body, and therefore its mortality. But an indirect result of this proof of the soul's mortality is that the body's fragility is thrown into relief: it is merely a vessel, easily shattered. The poet's account thus tends to identify the wholeness of the individual, "man himself," with his perishable, precarious mortal shell. The equation of *homo ipse* and *vas,* the "man himself" and the "vessel," is implicit too in the parallelism of *homo ipse* and *corpus* in 554–55: *sine corpore et ipso / . . . homine.*

Lucretius can use this tension between part and whole to create sometimes powerful, even macabre, effects. The account of the severed limbs of the scythe-armed chariot, for example, culminates (naturally enough) in the head (654–56):

> et caput abscisum calido viventeque trunco
> servat humi vultum vitalem oculosque patentis,
> donec reliquias animai reddidit omnis.

(And the head cut off of the warm and living trunk keeps its living countenance on the ground and its wide-open eyes, until it has given up all the remains of the soul.)

The lines juxtapose the visual horror of the severed head with the invisible remains of the *anima* that slip off into the air. They also explore, indirectly, the problem of the physical details that we recognize as the "life" of the living man. The phrase *vultum vitalem* ("the expression of life," in Kenney's translation; "the look of life" in Bailey's), especially following closely upon the *vivente trunco* of the previous verse, suggests the living configuration through which we most immediately perceive the "aliveness" of others as whole persons and of course feel our own aliveness as well.[21]

In focussing on just this point of crossing between a generalized life-consciousness and the separated limbs, Lucretius indirectly touches on one of the principal anxieties about death, the dissolution or disappearance of our total consciousness as a self. His concern with the separable limbs and organs of the body corresponds to what Jacques Lacan calls "le corps morcelé," the feeling of the fragmentation of or even the alienation from a central self in ego neuroses.[22] But rather than try to trace the origins of this stylistic feature of Lucretius's poem to any personal neurosis, I would insist on the general sense of mortality that such passages imply. As in metamorphosis, the sensation of the separability of limbs and organs portrays, and to some extent arouses, anxiety about the status of our physical being as a *thing*. When we contemplate our physical being

[21] As commentators point out, Lucretius is adapting Ennius, *Annales* 472–73 Vahlen (ed. 2), *oscitat in campis caput a cervice revulsum / semianimesque micant oculi lucemque requirunt.* Cf. also Virgil, *Aeneid* 10.394–96. The detail of *vultum vitalem* seems to be Lucretius's own, particularly as he is fond of the adjective *vitalis*, which occurs more than twenty times in the poem. On *vultus* see also Chapter Two above. The description of the chopped-up snake in this passage (3.657–63) even the sober Boyancé calls "un réalisme plutôt sinistre et macabre": Pierre Boyancé, "La théorie de l'âme chez Lucrèce," *Bulletin de l'Association G. Budé, Lettres d'humanité* 17 (1958): 44.

[22] Jacques Lacan, "Le stade du miroir comme formateur de la fonction du Je," *Ecrits* 1 (Paris 1966): 94.

in this way, we become aware of our body as an object that exists independently of our mental consciousness about our life or our selfhood.[23]

This "thingness" also means that the body can be made into a heap of scattered pieces. The tension between this awareness of the possible piecemeal fragmentation of our corporeal substance and our generalized sensation of a unified consciousness appears, as suggested above, in the contrast that Lucretius often develops between the whole person and the organic components. As we have observed, he often enumerates the separate elements of the body in contexts where he is discussing the loss of consciousness. The extreme violence associated with these separations of the bodily parts, in turn, is a displaced form of fears about violence done to the integrity of our physical being, of which the most extreme form is dying.

[23] See my "Ovid," 57–58, with 62 n. 12.

Chapter Seven

THE VIOLATION OF CORPOREAL
BOUNDARIES, 2

PUTREFACTION

We fear death, Epicurus and other Hellenistic philosophers argue, because we fear what will happen to our body after death, forgetting that this body is no longer "ours" or "us." Both the authors of Cynic diatribes like Teles and later Epicureans like Philodemus delight in enumerating how little it matters to us whether this body is burned, buried, mangled by beasts, or eaten by worms or fish.[1] In such attacks on the integrity of the self, putrefaction has a role akin to that of dismemberment. In other periods of Western culture too, where there is high anxiety about death, the decay and corruption of the body bulk large in the literary or visual representations of death, for example in early and classical Greek poetry and in the writings, sculpture, and painting of Europe from the fourteenth to the seventeenth centuries.[2]

Lucretius reproduces many of the Hellenistic arguments about the worthlessness of the body after death, utilizing the rhetoric of the diatribe. Curiously, these sources rarely include

[1] See Philodemus, *De Morte* 32.35ff.; Teles, *De Exilio*, in the *Epitoma Theodori* in Otto Hense, ed., *Teletis Reliquiae*, 2nd ed. (Leipzig, 1909), 31: "What difference does it make to be consumed by fire or to be devoured by a dog or if above the earth by crows or, if buried, by worms?" Hense (ad loc.) cites parallels from Epictetus, Seneca, Petronius, and others. For further discussion, see Wallach, *Lucretius and the Diatribe*, 30–33.

[2] See, for example, Ariès, *Western Attitudes toward Death*, 39–44, and *Hour of Our Death*, 110ff.; also the classic work of Johan Huizinga, *The Waning of the Middle Ages* (1919; English trans. 1949; reprinted, Garden City, N.Y., 1954), esp. 138–51. For early Greece, see, for example, Homer, *Iliad* 22.509 and *Odyssey* 12.45–46; in general, James Redfield, *Nature and Culture in the Iliad* (Chicago, 1975), 167ff., 183ff.

putrefaction in the list of the post-mortem tribulations of the body, although Philodemus refers to physical decay in extreme illness and briefly refers to the body being "hidden away by worms and maggots" (*De Morte* 29.27–30, 33.1–9). That this argument is in fact part of the Epicurean armory, however, is rendered likely by the pseudo-Platonic *Axiochus*, which is probably inspired by Epicurean sources. Axiochus there expresses his fear that he will "lie there, rotting away, turning into worms and snakes" (365C). And Socrates answers with the Epicurean argument of *anaisthesia*, that he will not in fact perceive any of this.[3] At the point where Lucretius himself addresses the anxiety about the actual state of the body after death, he gives only half a line to putrefaction (3.871): *fore ut aut putescat corpore posto.* Instead, he seems to displace these anxieties into metaphors of "wasting away" with grief (e.g., *tabescere luctu*, 911) or the general decay of old age (cf. *marces*, 946, 954). Where he does make heavy use of the motif of putrefactive decay, it is not for the dead body but for the process of dying. Thus he draws one argument for the mortality of the soul from the corruption of the body in the process of death (3.580–85):

> denique cum corpus nequeat perferre animai
> discidium quin in taetro tabescat odore,
> quid dubitas quin ex imo penitusque coorta
> emanarit uti fumus diffusa animae vis,
> atque ideo tanta mutatum putre ruina
> conciderit corpus. . . .

(Finally, since the body cannot endure the splitting off of the soul without wasting away in foul stench, why do you doubt that the force of the soul, poured forth like smoke, has flowed out, rising up from deep within, and for that reason the body falls crumbling, changed by so great a collapse?)

The foul smell of decay at the beginning of the process (*taetro tabescat odore*, 581) is reinforced by the crumbling ruin of the

---

[3] See Bailey, *T. Lucreti Cari*, 2:1140.

body's material substance when the process of death is complete.

The root *putr-*, cognate with Latin *pus* ("pus") and Greek πύθειν, ("to rot"), has a secondary meaning of "crumbling" (especially of soil and stone), in addition to its primary sense of stench and rot. Lucretius uses this secondary meaning several times and is especially fond of various combinations of *putris* and *ruina*. In this secondary meaning, as we have noted in Chapter Five, *putris* and related words associate the death of the human body with the inevitable disintegration of all parts of the world as atomic compounds eventually dissolve into their constituent atoms. Thus we may compare the collapse of the "walls of the world" into *putris ruinas* in 2.1145 with the body's fatal "crumbling away" in ruinous change at the soul's departure in 3.584 (*tanta mutatum putre ruina*; cf. also 2.859–63, 5.832–36). In 5.307, to prove the mortality of the world, Lucretius draws an analogy with the "collapse" of towers and the "crumbling" of stones: *altas turris ruere et putrescere saxa*. Here too, as in the other passages above, he combines the roots *putr-* and *ru-* to reinforce the effect of physical collapse. Later in the book, the verb *putrescere* again describes the universal processes of destruction and renewal, with no specific idea of putrefaction (5.832–33): *namque aliud putrescit et aevo debile languet / porro aliud succrescit.* Closely related, though more emphatic, is the shaking and collapse of the limbs at the soul's departure in death (3.343): *penitus pereunt convulsi conque putrescunt.* Here the underlying metaphor seems to be of a building that crumbles, as in an earthquake, rather than a decay.

It is revealing to compare Lucretius's treatment of the fears about beasts tearing the body here with the reverse situation in book 6, where beasts avoid the bodies of those who have perished of the plague:

> vivus enim sibi cum proponit quisque futurum,
> corpus uti volucres lacerent in morte feraeque,
> ipse sui miseret; neque enim se dividit illim
> nec removet satis a proiecto corpore et illum
> se fingit sensuque suo contaminat adstans.

(For when each, in life, supposes to himself that birds and wild
beasts will tear his body in death, he pities himself; nor does he
separate himself off from there, nor remove himself sufficiently
from the laid-out body, but imagines that that [body] is himself,
and standing there he taints it with his own sensations.)
(3.879–83)

> spiritus ore foras taetrum volvebat odorem,
> rancida quo perolent proiecta cadavera ritu.

(The breath rolled forth a foul stench, in the manner that foul-
smelling bodies that have been cast forth stink.) (6.1154–55)

> multaque humi cum inhumata iacerent corpora supra
> corporibus, tamen alituum genus atque ferarum
> aut procul absiliebat, ut acrem exiret odorem,
> aut, ubi gustarat, languebat morte propinqua.

(Even though many unburied bodies lay on the ground, body
piled on body, nevertheless the race of birds and wild beasts ei-
ther leapt far away from them, in order to get away from the
sharp stench, or else when they had tasted them lay faint in a
death soon to come.)   (6.1215–18)

In the third passage the power of corruption is so forceful that
the wild creatures "leap away" from the decaying bodies (*ab-
siliebat*, 6.1217). In both of the descriptions in book 6, too,
the smell of decay is intimately associated with the "languish-
ing" of the forces of life, for in both cases the reference to
corruption leads directly into a general statement of a wide-
scale defeat of life-energy:

> atque animi prorsum vires totius et omne
> *languebat* corpus leti iam limine in ipso.

(But the strength of the whole mind and the entire body *was
faint*, now in the very threshold of doom.)   (6.1156–57)

> aut, ubi gustarat, *languebat* morte propinqua.
> . . . nec tristia saecla ferarum
> exibant silvis. *languebant* pleraque morbo
> et moriebantur.

(Or else when they had tasted them [they] *lay faint* in a death soon to come. . . . Nor did the sad races of wild beasts go forth from the forests. For the most part they *lay faint* with disease and died.)   (6.1218–22)

The disgusting smell of the decaying corpse in book 6 plays no role in the concern or the indignation of the man contemplating his post-mortem body in book 3. The full horror of corruption, however, has emerged earlier in the book, in a passage discussed above; and here the reference is not only to the body after death but to the rotting of severed limbs as part of the painful process of dying (3.551–55):

> et veluti manus atque oculus naresve seorsum
> secreta ab nobis nequeunt sentire neque esse,
> sed tamen *in parvo liquuntur tempore tabe*,
> sic animus per se non quit sine corpore et ipso
> esse homine, illius quasi quod vas esse videtur. . . .

(And just as the hands and eye or nostrils separated off from us cannot have sensation or exist but still *are melted with decay in a short time*, so the mind cannot exist without the body and the man himself, because he seems to be, as it were, the vessel of the mind, or something even more closely joined if you care to imagine it, since the body clings to it in close intertwining.)

The small detail of *liquuntur . . . tabe* adds liquefaction to the foul smell mentioned in the passages cited above from book 6. This passage too shows the close connection of putrefaction with dismemberment or mutilation: both are parallel forms of primary boundary violation.

Continuing this line of argument, Lucretius adds the soul's dispersion throughout the body as further proof of its mortality (3.580–91). From a strictly scientific point of view, dying is the neutral, even gentle process of the soul's diffusion into the air, like smoke (3.583, 590–91). But in the same context, Lucretius also shows death as a harsher physical process, one that deforms the body by the "change" into a condition of rotting decay (3.584–85): *tanta mutatum putre ruina / conciderit corpus.* . . . The enjambment of the verb *conciderit* stresses the physical nature of the body in its "fall." *Putre* in

584 also harks back to the more elaborate description of decay just preceding (580–81):

> denique cum corpus nequeat perferre animai
> *discidium* quin *in taetro tabescat odore.*

(Since the body finally cannot endure the *splitting apart* of the soul without *wasting away in foul stench.*)

These two lines combine "splitting apart" and malodorous decay, the two forms of primary boundary violation that Lucretius also brings together in 551–55.

As in the case of mutilation, there is an escalation of the physical ugliness of wounded or mortified flesh as the book continues, for shortly after the detailed horror of dismemberment in 642–45 occurs the most detailed account of putrefaction in the book. The presence of maggots in the dead body, Lucretius argues, is due to small remnants of *anima* in the corpse (3.717–21):

> sin ita sinceris membris ablata profugit
> ut nullas partis in corpore liquerit ex se,
> unde cadavera rancenti iam viscere vermis
> exspirant atque unde animantum copia tanta
> exos et exsanguis tumidos perfluctuat artus?

(But if the soul, taken away, flees forth from the limbs so that it has left in the body no parts of itself, whence do the bodies breathe forth worms in the now-rotting flesh and whence does so great an abundance, boneless and bloodless, of living creatures seethe throughout the swollen limbs?)

The point is useful for Lucretius's argument as he is trying to prove the materiality and divisibility of the *anima*. There is, however, a poetic overkill: his wealth of gruesome detail goes far beyond what strict logic requires.[4] The reference to "flesh" in the phrase *rancenti viscere* once again points up the separated state of the parts of the body. It also reminds us of the vulnerability of the vital organs and the exposure of the inte-

---

[4] In a lost work *On Diseases and Death* (frag. 18 Arrighetti = *P. Herc.* 1012, col. 22) Epicurus refers to the worms that result from corruption, but the context and degree of detail are uncertain.

rior cavities of the body. This "flesh," furthermore, is already fully in the grip of decomposition, in its physically offensive, ugly form (*rancenti*). *Exspirant* and *perfluctuat* vividly depict the physical process by which the flesh liquifies to its puffy, putrescent state. *Copia tanta exos et exsanguis* ("so great a boneless and bloodless abundance") calls attention to the specifically worm-like quality of the pullulating new life in the maggotty remains; and *tumidos artus* reminds us, grimly, that these are (or were) the limbs of a human body, now distorted in their subjection to the inexorable natural decay.

By the details of these carefully chosen verbs and adjectives, Lucretius presents the integrity of the body as violated simultaneously from within and from without. The external outline of what were initially "whole limbs" (*sinceris membris*, 717) is deformed by their bloating with worms (*tumidos artus*, 721). The soft internal organs now consist of *rancenti viscere* and are inhabited by a "great abundance" (*copia tanta*) of living things which, however, are "bloodless and boneless," that is, lack the expected solidity and outline of the familiar human or even mammalian body. Indeed, the "bloodlessness" of these "living things" suggests that even this life has an ambiguous quality. The hypallage of "boneless abundance of living things" (*animantum copia tanta / exos*) has a horrifying brilliance worthy of Baudelaire's "La Charogne."

Just as these living creatures are ambiguously without blood, so the normal life process of breathing is distorted into a macabre form, virtually animating dead men as the corpses "breathe forth worms" (*exspirant*). The plural magnifies the effect. The life process here produces the signs of its opposite, the marks and the very agents of decay. The degree of the horror may be measured against the expansive beauty that Lucretius elsewhere attributes to breathing, as in 3.405: *vivit et aetherias vitalis suscipit auras* ("lives and takes in the vital winds of the upper air").

Lucretius has already laid the scientific basis for his argument about putrefaction in book 2, but the difference of emphasis between the two discussions brings out the greater concern of book 3 with the physical horror of dying. In 2.871–78, as part of the endless process of atomic change, "living worms come forth from foul dung" (*vivos exsistere vermis / stercore de tae-tro*, 2.871–72). But the same processes also produce less threatening transformations (2.871–78):

> quippe videre licet vivos exsistere vermis
> stercore de taetro, putorem cum sibi nacta est
> intempestivis ex imbribus umida tellus;
> praeterea cunctas itidem res vertere sese.
> vertunt se fluvii frondes et pabula laeta
> in pecudes, vertunt pecudes in corpora nostra
> naturam, et nostro de corpore saepe ferarum
> augescunt vires et corpora pennipotentum.

(For one may see living worms come forth from fetid dung when the earth, wet after heavy rains, has gained a rich rotting for itself; all things transform themselves in like manner. Rivers, foliage, and the joyful fodder transform themselves into cattle, cattle change their nature into our bodies, and often from our body the strength of wild beasts and the bodies of feathered birds gain increase.)

Lucretius here is emphatic about the process of dung, heat, moisture, and decay that generates worms (2.871–73). But he does not use this motif to threaten our sense of bodily integrity, as he does in 3.717–21. The changes of "our bodies" (2.876) involve only birds and beasts, and the details of blood, bone, and limb found in 3.721 are absent here. At this point in book 2, Lucretius's concern is not death for the individual but the movements of atoms that pervade "all things" (*cunctas itidem res*, 2.874). Thus the transformative processes in "our bodies" are due to the impersonal *corpora* whose movements make and unmake all living substance. A little later Lucretius makes a similar point apropos of the generation of worms after rain, and again his concern is the rearrangement of atoms, not rotting corpses (2.898–901):

> et tamen haec, cum sunt quasi putrefacta per imbris,
> vermiculos pariunt, quia corpora materiai

antiquis ex ordinibus permota nova re
conciliantur ita ut debent animalia gigni.

(And yet these [bodies], when they have been, as it were, putri-
fied through rains, give birth to little worms, because the bodies
[atoms], moved from their old arrangements by the new thing,
are brought into union in such a way that animals are begotten.)

In book 3, however, Lucretius the physicist/biologist has be-
come Lucretius the moralist, and the atomic processes are re-
focussed on personal death and our primary boundary anxie-
ties about the body.

In its miniaturized horror, 3.717–21 surpasses a good deal
of the gruesomeness of the plague in book 6. Its details, how-
ever, are not reported as a possible subject of anxiety but are
merely given as objective fact. A little later Lucretius offers as
a minor proof of the soul's mortality the ironical suggestion
that the soul might be afraid of being enclosed in a decaying
body (*an metuit conclusa manere in corpore putri*, 3.773).
This "fear" is perhaps not only that of the hypothetical *anima*:
it may belong to the thoughtful person who contemplates the
reality of his body in death. Glancing back some fifty lines
earlier to the description in 717–21, such a reader knows what
lies in store for his *corpus putre*.

ENCLOSURE AND CONSTRICTION

As 3.773 indicates, anxiety about death may also take the dis-
placed form of imprisonment, entrapment, or constriction (cf.
metuit conclusa manere in 773). The anxieties about the body
after death include suffocation in honey (*in melle situm suf-
focari*, 3.891), darkness (1011), and imprisonment (*carcer*,
1016). These are standard topics in Epicureanism and in the
Cynic diatribe against worrying about your corpse.[5] Else-
where, however, Lucretius changes the focus of this concern

---

[5] Compare, e.g., Philodemus, *De Morte* 32.2–33.25; cf. Wallach, *Lucretius
and the Diatribe*, 31ff.

from the state of death to the process of dying, where constriction or enclosure is often prominent.

Anxiety generally in Lucretius consists in the acute physical sensation of internal constriction. In its two occurrences in the poem the vivid phrase *anxius angor* is closely associated with death.[6] In book 3, it describes the allegorical significance of Tityos's punishment. The eating of his liver in Hades really points to the anguish of the lover's anxiety in this life (*exest anxius angor*, 3.993). In book 6, however, the subject of this *anxius angor* is the direct confrontation with dying as the "body languishes at the very threshold of death" (6.1156–59):

> atque animi prorsum vires totius et omne
> languebat corpus *leti iam limine in ipso.*
> intolerabilibusque malis erat *anxius angor*
> *adsidue comes* et gemitu commixta querela.

> (And at once the strength of the whole mind and all the body lay fainting *now in the very threshold of doom.* And *companion constantly* to the unbearable woes were *constricting anxiety* and lamentation mingled with groans.)

Here the constricting anguish of the fear of death is virtually personified as a "companion" and stands among the "unendurable sufferings" of this affliction. Physical constriction is present along with the figurative, psychological enclosing, for Lucretius goes on to the incessant heaving of breath (*singultus*) that seizes and compresses the limbs (*membra coactans*, 6.1161).

The disturbed passion of violent love in book 4 produces this same constricting effect of *angor*. Here this "anxiety" appears only in a verbal form (*angat*), as a vague "something"

---

[6] Besides 3.993 and 6.1158, see *angor* in 3.853. See generally Stork, *Nil igitur mors est*, 3–4. Lortie, "Crainte anxieuse," 49, n. 11, quotes a psychological description of anxiety (made without reference to Lucretius) that is relevant: anxiety is "une émotion characterisée par un état de douleur morale et d'incertitude, avec sensation fréquente de *constriction physique. Cette sensation physique de resserrement* constitue à proprement parler l'angoisse" (my emphasis).

that "chokes" the lover "in the very midst of the fountain of delights" (4.1133–34):

> nequiquam quoniam medio de fonte leporum
> surgit amari aliquid quod in ipsis floribus *angat*.

(All in vain because in the midst of the fountain of delights there rises up something bitter that chokes amid the flowers themselves.)

However different in their contents and objects, all the dangerous passions have a fundamental similarity in the deleterious effects on the health and peace of the soul.

The cure for the internal entrapment of *angor* is the expansive vision that philosophy can provide. Thus, to return to book 3, if men were to have a clear vision in their minds of the Epicurean truth about death, their spirits would find "release" from gripping fear (3.902–3):

> quod bene si videant animo dictisque sequantur,
> dissoluant animi magno se angore metuque.

(But if they should see this in their mind and pursue it with their words, they would release themselves from great anguish and terror of mind.)

The freedom of this "vision" of the mind corresponds to the philosopher's broad vision of the "world's walls" in the proem of book 3. Here the poet (speaking in the first person) hears Epicurus's doctrine, as if in a personal communication (*ratio tua coepit vociferari*, "your system began to shout forth," 3.14) and beholds the truth of atom and void (3.16–17):

> diffugiunt animi terrores, moenia mundi
> discedunt, totum video per inane geri res.

(The fears of the mind scatter in flight, the walls of the world make way, and I see things at work throughout the void entire.)

Shortly before the passage about the mind's release from its *angor* and *metus* in 3.902–3, Lucretius returns to this imagery of broad, liberating vision. Seeing (*respicias*, 854) the "whole past extent of time measureless" that precedes our birth should provide a freedom analogous to the Epicurean vision beyond the *moenia mundi* in the proems of books 1 and 3. Lucretius in fact observes that in such moments we become free of *angor* (3.852–56):

> et nunc nil ad nos de nobis attinet, ante
> qui fuimus, nil iam de illis nos adficit *angor*.
> nam cum *respicias immensi temporis omne*
> praeteritum *spatium*, tum motus materiai
> multimodis quam sint, facile hoc accredere possis.

> (And now we have no concern at all about the "we" who were before, no *anxiety* at all moves us about those persons. For when *you look back over the entire past expanse of measureless time*, then at the movements of matter, how multifarious they are, easily could you come to this belief.)

This larger view frees us from the narrowing limits of obsessive passions and counteracts the fear that "encloses in nets" (*circumretit*, 5.1152) or "contracts" our minds with superstitious fear (*animus formidine divum / contrahitur*, 5.1218–19) or keeps us on the "narrow road" of greed for wealth and power (*angustum iter*, 5.1131–32). By contrast, the truths of philosophy open wide vistas before us (3.16–17, 854–55; cf. 1.62–79).

Epicurus had warned that as far as death is concerned we all live in an unwalled city (frag. 339 Usener). As wealth and power increase, men, unable to ward off death, seek the artificial enclosure of "strong towers" (*validis saepti . . . turribus*, 5.1440).[7] But, paradoxically, the only true "defense" is the broad views offered by the peaceful *templa* constructed, figuratively, by the *doctrina* of philosophy (2.7–10):

> sed nil dulcius est, bene quam munita tenere
> edita doctrina sapientum *templa serena*,

---

[7] For the motif of towers and fortification against death, see above, Chapter Five.

> *despicere* unde queas alios passimque *videre*
> errare atque viam palantis quaerere vitae.

(But there is nothing more sweet than to hold the fortified, *tranquil precincts* raised aloft by the teachings of the wise, whence you can *look down* and *see* men wandering far and wide and, in their straying, seek the road of life.)

To live a life oppressed by such anxieties is to live like a small, frightened boy in a dark room (3.87ff.).[8]

Of these constricting and darkening terrors, fear of death is the most powerful. Hence it is significant that the lines on Epicurus's own death near the end of the book not only use the hyperbole of solar imagery (3.1043–44) but, in the phrases *decurso lumine vitae* and *superavit* (1042–43), also recall the philosopher's victorious journey to the world's limits to defeat superstitious fear in the first proem (3.1042–44):

> ipse Epicurus obit decurso lumine vitae,
> qui genus humanum ingenio superavit et omnis
> restinxit, stellas exortus ut aerius sol.

(Epicurus himself met his end when he had traversed the light of life, he who surpassed the race of mankind in intellect and outshone them all, as the sun risen forth to its place in the heavens [outshines] the stars.)

Epicurus the philosopher is suffused by the radiance of triumphant light, even as Epicurus the mortal man (*ipse Epicurus*, 1042) confronts the darkness of death. This collocation of light and darkness harks back to the imagery that opens book 3: the light that shines in the darkness of ignorance (*e tenebris tantis tam clarum extollere lumen / qui primum potuisti*, "You who were first able to raise so bright a light forth from darkness," 3.1–2)[9] and the cloudless sky of the Epicu-

---

[8] For the contrasts of enclosure and open vision, see DeLacy, "Distant Views," 54–55; also Michels, "Death," 165 and 168; Schrijvers, *Horror*, 18–19. See also the remarks of William Fitzgerald, "Lucretius's Cure for Love in the *De Rerum Natura*," *Classical World* 78 (1984–85): 79.

[9] For the question of the reading in 3.1, see Chapter Four, note 12.

rean gods that smiles with true light there (*semperque innubilus aether / integit et large diffuso lumine ridet*, "The ever-cloudless aether covers it, and it smiles with its light poured widely forth," 3.21–22; cf. also 1.8–9). To Epicurus death is indeed nothing, for his spirit has soared far beyond all mortal constraints. But the first two-thirds of book 3, even as it presents the Master's liberating proofs of the soul's mortality, dwells on those corporeal constrictions in which we most fully, and "anxiously," experience the fears that our mortality holds.

As *angor* includes both physical and emotional constriction, so the images of enclosure prior to the diatribe against the fear of death at the end of book 3 shift between literal and figurative usages. These images of constriction also operate both from the inside out and from the outside in. In the latter case the body appears as a vessel that contains and protects the precious essence of life, the fine, airy, labile *anima* and *animus* (see 3.396–444). Hence the expression *vitai claustra*, "the fastenings of life," which Lucretius uses once in this book and once again in the account of the plague (3.396 and 6.1153), conveys the notion of the body as the protective enclosure of the vulnerable *anima*. In both of these passages, however, the context also stresses the weakness of this corporeal container. In 3.396–401 the *animus vitai claustra coercens* ("the mind that keeps together the enclosures of life") all too easily slips off into the winds (400) and "leaves behind the limbs chilled in death's cold" (401). In 6.1151–53 the destructive power embodied in the plague (*morbida vis*) flows into the breast so that "all the fastenings of life totter and fail." The "vessel" that is the body is, in effect, too leaky and too easily perforated to offer much security to the fragile substance that contains our life (3.434–35, 440–44, 554–57).

Swooning into a coma, as noted earlier, is experienced as sinking into dark waters (*in nigras lethargi mergitur undas*, 3.829). Drowning here occupies a place intermediate between literal event and metaphor. In its metaphorical value, it is the opposite of Lucretius's determination, stated in the proem, to confront and defeat the fear of death by the illuminating vision of his poetry (3.35–40):

> . . . hasce secundum res animi natura *videtur*
> atque animae *claranda* meis iam versibus esse
> et metus ille foras praeceps Acheruntis agendus
> funditus humanam qui vitam turbat *ab imo*
> *omnia suffundens mortis nigrore* neque ullam
> esse voluptatem *liquidam puramque* relinquit.

(After these matters the nature of the mind and soul must be *illuminated* now by my verses, and that fear of Acheron that stirs human life up *from the very depths* must be driven forth headlong, that fear that *covers over everything with death's blackness* and leaves behind no pleasure to be *clear and pure*.)

The figurative radiance of truth vanquishes both the physical blackness of death and, by implication, the fabled darkness of Acheron.

As in the descriptions of Epicurus at the beginning of books 1 and 3, darkness and ignorance are associated with entrapment, light and knowledge with energetic movement outside, be it the lofty *templa* of knowledge or the flowery river banks enjoyed by the wise at the opening of book 2 or the infinite reaches of the universe attained by the Master himself at the beginning of book 1. Here in the proem of book 3, fear's dark, liquid entrapment of all of life's goods (39–40) comes up against the poet's vigorous "thrust" to send it away, "outside" (*foras*), in "headlong" flight (*metus ille foras praeceps Acheruntis agendus*, 37). The verbal play between *funditus* and *suffendens* here in 3.38–39 reinforces the implicit definition of fear as something that does its work in the dark, lower strata of our lives (cf. *ab imo*, *suf-fundens*). In this respect it shares the subterranean qualities of the "dark goad" beneath our hearts later in the book (*sub-esse / caecum aliquem cordi stimulum*, 3.873) and of the goads of dangerous erotic passion in book 4 (*stimuli sub-sunt*, 4.1081–82). In this latter passage, as in 3.40, the contrasting term is *pura voluptas*, associated with light and clarity. Victory over the fear of death in book 3, like its paradigm, the victory of Epicurus over *religio* in the proem of book 1, consists in attaining the open air and forcing the dark, hidden thing out into the light, where it will vanish in the bright rays (cf. *e tenebris tam clarum extollere lumen* . . . , 3.1ff.; also 3.1042–44, *supra*).

The metaphors of drowning and immersion in 3.39–40, therefore, need to be allowed their full, concrete force. In the plague of book 6, that force is even more tangible and physical. Drowning here is not just the metaphor of 3.39 or 3.829; it is the actual cause of death: *interclusa anima nimia ab dulcedine aquarum* ("life cut off by the excessive sweetness of the water," 6.1266). The expressive compound *interclusa*, which occurs only here in Lucretius, also conveys the notion of suffocation. The sweetness of water becomes a cloying substance that closes off the breath, not unlike the suffocating honey of embalming that the foolish man fears for his body after death (*in melle situm suffocari*, 3.891). In comparing primitive and modern man in book 5, Lucretius shows his contemporaries "drowning" in the cloying superfluities of the present day: *nunc rerum copia mersat* (5.1008). We may recall too the misery of the impassioned lover, "choked" in the very flowers of his delight by something bitter that rises up from the liquid "fountain" of his pleasure (4.1133–34). In the plague at Athens, men greedily come with "gaping mouth" to these literal "fountains" or wells, but nothing can assuage the terrible thirst that, paradoxically, "drowns" their bodies (6.1172–77):

> in fluvios partim gelidos ardentia morbo
> membra dabant nudum iacientes corpus *in undas.*
> multi praecipites lymphis putealibus alte
> inciderunt ipso venientes *ore patente*:
> insedabiliter sitis arida, *corpora mersans,*
> aequabat multum parvis umoribus imbrem.

(Some gave their limbs burning with disease to the cold streams, hurling their naked body *into the waves.* Many dived headlong deep in the waters of wells, coming with their *mouth all agape*: the thirst, unquenchably parching, *drowning their bodies*, made great waters [seem] equal to small moisture.)

There is a special horror in the plague's combination of the literal constriction of the throat in its physical symptoms and the psychological constriction of the *anxius angor* at the terror of death. In 6.1151–53 the plague's virulent force "filled up the breast through the wind-pipe" and then "flowed into the sad heart" so that "all of life's fastenings give way in collapse":

> inde ubi *per fauces* pectus *complerat* et ipsum
> morbida vis in cor maestum *confluxerat* aegris,
> omnia tum vero vitai *claustra* lababant.

The repeated prefix in *com-plerat* and *con-fluxerat* underlines the strangling effect of the accumulating liquid passing "into the breast." There is a tension, almost an oxymoron, between the interior and exterior effects of this settling of liquids in the chest, for the result of the constriction is the weakening of the "fastenings" that contain life (*vitae claustra*, 1153). The constriction from within (*pectus complerat, in cor . . . confluxerat*) is a particularly disturbing form of the violation of the body's boundaries. It is, in fact, a physical equivalent of the *anxius angor* that characterizes the fear of death and occurs a few lines later (6.1158).

In this passage the boundaries of the body are attacked both from within, by implosion (*per fauces pectus complerat*), and from without, by destruction of the *claustra* that protect life from the hostile forces outside, the atoms that are always hammering away at us as they impinge constantly on the outer edges of our frame. This double process corresponds, in microcosm, to the destruction of worlds described in 2.1118–49. In the two-sidedness of this attack on the body, the deadly force of constriction reverses itself, shifting the focus from the exterior to the interior. After the force of the disease has "filled up the breast," coming from the outside to the inner organs, it proceeds to weaken the "enclosures" that keep the life of the body safe within (*omnia tum vero vitai claustra lababant*, 6.1153).

Related to the emotional constriction of *anxius angor* is the other great evil of the human emotional life, passionate love.

Its dangerous effects too often take the form of a trap or net in which the lover is "caught" and tied as in the "toils of Venus": *captum retibus ipsis . . . Veneris nodos* (4.1147–48); *quos retinere volunt adstrictosque esse in amore* ("whom they wish to hold and to be constrained in love," 4.1187); *mutua saepe voluptas / vinxit, ut in vinclis communibus excrucientur* ("often mutual pleasure has bound them so that they are tormented in common bonds," 4.1201–2); *validis Veneris compagibus haerent* ("they are stuck fast in the snares of Venus," 4.1205).

The common imagery that unites the anxieties of death and the entrapment of passionate love reveals the basic affinity among all the dangerous passions. The nets of love resemble the suffocation of death. In the account of the plague, death is like a wild beast that holds its victim in an enfolding grip, *implicitum morbo* (6.1231). The disease thus reduces man at the height of civilization (Periclean Athens) to the helplessness of his savage ancestor in the wild (5.990). So too the murderous "embrace" of the wild lioness enfolds her victims and holds them fast with her teeth and claws (*deplexae . . . morsibus adfixae validis atque unguibus uncis*, 5.1321–22). Just as the infatuated lover is held fast as he clings (*haeret*) to the "strong bonds of Venus" (4.1205), so the man fearful of death "clings" to the self that is the source of his trouble, even though he "hates" it (*haeret et odit*, 3.1069). Going in and out of his house or driving madly to his country house, he finds that in his journey outside the city he cannot get outside himself (3.1060–67; cf. especially *saepe exit foras* and *foris* in 1060 and 1062).[10] The impassioned lover, shut outside the door that he covers with flowers and anoints with perfumes, sees only the exterior in every sense; if he could see within, he would be glad to "go out" and never return (4.1177–81).[11]

---

[10] Analogous to the hopeless flight of the bored man here is the vague inner wandering that marks the emotional unsoundness of the lover who *fluctuat incertis erroribus* (4.1077; cf. 3.1052). On the negative value of "wandering," see Schrijvers, *Horror*, 18; also Logre, *L'anxiété*, 201; Pigeaud, *Maladie de l'âme*, 205.

[11] The "foul odors" (*taetris odoribus*) of the woman in this passage

Neither the bored man nor the lover understands that the abandonment of his passion through Epicurean philosophy is the only possible release. To escape this inner bondage and darkness one must expel "outside" the fear of death (*foras praeceps agendus*, 3.37). Those who are "compelled," literally "driven together," inwardly by the fear of death are looking in the wrong direction when they attempt the most remote flight possible and only multiply the miseries of their and others' lives (3.68–70):

> unde homines dum se falso terrore coacti
> effugisse volunt *longe longeque* remosse,
> sanguine civili rem conflant. . . .

(While men, compelled by false fear, wish to flee *far* from these and remove themselves *far away*, they bring together wealth by civil bloodshed.)

Lucretius implies a similar contrast between the hidden and dark goads that lurk beneath us (3.873–74) and his own philosophical vision. In the latter case, the act of flight is not irrational avoidance but the result of enlightenment. The contemplation of Epicurus's eternal wisdom opens the "flowery meadows" of our peaceful joy (*floriferis ut apes in saltibus*, 3.11, possibly implying Epicurus's "garden") to the infinite horizons of the universe. It is here that the "soul's terrors" flee; and all the constraints upon human vision, including the confining "walls of the world," fly apart (3.16–17).

Epicurus's intellectual triumph is in effect a victory over constriction and enclosure. In the first proem he is able to resist the inhibiting pressure (*compressit*) that comes from fears about the gods and celestial phenomena (1.68–69); and he is able to "break down the tight fastenings of nature's gates" (*effringere . . . arta naturae . . . portarum claustra*, 1.70–71). Lucretius continues the Master's work, defining his task as "unloosing the mind from the tight knots of religious super-

---

(4.1175; cf. *aura una modo*, 1180–81) may also recall the rancid smell of putrefaction; if so, they help establish another link between the errors of passionate love and the folly of fearing death.

stitions" (*artis / religionum animum nodis exsolvere*, 1.931–32). Complementing this image of the "knots" of love or fear is Lucretius's assertion that the soul, being of mortal origin, is "not released from the law of doom" (*nec leti lege solutas*, 3.687). Paradoxically, this denial of the soul's "release" is part of the larger purpose of "releasing the mind" from its bonds of anxiety.

OPPRESSIVE WEIGHT

As the forcefulness of his *angor* metaphor suggests, constriction is the most physical of the bodily sensations that Lucretius associates with anxiety. Weight and heaviness, however, are a close second. In the first proem, *religio*, "heavy superstition," has held human life "pressed down to earth" (*in terris oppressa gravi sub religione*, 1.62), just as the individual human victim, Iphigeneia, is "pushed to earth on her knees" in terror of the sacrificial knife (*muta metu terram genibus summissa petebat*, 1.92). Epicurus, however, who "dared to raise up his eyes and first take his stand against" this force (1.66–67), has left *religio* "crushed underfoot in its turn, and his victory makes us equal to the heavens" (1.78–79):

> quare religio pedibus subiecta vicissim
> obteritur, nos exaequat victoria caelo.

Book 3 opens with an echo of this passage, praising Epicurus for "raising up the clear light from the darkness" (3.1–2); and we have already noted the echo of the *triumphator* theme of book 1 in the surpassing brilliance of Epicurus even in his death (3.1042–44; 1.75 and 79).[12] Airy lightness and upward soaring characterize his fame (*exortus ut aerius sol*, 3.1044; cf. *ad caelum gloria fertur*, 6.8). Lacking the "heart set at peace" that his wisdom brings (5.1203), men who look up at the sky fall back to earth, prostrating themselves in religious fear (*procumbere humi prostratum*, 5.1200) because anxiety about celestial phenomena creeps "into hearts weighed down

---

[12] On Epicurus as *triumphator*, see Buchheit, "Epikurs Triumph," passim.

by other woes" and there "begins to raise up its head" (*aliis oppressa malis in pectora cura / . . . caput erigere infit*, 5.1207–8). Similarly, a little later, "some hidden force crushes human affairs" (*usque adeo res humanas vis abdita quaedam / obterit*, 5.1233–34).

These metaphors of weight are very much alive for Lucretius and need to be taken seriously. They exemplify the somatic sensitivity to emotions, and especially emotions of fear, worry, and anxiety, that we have been tracing in book 3.[13] They also play a prominent part in the fear of death, both as a literal weight and as the metaphorical weight of anxiety and fear. But, as we have suggested, even the metaphorical heaviness or the constriction of anxiety has, for Lucretius, the status of a strong, physical sensation. And of course this material basis of emotions is fully in accordance with his atomic theory.

In his atomistic psychology, even very fine sensations, like seeing light, have a material basis. Thus some visual sensations have attributes of weight or mass. In 4.337ff., for example, darkness—one of the poem's favorite metaphors for ignorance and folly—results from the heavy "thickness" that enters our eyes and "fills up their pores and besieges their paths," so that the *simulacra* are unable to move (4.348–52):

> quod contra facere in tenebris e luce nequimus
> propterea quia posterior caliginis aer
> *crassior insequitur* qui cuncta foramina *complet*
> *obsiditque vias oculorum*, ne simulacra
> possint ullarum rerum coniecta *movere*.

(But on the other hand we cannot do this [i.e. see] [coming] from light into darkness because the air of misty dark, *thicker, follows after*, and this *fills up* all the passageways and *blocks the paths of the eyes*, so that no images of any objects, thrown forth, are able to move.)

---

[13] On the physical sensation of weight in such emotions, see Perelli, *Lucrezio*, 38, apropos of 3.1053–59; also Pigeaud, *Maladie de l'âme*, 205–6, who rightly objects to Logre's transposing of these symptoms of ennui to a pathological state of melancholia in Lucretius himself.

Darkness, therefore, is associated with this *crassior aer*, whereas light is finer, moves more quickly, and has a cleansing effect on the "black shadows" around it (4.340–41):

> insequitur candens confestim lucidus aer
> qui quasi *purgat* eos et *nigras discutit umbras.*

(There follows at once the clear, shining air, which as it were *cleanses* them [i.e., the eyes] and *scatters away the black shadows.*)

This passage, we may add, begins with the phrase *e tenebris* (4.337), the same phrase that rings in the praise of the light-bringing Epicurus in book 3 (3.1).

The strongest of the feelings of weight that Lucretius associates with death is the foolish man's anxiety about the heaviness of earth resting upon his lifeless body. This fear comes last in the series of fears about the afterlife, and it is immediately preceded by the related notion of suffocation in honey and its near opposite, lying on cold stone (3.891–93):

> aut in melle situm suffocari atque rigere
> frigore, cum summo gelidi cubat aequore saxi,
> *urgerive* superne *obtritum pondere terrae.*

(Or else placed in honey to be suffocated and to stiffen with cold when he lies on the top surface of chill stone, or to be *pressed upon* from above, *crushed by the weight of earth.*)

Lucretius is, of course, utilizing the language of the traditional funeral prayer, "May the earth lie light upon you," as well as drawing upon the moralizing rhetoric of Epicureans and Cynics.[14] But the feeling of physical weight also stands in close relation here to the psychological oppression of anxious thoughts. *Obtero* is in fact one of the words that Lucretius uses for the irrational force of false desires that "crushes human affairs" in 5.1233–34. In 1.78–79 it describes Epicurus's reverse effect on *religio*, now triumphantly "crushed" instead

---

[14] See Kenney, *Lucretius III*, ad 3.893; Wallach, *Lucretius and the Diatribe*, 33 and 45. Cf. Philodemus, *De Morte* 33.2–3. For another inversion of the formula of "light earth" in burial, see Seneca, *Phaedra* 1279–80.

of crushing us (*obteritur*). *Urgeor* in 3.893 recurs twice later for the quasi-metaphorical weight of fear: first it describes the crushing fear of the gods in Lucretius's allegorical interpretation of Tantalus's punishment (*sed magis in vita divum metus urget inanis*, "But rather the empty fear of the gods presses on us in life," 3.982); later it describes the bored and troubled man who "wastes" (literally, "wears down," *conterit*, 3.1047) the greater part of his life in sleep and is "pressed down by anxieties on every side" (*urgeris multis miser undique curis*, 3.1051).[15]

In both of the *urgeor* passages, the context makes clear the special connection of the psychological with the physiological or material oppression. The first passage points up the groundlessness of such fears of the gods by the oxymoronic juxtaposition of *urget* and *inanis*, "press down" and "empty" (3.982): what crushes us with such heavy weight, like the stone that benumbs Tantalus (cf. *formidine torpens*, 981), is in fact "empty." The second passage analogously juxtaposes the paralyzing oppression of anxiety (cf. 981) and the lightness of aimless, unstable wandering in the following line (*animi incerto fluitans errore vagaris*, 3.1052). Turning from his second-person address to "men" in general (*si possent homines*, 1053), Lucretius pinpoints ignorance as the cause of the heavy burden of anxiety that tires us with its "weight" (*pondus inesse animo quod se gravitate fatiget*, 1054). From this source too comes the "mass of suffering" that "sits on the chest" (*tanta mali tamquam moles in pectore constet*, 1056). The "weight" that should most concern us is not that of earth over our body in death but the *pondus* in the mind (1054) that oppresses us while we live. Those who persist in this ignorance will never be able to throw off the "burden," no matter how much they move around (*quaerere semper / commutare locum quasi onus deponere possit*, 1058–59). The change of place is like the unstable floating of 1051–52: when the source of the

---

[15] The uses of *urgeo* in book 3 are the only metaphorical usages of the verb in the poem. Elsewhere it describes the tangible mass of cloud or water pushing down from above: 2.197, 6.191–93, 480–81, 510–12, 558.

trouble is untreated because unknown, the flightiness of excessive motion comes to the same thing as immobility beneath oppressive heaviness.[16] Similarly, driving horses at breakneck speed is, from the Epicurean point of view, paradoxically equivalent to the action that follows it, going off into sleep, in heavy immobility (1063–67; *abit in somnum gravis*, 1066).

Through these repeated metaphors of weight, Lucretius arrives at a psychological reading of human anxiety that goes far beyond the Hellenistic diatribe, or even the earlier Epicurean arguments against fearing death because of worries about the mass of stone or earth on our buried corpse (cf. 3.888–93). These metaphors gain a special force from the contrast with the preceding description of Epicurus in 3.1042–44. That thinker's vast journey of spirit to the limits of the world, here evoked in the celestial imagery of 1043–44, is the valid paradigm of travel and shows where rationally directed mental energy can lead us. In contrast to the life of the bored man, floating unanchored in directionless inertia, the mission of the savior of mankind is sure in its goal and radiantly expansive in its results. In contrast to the paralyzing and immobilizing weight of fear, Epicurus soars freely above all mortals, figuratively "rising" like the sun into the heavens (*exortus ut aerius sol*, 1044).

Earlier in the book, oppressive weight has a more direct and harsher physical form. It accompanies not just the fear of death but the actual process of dying. In this shift it resembles some of the other physical sensations that we have examined. The vividly described coma of 459–69 is "heavy" (*gravis*), and in its context seems to contribute to holding the victim down in the deep sleep in which he is carried off (*gravi lethargo fertur in altum / aeternumque soporem*, 465–66). A few lines later, after mentioning terminal illness (*morbus leti fabricator*) and "the death of many" (*multorum exitium*), Lucretius comes to "wine's force" that causes "heaviness of the limbs"

---

[16] Cf. 4.1077. Logre, *L'anxiété*, 201, would find in these metaphors the clinical symptoms of a pathological condition, like "l'onirisme alcoolique." If so, Lucretius evinces a remarkable ability to transform his (or others') psychosomatic illness into a large view of the human condition.

(*gravitas membrorum*, 478). When men worry that the pun-
ishments after death may "grow even heavier" (*magis haec ne
in morte graviscant*, 1022), their anxiety already has a physi-
cal basis in the "heavy" sufferings of the body as it approaches
death (465–66) or is in a physically debilitated state (479).
Akin to this overlapping of physical and psychological "heavi-
ness" is the ancient metaphor of the wound of love in book 4.
This begins as an ulcerated sore (*ulcus*) that "lives and grows
by taking nourishment" until its "pain grows heavy" (*ulcus
enim vivescit et inveterascit alendo / . . . atque aerumna gra-
vescit*, 4.1068–69).

The movement toward the psychological "constriction"
and "weight" at the end of book 3 tends to shift the emphasis
from the physical (and often fatal) sufferings given in the
proofs of the mortality of the soul in the first half to more
figurative and more inward sufferings. This shift of emphasis
also reinforces the point of the proem (strongly reasserted in
the proem of book 5) that Epicurus's relief of emotional suf-
fering is more important to human happiness than healing the
body's physical ills. Thus the images of decay and putrefaction
earlier become the gentler, more emotionally defined "wasting
away in grief" in 3.911 (*tabescere luctu*). The ugly degenera-
tion of old age, organ by organ, in 3.451ff., becomes general-
ized to the single verb *marces* in 956 and to the non-specific
references to "body" and "limbs" in 946–47 (*corpus iam mar-
cet et artus confecti languent*; Lucretius uses *marceo* only in
these two passages).

The gentlest description of old age Lucretius reserves for the
great thinker, Democritus, who in his fearlessness "of his own
will himself offered his head to death when ripe old age told
him that the remembering movements of his mind were be-
coming sluggish" (1039–41):

> denique Democritus postquam matura vetustas
> admonuit memores motus languescere mentis,
> sponte sua leto caput obvius obtulit ipse.

For the philosopher, death, far from being the physical dete-
rioration grimly detailed in the first half of the book, is itself a

process of telling and understanding (*admonuit*), almost a co-operative dialogue between body and mind rather than a con-flict. It is noteworthy that in this case no part of the body is mentioned except the head, which the thinker offers volun-tarily to death (1041). Old age itself appears in its vaguest, most abstract, and least corporeal form, as a *matura vetustas* that itself seems to "give advice." In the lines that follow, on Epicurus himself, the body does not appear at all (1042–44). The course of physical life is itself a "road to light," an image appropriate to a philosopher: one is reminded of Parmenides's journey, led by the Daughters of the Sun. Death itself is a tri-umphant rise above, into the stars.

For all of the note of triumph here, it is important not to let the poetic brilliance and engaging energy of the last third of book 3 make us forget the numerous descriptions of disease, mutilation, deterioration, and putrefaction in the earlier por-tion. Through such descriptions Lucretius does confront, if only indirectly at this point, the fears about the agony of dy-ing. The descriptions of violent death in this section of book 3 and later in book 5 are as vivid as one would expect them to be in an age before antibiotics, morphine, or even distilled al-cohol. Lucretius reserves the full confrontation with these fears until the finale of his poem, the plague at Athens.[17] But he prepares the way for that confrontation through the de-tailed physical descriptions in the first half of book 3, and also through the examples of Epicurus and Democritus. These are

---

[17] I tend to agree with Clay, *Lucretius and Epicurus*, 266, and Minadeo, *Lyre of Science*, 107–10, that the plague at the end (as the finale intended by Lucretius) presents the reader with the opportunity "to face the final test of his mastery of the poem" and "to contemplate the ugliest face of an indiffer-ent nature that has destroyed, even as it created, the highest form of human civilization." I would add, however, the close connection of this final "test" with book 3 and the gradualness of the preparation for the horrors of physical disintegration in the first part of book 3. For Pigeaud (*Maladie de l'âme*, 237ff.), the plague is the culminating statement of Lucretius's anti-teleological and anti-providential world view. By ending with historical fact, not myth, in contrast to Plato and Cicero at the end of their respective *Republic*s, he sharp-ens his challenge to personal, providential gods.

the thinkers who in some way triumphed over their bodies' fragility and who thus provide the model for the only way in which mortal man can defeat the processes of death and decay going on incessantly around him. It is these figures to whom we must next turn.

Chapter Eight

GENERALS, POETS, AND PHILOSOPHERS: DEATH IN THE PERSPECTIVE OF TIME AND ETERNITY

WAR-HERO AND PHILOSOPHER-HERO

The closing section of Lucretius's diatribe against the fear of death in book 3 is carefully organized. *Hoc etiam* in 3.1024, which introduces the need to accept death as the universal mortal fate, answers *hoc etiam* in 3.912, which introduces the common man's complaint of the brevity of life's joys. After Natura's speech and Lucretius's comment (931–77), the poet gives his celebrated allegorical interpretation of the punishments in Hades (978–1023). The repetition of "Acheron" at the beginning and end frame this section as a discrete unit (*Acherunte profundo*, 978, and *Acherusia vita*, 1023).

The mythological examples of Tantalus, Tityos, Sisyphus, and the Danaids, with their sources in Greek poetry from the *Odyssey* on, are an obvious preparation for the literary evocations of Aeschylus's Xerxes in 1029–32 and for the literary quotations from Ennius's epic about Ancus Martius and (probably) Scipio. Thus the remote past of Greek myth is balanced by the remote past of history, both Greek and Roman. Mythical heroes and warriors are also answered by the philosophical "heroes," Democritus and Epicurus.

By combining both Greek and Roman exempla, Lucretius is obviously underscoring the universality of his subject and its relevance to *all* the races of mankind.[1] He is also suggesting the shortcomings of the existing literary and mythical models

---

[1] On this point, see Minyard, *Lucretius and the Late Republic*, 37–38.

for noble behavior, intelligent action, and insight into the nature of human motives. Not the epic and dramatic poetry of the Greeks, but the philosophy of Epicurus (and implicitly the philosophical poetry of Lucretius) is the correct mode of representing the nature of man, and it provides the proper means for arriving at the essential truths about the human condition.[2] Not Achilles or Hercules but Democritus and especially Epicurus are the true "heroes" in man's struggle against meanness and savagery. They, therefore, are the stuff of which the myths and poems of enlightened mankind will be made.

The proper names, mythical and historical, emphatically placed throughout the entire passage (978–1044), develop a gradual progression from myth to history (Tantalus, Scipio); from the fantasies of Greek poetry, far removed from truth, to the founding figures of the true philosophy, Democritus and Epicurus; and from the darkness of "deep Acheron" (978) to the celestial radiance of Epicurus (1043–44). Lucretius also self-consciously fuses Greek and Roman, not only in the juxtaposition of Greek myth and Roman history, but also in the combination of Ennian and Homeric epic.[3] Beside the themes of the Odyssean Nekyia in the previous passage (3.980–1012) stands the Iliadic and characteristically Achillean motif of the universality of death (cf. 3.1026 and *Iliad* 21.106–7).

Lucretius's juxtaposition of the great epic poets of the two cultures asserts the power of death over the most majestic of the ancient literary genres. This perspective on death is generic (in the literary sense) and synchronic. By assimilating material from different chronological periods, Lucretius also places the universality of death into a diachronic perspective. Each of the two series of specific exempla—Ancus Martius, Xerxes, Scipio; and Homer, Democritus, Epicurus—forms a chronological progression. In the latter group, Lucretius brings Homer and Epicurus into contact with one another, each men-

---

[2] Thus Lucretius often refers contemptuously to Greek myths' remoteness from truth: 1.102–3, 2.600 and 655–60, 5.405–6; see also 3.629–33, 4.590–94.

[3] For this feature of Latin poetry generally, see Gordon Williams, *Tradition and Originality in Latin Poetry* (Oxford, 1968), ch. 5.

tioned by name here for the only time in the poem. Epicurus, however, is praised in terms adapted from the Hellenistic epigram of Leonidas of Tarentum in honor of Homer (*Anthologia Palatina* 9.24). And Homer, for all that he possessed the "scepter" of poetry, fell into the same fatal "sleep" as all the others. This point is emphasized by the mild paradox of *unus . . . eadem aliis* (1037–38).[4] In the verbal microcosm of phrasing, as in the argument as a whole, death levels uniqueness to sameness, diachrony to synchrony.

This contrast between the poet and the philosopher has a pendant in the contrast between the warrior and the philosopher. Scipio, although he is the "thunderbolt of war" (*belli fulmen*, 1034), nevertheless gave his bones to the earth (1035). Though a man of power, he suffered the same fate as the "lowest" slave (*infimus*, 1035). Epicurus, who of course also dies, nevertheless won a far wider victory than either Xerxes or Scipio: *genus humanum ingenio superavit* ("he surpassed the human race in intellect," 1043); and he rose to the highest place in our world. We may also contrast Epicurus, *exortus ut aerius sol* ("rising like the sun in the heavens," 1044), with Scipio, *terrae . . . infimus* ("lowest on earth," 1035).

The greedy conqueror Xerxes with his seaborne legions recalls the ambitious generals of 2.40ff. and anticipates those of 5.1226ff.—foolish men whose martial panoplies cannot free them from crushing anxiety about death. This juxtaposition of war-hero and philosopher also resumes major themes within the poem: the contrast of the war-god Mars, "defeated by the eternal wound of love" (*aeterno devictus vulnere amoris*, 1.34) with Epicurus as *victor* and *triumphator* in 1.72–79; and the contrast of Epicurus, the hero of philosophy, with the culture-hero of force, Hercules, in the proem of Book 5.

---

[4] On 1037, see Giussani, *T. Lucreti Cari*, ad loc.: "*Unus* serve a far sentire il contrasto fra la singolarità della persona e la communanza del destino." In my opinion, Francesco Giancotti, *Il preludio di Lucrezio* (Messina and Florence, 1959), 85, takes too positive a view of Lucretius's treatment of Homer's fate here, arguing that the universality of death is balanced by the aesthetic value of the poetry.

Lucretius's list of the memorable kings and generals of our passage juxtaposes the "good Ancus" and the evil tyrant, Xerxes, unnamed. The Roman general, fighting for what Lucretius's audience would certainly consider a worthy cause, also stands beside the evil Xerxes. The power-hungry Xerxes seems to meet a violent end, pouring forth his soul from his dying body (*lumine adempto animam moribundo corpore fudit*, 1033). His *moribundum corpus* reminds us of the soldier whose *moribundus pes* has been sheared off by the scythe-bearing chariot of 3.653—a detail that occurs in one of the bloodiest descriptions of the mayhem of war in the poem. Scipio, to be sure, also dies, but in a gentler way. "Giving his bones to the earth" (*ossa dedit terrae*, 1035), he performs a quasi-voluntary act that marks at least a small step in the direction of Democritus who "of his own accord put his head in the way of death" (1041). So also Ancus, whose death seems to have been utterly unremarkable,[5] simply "left the light" (*lumina sis oculis . . . reliquit*, 1025). Lucretius does not use these contrasts to make an explicit moral judgment. His silence on this point serves to underline the universality of death. The individual descriptions nevertheless point up real differences in the ways in which these men meet their respective ends.

Xerxes has a pivotal place in this list of the famous dead. He is juxtaposed with Ancus on the one side, as bad king to good, and with Scipio on the other, as evil general to good. His total loss of light in death (*lumine adempto*) also contrasts with Ancus, who (as the phrasing of 1025 suggests) possessed the light of vision to the very end (*lumina sis oculis reliquit*), and more markedly with Epicurus himself, whose very life is "a course of light," as the metaphor of *decurso lumine vitae* in 1042 implies. In the next line, in fact, Epicurus rises like the sun in the sky (1044). Epicurus thus as much surpasses the good Ancus, who "left the light" (1025), as Ancus is superior to Xerxes, who had the light "taken away."

Beyond these there is an overarching contrast between the

---

[5] On Ancus's unremarkable end, see Cicero, *Rep.* 2.20.35; Livy 1.35.1; Dionysius of Halicarnassus, *Roman Antiquities* 3.45.2.

two generals, Xerxes and Scipio, on the one hand, and all of the "discoverers of the arts and sciences," philosophers included, on the other (3.1036). Even Scipio is a man of violence, as the epithets of *fulmen* and *horror* imply, whereas the death of the "Muses' companions" is as peaceful as sleep (*eadem aliis sopitu' quietest*, 1038). And sleep, as Lucretius has pointed out earlier, is the model for a death that is free of fear; "Just as you are asleep in death (*leto sopitus*), so will you be for all the rest of time separated from all painful sufferings" (3.904–5; cf. also 3.976–77).

Democritus's death is not only a voluntary act (1041); it is even an intellectual act: his "ripe old age" gives the necessary advice (*admonuit*) to the "mindful movements of his mind" (1040). When he comes to Epicurus, Lucretius keeps the reference to death as neutral as possible: *ipse Epicurus obit decurso lumine vitae* ("Epicurus himself met his end when his life's light had run its course," 1042). Epicurus thus stands at the furthest extreme from the physicality of Xerxes's death. His end also contrasts with Democritus's suicide in the previous line. The neutral *obit* of Epicurus's passing recalls but also sharply differs from his predecessor's vivid gesture of offering his head to *letum* in the previous line: *caput obvius obtulit* (1041; cf. 1079). In Epicurus's case, the emphasis falls not upon death but rather on the unique solar brilliance in his "course of life" (1043–44). Epicurus's privileged place is reflected also in the phraseology. Democritus, introduced by *denique* ("finally," 1039), is in a sense the last real exemplum of the universal subjection to death. Epicurus, added in asyndeton, is a massive a fortiori capstone to the entire argument: *ipse Epicurus . . . qui . . . omnis restinxit* ("Epicurus himself whose light extinguished all others'," 1042–44).

LITERARY ECHOES: ENNIUS, HOMER, AND OTHERS

In addition to these contrasts and symmetries within 3.1024–44, there are important connections with two other passages in the poem. The allusions to the *Heliconiadum comites* and to the *sceptra* that Homer possessed in 1037 belong to the same order of self-conscious literariness as the "crown of ever-fresh foliage" that "our Ennius" once brought down from Helicon as the token of his lasting glory among the Italian people (1.117–19):

> Ennius ut noster cecinit qui primus amoeno
> detulit ex Helicone perenni fronde coronam,
> per gentis Italas hominum quae clara clueret.

(As our Ennius sang, who first brought down from pleasant Mount Helicon the crown of lasting leafage to be brilliant in fame among the Italian races of men.)

In the next lines, however, Lucretius goes on to criticize Ennius (cf. *tamen*, 120) for reporting false tales about Acheron (*Acherusia templa*) in his "immortal verses" (*aeternis versibus*, 120–21). As we have noted, the motif of Acheron is important in our passage too (cf. 3.978 and 1023). Ennius's dream of Homer's shade "rising up" from Hades (*exortam speciem*, 1.124–25) is a very different rising from Epicurus's ascent into the heavens in 3.1044 (*exortus ut aerius sol*). The contrast is all the more pointed because the lines comparing Epicurus to the sun are adapted from Leonidas's epigram in honor of none other than Homer. Just as the fiery sun dims the light of the stars and the moon, Leonidas wrote, so Homer surpassed all other poets "holding up the most brilliant radiance of the Muses."[6] That comparison may have been something of a literary commonplace (cf. Ps.-Longinus, *De Sublimitate* 9.13), but Lucretius adapts it to a new use.

The "rising" of Homer in Ennius's poetry has as its background the old myths of "Orcus's shadows and vast chasms" (1.115), whereas Epicurus's "rising" belongs entirely to the clear light of the heavens. Poet and philosopher thus contrast in terms of darkness and light, which of course are Lucretius's favorite terms for the contrast of ignorance and truth (e.g., 1.146–48, 1.1114–17, 2.54–61). His description of Ennius in book 1, in fact, begins with a warning about the fear-inspiring

---

[6] Leonidas, *Palatine Anthology* 9.24. See Bailey, *T. Lucreti Cari*, ad 3.1044; Wallach, *Lucretius and the Diatribe*, p. 96 with n. 116.

language of poets (*vatum terriloqua dicta*, 1.102–3). Poets are
the purveyors of just those "threats and superstitions" about
the soul's life after death that Lucretius's own poetry should
help us "resist" (*religionibus atque minis obsistere vatum*,
1.109; cf. *obsistere contra*, of Epicurus himself, in 1.67).

Just as Lucretius transfers Leonidas's honorific epigram
from Homer to Epicurus, so in the second proem he transfers
to himself the ancient and conventional imagery of the Muses'
haunts, fountains of song, flowers, and garlands (1.921–30).[7]
The subject of these verses, however, is not myth but philoso-
phy. Lucretius's task is the very opposite of Homer's and En-
nius's, namely to "free the mind from the tight knots of super-
stition" (*religionum animum nodis exsolvere*, 1.932) rather
than to perpetuate those old tales as Ennius did (1.120–21, cf.
102–3 and 109). Lucretius sees himself also as a teacher (cf.
doceo, 1.931) rather than a teller of tales. Thus his *musaeus
lepos* ("grace of the Muses," 1.934) will differ fundamentally
from the *lepores* that Homer discovered (cf. *repertores doctri-
narum atque leporum*, "discoverers of teachings and artistic
graces," 3.1036).

The parallels with book 1 cast light on the intense literari-
ness of 3.1024–44. Lucretius incorporates verses from both
Ennius and Homer in consecutive lines (3.1025 = Ennius, *An-
nales* 149 Vahlen; 1026 = *Iliad* 21.106–7). Then, coming to
Scipio, he again looks to Ennius (*Annales* 312–13, Vahlen),
but also glances at the shade of Achilles in *Odyssey* 11. With
proinde ac famul infimus est in 3.1035 ("just as if he were the
lowest of slaves") we may compare Achilles's famous remark
in *Odyssey* 11.489–91: "I would wish to be a serf to another
man, one who had no ownership and small living, as a plow-
man of his field, rather than rule over all the corpses of per-
ished men."

Moving on to the *repertores doctrinarum atque leporum*,
Lucretius names Homer, in a phrase that is itself a Greek epic

---

[7] For the association of flowers and poetry in Lucretius, see Schrijvers, *Hor-
ror*, 75–76 and 80–81. For the Callimachean and other literary echoes in this
passage, see my "Poetic Immortality," with the bibliography there cited.

locution, as Gian Biagio Conte has pointed out (cf. *quorum unus* and the Homeric οἷος τῶν).[8] Yet the word *Heliconiades* in 1037 (which occurs only here in Lucretius) and the allusion to the "scepter" in the next line combine Homeric epic with references to the didactic hexameter poetry of Hesiod (*Heliconiades: Theogony* 1 and 100; poet's "scepter": *Theogony* 30). The praise of Epicurus soon after (1042–44) may be utilizing the old Roman dramatic poetry of Pacuvius; and the stars/sun comparison is an ancient encomiastic convention familiar from lyric poets like Alcman and Sappho.[9] But, as we have noted earlier, these lines have their closest affinities with Leonidas's epigram in praise of Homer.

The passage then, is a literary tour de force by Lucretius at his most *doctus*.[10] Within the short space of some twenty verses Lucretius manages to pack in allusions to or adaptations of the *Iliad* and *Odyssey*, Hesiod, Aeschylus's *Persians*, Ennius's *Annals*, Greek encomiastic or choral conventions, and Hellenistic epigram. There are also other epic locutions, pointed out by Conte, like *magnis qui gentibus* . . . and *ille quoque ipse . . . qui quondam* ("who ruled over great peoples," 1028; "he too who himself once led . . . over the seas," 1029).[11]

By bringing these disparate allusions together in so short a space of text, Lucretius produces a peculiar distortion, an almost manneristic foreshortening. He borrows, and indeed quotes verbatim, from Ennius; but he names only Homer.

[8] See Conte, "Trionfo della morte," passim, esp. 126. Taking his cue from Conte, Schrijvers, *Horror*, 231–34, points out the importance of poetic periphrasis in this passage.

[9] E.g., Alcman 1.40–43 Page; Sappho 96.6–9. On the echo of Pacuvius (frag. 347 Ribbeck) in 3.1042–44, see West, *Imagery and Poetry*, 45. Other Ennian echoes, possibly in connection with Scipio, are suggested by Alessandro Perutelli, "Scipione ed Epicuro," *Atene e Roma* 25 (1980): 23–28, esp. p. 27, citing *Varia* 21–24 Vahlen.

[10] See Kenney, "Doctus Lucretius," esp. 372–80, on Lucretius's self-conscious criticism of Ennius's claim to poetic authority; also Gordon Williams, "Roman Poets as Literary Historians: Some Aspects of *Imitatio*," *Illinois Classical Studies* 8 (1983): 224–28.

[11] Conte, "Trionfo della morte," 123.

Homer's epithets of praise are borrowed (at least in part) from Hesiod, whereas the praise of Epicurus is adapted from an epigram in honor of Homer. This telescoping and re-mixing of literary history belongs to the self-conscious artistry of the passage, and also, as Conte suggests, helps transform the low style of the Cynic-Stoic diatribe into the sublime style of epic and didactic hexameters,[12] particularly as the writers in the background are respected exemplars of grandeur and learning. But the total effect does more than just show off stylistic virtuosity. It also reinforces the deliberate thematic progression from poetry to philosophy, from myth and fable to the truth of the *vera ratio*.

This mosaic-like accumulation of literary allusions and motifs either directly enacts the commemorative power of poetry or else alludes to that power indirectly. The line *Scipiadas, belli fulmen, Carthaginis horror*, for instance, has the sculptural solidity and monumentality of a verse on a tombstone ("scion of Scipios, thunderbolt of war, terror of Carthage," 1034). The lines on Epicurus (as noted earlier) are in fact derived from commemorative epigram. Lucretius, however, places his own distinctively Epicurean stamp on that commemorative tradition, and thereby recasts it into a form that is particularly relevant to his present argument, the universality of death.

The truly deserving recipient of poetic immortality, he suggests, is not the poet praised by Leonidas's epigram on Homer, but rather the thinker who has reflected on the true significance of death and given us a means for overcoming it that is more efficacious than the verse memorials of the literary tradition. The very meaning of "immortality" in such a situation becomes problematical, as Lucretius implies in his verse on "death eternal" at the end of the book (3.1091): *mors aeterna tamen nilo minus illa manebit* ("That death will remain, nonetheless, eternal"). This verse too recalls the commemorative tradition of archaic Greece, e.g., the so-called Cleobulus epigram on King Midas's tomb (*Anth. Pal.* 7.153.2–3): "Re-

---

[12] Conte, "Trionfo della morte," 127; also his "*Hypsos*," 359ff.

maining here on this much-bewept tomb, I shall announce to passersby that Midas is buried here."

LITERARY IMMORTALITY AND ETERNAL DEATH

As the first Latin poet of Epicureanism (counting Virgil and Horace as at least partly Epicurean), Lucretius places himself alongside the great poets of the past. He allusively evokes the literary tradition from Homer to Ennius, in part to pay his debt of admiration to Ennius, but also in part to assert the errors of his predecessors and, therefore, to claim for himself a privileged place within that tradition. He is superior to his predecessors precisely in his truer knowledge of death and the afterlife. He self consciously substitutes Epicurus for Homer, just as earlier he implicitly put his poetry in the place of Homer's and Ennius's (cf. 1.102–35). As Epicurus's philosophical journey had carried him beyond all previous philosophers (1.63–79), so Lucretius has traveled beyond all previous poets (1.926–50; and cf. *peragravit* of Epicurus in 1.74 and *peragro* of himself in 1.926).

In transcending the poets of the past, however, Lucretius, as an Epicurean, also faces the problem of transcending the immortality of fame that poets traditionally claim for themselves. The change from the ardent desire for fame in 1.922–25 to the acceptance of universal death at the end of book 3 reflects a dynamic movement within the poem, wherein the poetic voice itself participates in the progress from myth to philosophy and from the traditions of the poets to the truths demonstrated by Epicurus.

If we now read 3.1024–44 as a whole against the earlier evocations of the Homeric-Ennian epic tradition in Book 1, we can discern more clearly its relevance to the main themes of the poem. Lucretius is not only defining his level of style (high versus low); he is also taking on the whole of the literary tradition, from Homer through the later Greek epigram and the Roman historical epic, and (implicitly) declaring it superseded by his poetry of the *vera ratio*. Hence he can add the great poets and thinkers to the scrap heap of dead culture-heroes in the generalizing line, *adde repertores doctrinarum atque leporum* ("add the discoverers of teaching and of artistic graces," 3.1036). In making Epicurus eclipse Homer as the new "sun" of poetry, he provides a bright foil to "dark Tartarus" or "deep Acheron" in the grand epic myths (cf. 3.966 and 978); and at the same time, he renews his attack on Homer and Ennius in just this area (1.102–26).

When he mentions the poetic garland (1.928–29), Lucretius flirts with the traditional motif of the eternity of poetry, the poet's power both to confer and to receive immortal glory (the Homeric κλέος ἄφθιτον, "fame imperishable"). He also directly challenges his great predecessor in hexameter poetry, "our Ennius," with his Heliconian crown of eternal fame among the Italian peoples (1.117–19). There he even gave the epithet "immortal" to Ennius's verses about the fields of Acheron (*esse Acherusia templa / Ennius aeternis exponit versibus edens*, "Nevertheless Ennius set forth in the utterance of eternal verses that the regions of Acheron exist," 1.120–21). Yet as an Epicurean Lucretius knows that nothing is "immortal" except atom and void—and death, the main theme of book 3 (*mors immortalis, mors aeterna*, 3.869 and 1091). In book 5, when he avers the mortality of the world, sun and stars included (5.115), he speaks with the authority of another tradition, not poetic but prophetic (5.110–12):

> qua prius aggrediar quam de re fundere fata
> sanctius et multo certa ratione magis quam
> Pythia quae tripode a Phoebi lauroque prophatur . . . .

(Before I advance to pour forth sayings about this subject, in manner more sacred and with far surer reasoning than the Pythian priestess who gives prophecies from the tripod and laurel of Phoebus Apollo. . . .)

Here too Lucretius claims to be superseding the tradition that he is describing (*sanctius*, "more sacredly," 5.111; cf. 1.738–39). So, in our passage of book 3, he brilliantly and learnedly weaves into the fabric of his verse the many threads of a long tradition that asserts the immortality that poetry both pos-

sesses and confers. But even as he recreates this tradition, he
implies that it is false. Only death is eternal. Even his own
eternizing praise of Epicurus in 3.1043–44 stands next to his
assertion of the Master's death in 1042.

In the proud blazon of his own poetic achievement, and in
heavily traditional language in the so-called second proem
(1.921ff.), Lucretius asserts the novelty of his subject and his
priority and originality (1.926–30). But he stops just short of
declaring his poetic immortality. The "eternity" of Ennius's
verses in 1.121, we recall, stands in ironic juxtaposition with
their contents (the realm of death) and with their falsehood
(the soul's existence after death and the myths of "eternal"
punishment, 1.111).[13] Reminding us of the poet's claims to
immortality in our passage, Lucretius also exposes the false-
hood of those claims: only death is immortal (3.1091).

On the subject of poetic fame, however, the second proem
clashes sharply with the end of book 3.[14] In the former passage
Lucretius confesses that his heart is deeply stirred by "great
hope of praise" (1.922–30):

> sed acri
> percussit thyrso laudis spes magna meum cor
> et simul incussit suavem mi in pectus amorem
> musarum, quo nunc instinctus mente vigenti
> avia Pieridum peragro loca nullius ante

[13] There is probably an intentional juxtaposition of *Acherusia* and *aeternis*
in 1.120–21 and a deliberate contrast between Ennius's *aeterni versus* ("eter-
nal verses") here and the falsehood of his *aeternae poenae* ("eternal punish-
ments") in 1.111. Note too, by contrast, the *aeternum leporem* ("eternal
grace") for which Lucretius asks Venus in 1.28 and the *aeternum vulnus*
("eternal wound") by which Mars is defeated in 1.34. This section (1.102–
35) associates the falsehoods of the poets, religious superstition, the fear of
death, and mistaken views of dreams: see my essay, "Dreams and Poets in
Lucretius," *Illinois Classical Studies*, forthcoming.

[14] On the much-discussed problem of the poet's fame and Epicurean doc-
trine in this passage, see my "Poetic Immortality." For a clear statement of the
issues and a helpful review of earlier solutions, see J. H. Waszink, "Lucretius
and Poetry," *Mededelingen der Koninklijke Nederlandse Akademie van
Wetenschappen*, Afd. Letterkunde, N. R., vol. 17, no. 8 (Amsterdam, 1954),
243–57, esp. 245ff.

trita solo. iuvat integros accedere fontis
atque haurire, iuvatque novos decerpere flores
insignemque meo capiti petere inde coronam
unde prius nulli velarint tempora musae.

(But with its keen thyrsus, great hope of praise has smitten my
heart and at the same time has struck into my breast sweet love
for the Muses, and pricked on by this in forceful mind I now
wander over the pathless places of the Pierian Muses trodden by
the boot of no one else before. It is my joy to approach the un-
touched springs and to drink, my joy to pluck the new flowers
and to seek for my head a glorious crown from there whence the
Muses have crowned no man's temples before.)

In his final proem too (to be discussed more fully below), Lu-
cretius invokes the Muse for the last time with the wish to win
her "crown with its outstanding praise" (*te duce ut insigni
capiam cum laude coronam*, 6.95; cf. 1.118 and 1.929).

An earlier generation might have regarded the passionate
language of the second proem as the "anti-Lucretius," the poet
of strong feeling, at war with the wise and restrained philoso-
pher (especially *acri percussit thyrso, incussit, instinctus* in
1.922–25). Rather than surrendering to passion, however, Lu-
cretius, I suggest, is still very much in control. The tension be-
tween the second proem of book 1 and the end of book 3
needs to be more fully acknowledged than it generally is.

Through this tension, I suggest, Lucretius implies a dynamic
movement within the poem from the poetic persona who can
still be carried away by the thrill of fame and the persona who
in the last scenes of the work can confront death in its unre-
lieved horror. The recognition of the Master's own death and
of death's "immortality" by the end of Book 3 (*mors immor-
talis, mors aeterna*, 3.869 and 1091) marks an important stage
on this path toward freedom from the fear of dying and a con-
sequent diminution of the need for the immortality that poetry
brings to the writer himself. Instead of the pleasant springs of
flowers of the traditional poetic landscape of the second
proem, Lucretius is ready to confront the vast spaces that Ep-
icurus traversed at the beginning of the book (cf. *omne im-*

mensum peragravit mente animoque, "he traversed the mea-
sureless all with his mind and spirit," 1.74, and *avia Pieridum
peragro,* "I traverse the pathless places of the Pierian Muses,"
1.926). When the poet follows in his Master's footsteps, he
passes beyond the traditional *locus amoenus* of poetic inspi-
ration and looks down at the immensity of the void beneath
his feet (3.26–27). His emotions here are not Dionysiac pas-
sion or mere delight (cf. *iuvat . . . iuvatque,* 1.927–28), but
rather a thrill of awe, even terror, mingled with the "divine
pleasure" of philosophic enlightenment (3.28–30):

> his ibi me rebus quaedam divina voluptas
> percipit atque horror, quod sic natura tua vi
> tam manifesta patens ex omni parte retecta est.

(At these things a certain divine pleasure and shuddering awe
seizes me, because in this way by your force nature has been
revealed thus and laid open in every direction.)

There is, therefore, a development not only in Lucretius's re-
lationship with his reader, as Diskin Clay has convincingly ar-
gued,[15] but also within the poet's own persona—a point to
which I shall return later.

Even at the end of book 1, however, Lucretius, though ve-
hemently moved by the appeal of poetic immortality, still
stops short of allowing himself to be entirely carried away. He
speaks of "praise" rather than undying fame and of "hope"
rather than attainment (*laudis spes magna,* 1.923). By book 3,
the situation has changed. The examples of the great rulers,
generals, and poets who met death, including also the great
philosophers, modify his view of poetic fame (3.1024–45).[16]
When he repeats a large part of the second proem as the proem
of book 4, he omits the emotion-filled lines about the thyrsus

---

[15] See Clay, *Lucretius and Epicurus,* 212–25, 231, 266.
[16] On the exemplary status of the deaths of the great men at the end of book
3, see Charles Garton, "Conforming to the Great," *Classical World* 65
(1971–72): 73–76, who suggests that these are the "great men" referred to in
the often-emended 3.962, *aequo animoque agedum magnis concede: neces-
sest* ("Come, with calm spirit yield to the great: it is necessity").

and the intense longing for praise (1.926–50, repeated at 4.1–25, with the suppression of 1.922–25).[17]

In the final proem of the work Lucretius gives even less emphasis to the motif of poetic immortality. He echoes the lines on the garland and the praise from book 1, but the tone is markedly different (6.92–95):

> tu mihi supremae praescripta ad candida calcis
> currenti spatium praemonstra, callida musa
> Calliope, requies hominum divumque voluptas,
> te duce ut insigni capiam cum laude coronam.

(As I run to the white chalkmark of my designated goal, show me the course, O Calliope, clever Muse, peace of men and pleasure of the gods, so that with you as leader I may grasp the crown with its glorious praise.)

In contrast to the Dionysiac frenzy praised in the second proem (1.922–25), Lucretius now turns to a philosophic Muse (with strong allusions to Empedocles). She offers "rest" or "peace" to men, in contrast to the Venus of the first proem, who brings "pleasure" to both (*hominum divumque voluptas*, "pleasure of men and gods," 1.1). Calliope's *requies*, of course, signals the end of the poem, already marked by the racing metaphor of the preceding lines (92–93), and therefore also the poet's own "rest" from the enormous toil that he has undertaken (cf. *laborem*, 1.141). But *requies hominum*, "rest" or "peace of men," surely reaches beyond the poet. It can suggest the "catastematic" pleasure that is the true source of happiness. Thus it combines the notion of the "rest" that the poet has earned by his long journey (92–93) with that journey's purpose, peace of soul, ἀταραξία, both for himself and for his audience.

Free of the Dionysiac emotionality of the second proem, Lucretius has acquired the strength of the philosophic *ratio*, with

---

[17] The order of the proems has been much discussed, but with the majority of scholars I believe that Lucretius wrote 1.926–50 first and then transferred it to the beginning of book 4. See Bailey, *T. Lucreti Cari*, 1:36 and ad loc., 1:757ff.

which he is ready for what lies ahead, the triumph of death in the plague at Athens. In the prison of this polluted urban world, the waters into which the afflicted hurl themselves in desperation create an image of fountains at the opposite end of experience from those "pure springs" of the Muses in the second proem (cf. 6.1174–78 and 1.927–28). The calm beauty of that setting, however, was inherited from the traditions of the poets rather than earned through the lessons of philosophy. As Lucretius faced the Master's death with serenity at the end of book 3, so here he can confront the awful grip of death on the radiant city of the Master's birth (cf. 6.1–8).

As Clay has argued,[18] the whole course of the poem has prepared us for this moment and given us the wisdom to contemplate it without fear: *mors nihil est nobis*, "death is nothing to us." If we are attentive to the muting of the topos of poetic immortality from the first and second proems to the last, we can perhaps carry this argument a step farther. Not only is the reader strengthened to the point where he can confront the most terrifying of his fears, but there is a parallel evolution of the persona of the poet as well. The poet who was carried away in Bacchic excitement at the prospect of praise from future generations now calmly "grasps" the crown (6.95). The poet of the true doctrine about "eternal death" has left far behind those false myths about "eternal punishments" in the "eternal verses" of Ennius (1.111, 1.120–21). He claims immortality ultimately in the light of the deaths of Democritus and Epicurus, exempla of enlightened behavior and of the benefits of serenity and spiritual peace that come from understanding the place of death in the world order.

---

[18] Clay, *Lucretius and Epicurus*, 212–25, 231, 266.

Chapter Nine

WAR, DEATH, AND CIVILIZATION: THE END OF BOOK 5

THE FEAR OF DEATH not only causes us to make the dangerous and harmful substitutions of wealth, fame, and power for life, as Lucretius argues at the beginning of book 3; it also leads us to destroy life, our own and that of others.[1] In this respect the fear of death is causally related to aggression and destructiveness. Lucretius does not develop this point explicitly, but it is perhaps implicit in his discussion of the causes of civil war and fratricidal bloodshed at the beginning of the book (3.68–73). Because man is ignorant of the balance between destructive and creative processes in all of nature and in his own body, he is anxious and fearful about his own dissolution. The anxious, unhappy man will be mistaken about the ends of life and therefore is likely to reach out to the world aggressively rather than creatively. Such a man will be on the side of Mars rather than Venus, to use the mythical terms that Lucretius sets out in the first proem, with the resultant disturbances to self and society.

Although it would be an oversimplification to argue that Lucretius finds all of the sources of human aggression in the fear of death, he is certainly aware of the affinities between the two. Indeed, the connection of death and unlimited aggression is deeply imbedded in the classical literary tradition.[2]

[1] The original version of this chapter appeared in *Ramus* 15 (1986): 1–34, and it is reproduced here, in much revised form, by permission of Aureal Publications.

[2] In Homer, for example, the lust for killing goes hand in hand with a growing sense of the nothingness of human life and the levelling influence of mortality. Cf. Achilles' famous speech to Lycaon (*Iliad* 21.106–12): "So, friend, you die also. Why all this clamour about it? / Patroklos also is dead, who was better by far than you are" (Richmond Lattimore's translation), the prelude

As in the later Freud, the management of aggression and death go together; and Lucretius, as we shall see, even approximates the Freudian linking of aggressiveness and the death instinct. Unlike Freud, of course, Lucretius regards the pull toward death as an external, physical force rather than as an inseparable part of our inner being or psychic make-up. Thus he has a perhaps more optimistic attitude toward the possibility of overcoming these impulses and thereby achieving personal happiness. Like Freud, however, he believes that the analysis and understanding of the symptoms is essential to curing the malaise and thereby making a happy life possible.

A person with an incorrect attitude toward death turns from the calm joys of *vera voluptas* to false and deleterious pleasures, among which are the pleasures of violence. War in particular is the negation of the pleasurable calm that the poet envisages as the condition for creative work (1.41) and of the simple joys of country folk that he regards, nostalgically, as resembling the joys of mankind in its earlier stages (5.1379–1411). Early in the poem he calls on Venus, identified with both Epicurean pleasure and the principle of creative energy, to still the war-god Mars, "conquered by the eternal wound of love" (1.34). Venus does not succeed, and the imagery of war recurs throughout the poem to describe irrationality, folly, and situations of human suffering. The last scene in the poem is a bloody battle that would not have occurred if men had understood what death really is.

Lucretius's most probing and most disturbing discussion of war, violence, and self-destruction comes near the end of book 5. In tracing the origins of human civilization, he describes man's gradual invention of the skills necessary to survival:

---

to the poem's greatest surge of violence, Achilles' choking the river Scamander with corpses. Lucretius twice adapts this passage (3.1024–26, 1042–45), both times reversing the order of great man and little man. The truly great man, as the comparison with Homer implies, is neither the epic hero (Patroclus) nor the king (good Ancus Martius in 3.1025), but the philosopher, for his is the "true way" (*vera ratio*) to overcome the fear of death. Cf. also Achilles' prayer for universal destruction, including that of his own men, in *Iliad* 16.97–100, which sets the stage for the full unleashing of Achilles' murderous wrath.

shelter, cities, laws, religion, technology. The story is long and complex; and there are a number of disgressions, including an important account of the fear of the gods (5.1194–1240), which gives prominence to a general at sea, "with his strong legions and elephants" (1228). From here Lucretius turns to the discovery of metals, and this leads him, via iron (1281–96), into a vivid account of a moment when men tried to use wild beasts in war (1297–1349). This passage reaches such a pitch of nightmarish violence that even the sober Bailey is tempted by St. Jerome's story of the poet's madness; and another sober scholar, writing in 1985, is inclined to agree.[3]

Early men's weapons, Lucretius says, were hands, nails, and teeth, and later stones, branches, and fire. With their invention of bronze and then iron they reached a new level of power and destructiveness. "With bronze they plowed the earth's soil," but with that bronze they also "sowed vast wounds" (1289–90). Iron weapons were better. Then came the horse, chariots, scythe-bearing chariots, towers mounted on elephants. Men even tried to use bulls, boars, and lions in war. But these beasts turned against their trainers because "heated by the mingled slaughter in their savagery they threw the squadrons into confusion, making no distinction" of friend or foe (1313–14). The lions pulled men down from behind and attacked them with "strong biting and curved claws" (1321). The bulls tossed and trampled their own men and disembowelled horses. The boars "cut the allies with their strong tusks, dyeing the broken spears with their own blood" (1326–27). The horses and mules tried to avoid them, but to no avail, and they shook the earth as they fell, their sinews cut by the cross-ripping of the tusks (1330–33). Even animals that before seemed tame now "seethed in fury amid the wounds, shouts, flight, terror, and confusion" (1334–36). "Every kind of wild beast fled in all directions," Lucretius concludes, "just as now ele-

[3] Bailey, *T. Lucreti Cari*, ad 1308–49 (3:1529–30). G. B. Townend, reviewing Costa, *Lucretius, De Rerum Natura V* in *Classical Review* 35 (1985): 274, observes that the biographical explanation, the poet's subjection to hallucination and even mental derangement, "has never been satisfactorily refuted."

phants, badly injured by weapons, take flight when they have
done many savage deeds to their own side" (1339–40).

As if this outburst were not enough, Lucretius modulates
back to his main theme by taking the whole episode back, or
almost doing so: "But I am hardly persuaded that they could
not perceive in their mind and see that this general and fearful
woe would take place before it occurred" (1341–43). He then
concludes that these men unleashed the animals not to gain
victory but to harm their foes and "to perish themselves, for
they had no faith in their numbers and they lacked weapons"
(1347–49):

> sed facere id non tam vincendi spe voluerunt
> quam dare quod gemerent hostes, ipsique perire,
> qui numero diffidebant armisque vacabant.

The culture history then continues calmly, without even a con-
nective: "Knitted garments existed before woven clothing.
Weaving came after iron, because by iron the loom is fash-
ioned" (1350–51).

It is understandable that Bailey should consider this narra-
tive "perhaps the most astonishing paragraph in the poem."[4]
"Fantastic," "strange," "bizarre," "astonishing,"[5] the product
of "an intelligence fevered, perverted and cancerous,"[6] a dis-
play of "obsessive exaltation"[7]—such are the puzzled reac-
tions of scholars to these disturbing lines. Even scholars who
have sought to explain the passage rather than delete it as an
interpolation or an aberration wonder whether the poet "has
triumphed over the philosopher"[8] and therefore is called back
to a more sober reality by the "recantation" that he gives in

---

[4] Bailey, *T. Lucreti Cari*, ad 1308–49. For a survey of similar views, see
Saylor, "Man, Animal, and the Bestial," 310–11; McKay, "Animals," 124;
Costa *Lucretius V*, 143.

[5] So, for instance, Ernout and Robin, *Lucrèce*, ad 1341–49; Perelli, *Lucre-
zio*, 49–50.

[6] Beye, "Lucretius and Progress," 167.

[7] Bonelli, *I motivi profondi*, 238.

[8] McKay "Animals," 127. For Townend, "Original Plan," 110, the verses
of 5.1341–49 are "incoherent, though entirely Lucretian."

1341–49: such things probably did not happen but might have, given the infinity of possible worlds.

These difficulties should not be minimized; but, fortunately, thanks to a growing tendency to listen more sympathetically to Lucretius's underlying poetic "logic" at work, we are in a better position to make sense of this passage without throwing up our hands in astonishment, rage, despair, or suspicions of madness.[9] In particular, Lucretius's interest in mutilation, the body, and the physical details of death that we have been exploring casts, if not light, at least darkness visible on this passage.[10]

The apparent digression of 1308–49, I suggest, functions in a way analogous to one of Plato's myths: it contains a poetic truth that supplements, in an imaginative way, the surface logic of the exposition of Epicurean philosophy. That supplementation tends to be imagistic, metaphorical, and visual rather than literal or syllogistic. Familiar examples in the poem are the sacrifice of Iphigeneia, the cow seeking her lost calf, the Magna Mater, the aged farmer at the end of book 2, and of course the plague at Athens in book 6.

Such passages are what I would call emblematic. They crystallize a major underlying concern or theme into a poetic description rich in visual imagery, emotional power, and symbolic meaning. They often imply (as here) a psychological dimension of the subject, a symbolical psychohistory of mankind, for which Lucretius otherwise lacks the necessary vocab-

[9] Of recent studies the most helpful are Saylor, "Man, Animal, Bestial"; Schrijvers, *Horror*, 296–305; Kenney, "Historical Imagination" 19ff.; De Grummond "Interpretations." For a brief defense, see West, *Imagery and Poetry*, 20 and 54. The passage certainly exemplifies the Roman taste for physical violence, on which see Carlin A. Barton, "The Scandal of the Arena," *Representations* 27 (1989): 1–36; but taste cannot account for the place of this description here or its degree of detail.

[10] For Lucretius's use of associative patterns, verbal echoes, related sounds, and imagery, see Bailey, "Mind of Lucretius"; Friedländer, "Pattern of Sound"; Elder, "Lucretius 1.1–49," 93ff.; Anderson, "Discontinuity," passim; West, *Imagery and Poetry*, passim; Bollack, *Raison*, 268; Snyder, *Puns and Poetry*; Clay, *Lucretius and Epicurus*, 231ff., 241ff. For "poetic truth" in 5.1308ff., see Saylor, "Man, Animal, and Beast," 306 and 313.

ulary (cf. 1.136–39 and 5.97–106). He frequently marks such passages by adding a "palinode" or similar personal statement immediately afterward, and these take a variety of forms.[11] Such passages point not to a contradiction between Lucretius the Roman poet and Lucretius the Epicurean philosopher but to the pervasiveness of his poetic sensibility throughout. Lucretius wants to make the moral implications of his material come alive emotionally as well as intellectually.[12] Lines 1341–49, then, far from being a sign of incompleteness, late composition, or caprice, are Lucretius's signal to the reader that the preceding passage has the same metaphorical, emblematic significance as the sacrifice of Iphigeneia or the Magna Mater and involves a similar struggle of the poet-philosopher against the forces of violence and irrationality.[13]

Formally, the passage is related to the movement within the culture history as a whole through the motif of weapons. The last phrase of the passage, "they lacked arms" (*armisque vacabant*, 1349), harks back to the theme of "arms" in the preceding section (*arma*, 1283; *armatis*, 1292; *armis*, 1306).[14]

[11] See esp. 4.572ff. and 5.405ff.; in general, Regenbogen, "Lucrez," 370–75. Cf. also 5.526–30, where Lucretius contrasts this world and what might happen in infinite worlds. The long account of the sacrifice of Iphigeneia (1.82–100) is not followed by a palinode of the type mentioned above, but by a second-person address to Memmius, warning him of the dangers of being frightened by the myths of poets (1.102–6). This passage indicates the variety and flexibility of which Lucretius is capable in such palinodic passages. Lucretius is certainly capable of allegorical interpretation of others' myths: see 3.978–1023, and Bailey, *T. Lucreti Cari*, ad loc. (pp. 1157–58). Cf. also Philodemus, *De Morte* 33.10–30.

[12] Such a working together of intellect and imagination in Lucretius has been studied, from various points of view, by Amory, Anderson, Schrijvers, and West, among others.

[13] Schrijvers, *Horror*, 303–4 takes a different though complementary approach: the "recantation" serves to anticipate readers' doubts and also to signal Lucretius's use of "deception" in the service of Epicurean truth. For this kind of delicate balance between poetical use of the myths and Epicurean criticism or self-conscious allegorization, see Schrijvers's more recent study, "Critique des mythes," passim.

[14] Kenney, "Historical Imagination," 19. As he points out on p. 22, the repetitions, *facerent . . . factum . . . facere* (1341, 1344, 1347), indicate a well-thought-out, patterned progression of ideas.

The Carthaginian innovation of "snake-handed" elephants in war immediately preceding (1302–4) also forms a specific point of transition from the historical concreteness of an event located in time and place to the quasi-mythical, emblematic nature of 1308–49. The recurrence of iron in 1351 resumes the thread of the non-martial culture history that broke off with iron in 1281.

Lucretius clearly demarcates the transition between his imaginative reconstruction of early war and the "reality" of the present. The generalizing conclusion of the battle scene in the past, "Each and every kind of wild beast scattered in flight" (*diffugiebat enim varium genus omne ferarum*, 1338), is resumed with a specific focus on elephants in the present: "just as often now elephants, badly butchered by iron, scatter in flight, after they have done many savage deeds to their own men" (*ut nunc saepe boves lucae ferro male mactae / diffugiunt, fera facta suis cum multa dedere*, 1339–40). *Diffugiebat* ("scattered in flight"), in the past (1338), is answered by *diffugiunt*, also placed first in the verse, in 1340. The "savage deeds" (*fera facta*) of these exotic beasts sum up the savagery of the whole description and anchor it in the reality of war as actually fought in the present ("as often now," 1339).[15]

Mars here stands in proximity to the grim birth of whatever is fearful to mankind in arms (*horribile humanis quod gentibus esset in armis*, 1306);[16] and we may recall again the leitmotif of *arma* that led from the general line of culture history to war (1283). Taken in relation to what precedes, then, our passage reveals war as the culminating development of both human civilization and human savagery: *omnia cedebant armatis nuda et inerma* ("everything bare and unarmed yielded to what was armed," 1292). To be *armatus* is a sign of progress. The steady, onward march of civilization seems to leave

---

[15] The phrase *fera facta*, "savage deeds," at the end of the passage (1340) reinforces the theme of savagery that has been sounded three times by the word *saevus* ("cruel" or "savage," 1309, 1314, 1328). The trainers, too, are no less *saevi* than the beasts that they vainly try to control (*saevi magistri*, 1311).

[16] See Elder, "Lucretius 1.1–49," 115ff.

man (at times) not better but worse than the savage creatures that he has conquered.[17]

The apparent interruption to the flow of the argument in 1308–49 enables Lucretius to channel an underlying ethical message into a torrential flood of morally significant visual imagery.[18] The ancient arms, he tells Memmius as he introduces the discovery of iron, were hands, claws, and teeth, or else stones or branches (5.1281–85). But now we find man relying on claws and teeth (although not his own: 1322, 1326, 1330) and in fact enjoying no better success than his primitive ancestor when he tried to take shelter in a stony cave (cf. 5.984–87).

The very abruptness with which Lucretius pulls away from this bloodshed and reclaims his philosophical argument in 1341–49 reveals the disruptiveness of such violence for the poem and for mankind. It belongs to the *vis abdita quaedam*, the hidden forces that surface in human life as war and superstitious dread (5.1233ff.). It cannot be fully rationalized, either in life or in the philosophical frame of the work. It can only be symbolically located and artificially delimited by allegorizations like that of Venus and Mars or the Magna Mater, or else kept at a distance by uneasy intellectual formulations like that of 1341–49.[19]

Four major areas of tension or conflict are implicated in this passage and have important resonances in the book (and indeed the poem) as a whole. These are (1) the struggle between life and death; (2) the value of peace and calm over warfare and violence; (3) the contrast of agriculture and war, particularly within the early stages of man's development; and (4) the ambiguity of progress as Lucretius vacillates between an ide-

---

[17] For views along these lines, see Saylor, "Man, Animal, and the Bestial," 310 and 314; Kenney, "Historical Imagination," 23; De Grummond, "Interpretation," 53.

[18] On the importance of the visual imagination in Lucretius, see Bailey, "Mind of Lucretius," 285.

[19] See Bonelli, *I motivi profondi*, 243–44. For the importance of the irrational in Lucretius; see Perelli, *Lucrezio*; Regenbogen, "Lucrez," 349–50; Bradley, "Lucretius and the Irrational," 321.

alized, exemplary Golden Age simplicity ("soft primitivism") and a welcome escape from a savage existence of bare survival ("hard primitivism").

This last point is also important for the precarious balance that Lucretius maintains between viewing the past in terms of chronologically successive events or in terms of exemplary universals for the human condition. In our passage, 5.1308–49, Lucretius is placing the psychological above the historical reality. He gives us an emblematic account of the destructiveness and aggression that no amount of technological progress, in his day or in our own, has been able to eradicate from the human psyche.

LIFE AGAINST DEATH

The alternation between life and death, renewal and destruction, is an important part of the Epicurean principle of *isonomia*. For Lucretius it is both a basic scientific principle and a process that grips his poetic imagination as he contemplates the ceaseless formation and dissolution of men, animals, and whole worlds in the coming together and separating out of the atoms in infinite space. The child's cry as he sees "the shores of light" at birth mingles with the wail of the dying; and the succession of night and day, dawn and dusk is associatively drawn into the endless intermingling of birth and death (2.575–80). "Now here, now there the life force conquers and is conquered in turn" (2.574–75).[20] In this eternal "war" between creation and destruction, neither side gets the upper hand for long (2.573–74); and just this balance maintains the stability of the universe.

As an Epicurean, Lucretius accepts this process in its physical neutrality. But as a living being and as a poet and thinker who looks toward the future generations of men whom his work is intended to help, he also has strong sympathies (as well as vested interests) on the side of life, creation, and con-

[20] See also 2.944–62 and 1122–49. See in general Elder, "Lucretius 1.1–49," 106ff.; Anderson, "Discontinuity," 13ff.; Minadeo, *Lyre of Science*, esp. ch. 2; Perelli, *Lucrezio*, 41; Sikes, *Lucretius*, 18ff.

tinuity.[21] Thus he takes a special pleasure in pointing out that even though the individual compounds undergo endless alteration and therefore death, the totality of the universe can never dissolve into nothingness: "Something must survive intact, lest all things return to nothing and the abundance of things flourish as reborn from nothing" (1.672–74). "Flourish reborn" (*renata vigescat*) holds the center of line 674 (*de niloque renata vigescat copia rerum*), and the phrase shines with vivid life after the bare and abstract "to nothing . . . from nothing" just before. At the beginning of the next book, contemplating this process of renewal, Lucretius views the surviving creatures as handing on the torch of life. The fully anthropomorphic image recognizes the preciousness of the vital energies that they possess:

> Thus the totality of things is renewed always, and mortal creatures live among themselves in succession. Some races increase, others are diminished; and in a short space are changed the races of living things, and like runners they hand on the torch of life. (2.75–79)

It is hardly necessary to point out how deeply this contrast pervades the poem, from the opening invocation of Venus to the desolation of the plague at the end. One could draw up a formal alignment of values for the poem somewhat as follows:[22]

> Life versus Death
> Venus versus Mars
> Peace versus war
> Epicurean philosophy versus fear and superstition
> The serene life versus restless ambition
> Reproduction of life versus extermination or degeneration of life

Natura, as the process governing the physical world (cf. 5.78 and 1.21), includes both the formation and the disinte-

---

[21] For the influential formulation of this tension or balance in terms of "process" and "value," see DeLacy, "Process and Value," esp. 125–26.

[22] Amory, "Science and Poetry," 158–59, juxtaposes "love, pleasure, peace, a governing Nature, the reproduction of life" and "fear, superstition, war, death, and the degeneration of life."

gration of beings and substances. Yet Lucretius's poetry shows a particular commitment to the processes of creation and agglomeration that are implied in the root meaning of *natura* as "birth."[23] In book 5, where he is concerned with life's origins and unfolding, he lavishes some of the richest imagery in the poem on the beauty of fresh beginnings, the joyful energy of springtime and new life (5.737–40, 783–825). Even where he recognizes that this world of varied, abundant creation must come to an end (5.91–106), he prays that *fortuna gubernans* ("governing fortune," cf. *natura gubernans* in 5.78) may keep such an event far away from us (5.107–9). We should know it from philosophical deduction (*ratio*) rather than from the "thing itself," with the horror that such an experience would bring (cf. *horrisono fragore*, 109). A little later, when Lucretius blames the faulty construction of the world in his anti-teleological argument, he points out man's need to resist the encroachments of wild nature, "for the sake of life" (*ni vis humana resistat / vitai causa*, 5.207–8).

Man cooperates with the creative energies of the world as he "turns the fruitful clod with his plow" and moves the earth's soil upward toward the realm of light and birth (5.210–11). Heedless of man, earth and nature, in their multiplicity and variety, bestow on animals all that they need at birth (*omnibus omnia large / tellus ipsa parit naturaque daedala rerum*, 5.233–34), whereas the human infant is cast up "on the shores of light" like a shipwrecked sailor from "the cruel waves," in need of every assistance (222–27). This passage, in its sympathy for the newly born, as in its pointed question about the power of "untimely death" wandering about our world in the preceding line (*quare mors immatura vagatur*, 221), again reveals Lucretius's deep involvement in the struggle between the power of life's creation and the horror of death.

These themes continue into the second part of book 5, with its attention to the origins of life and the ever-present threat of death. In one of his frequent analogies between microcosm

[23] On this sense of *natura*, see most recently Clay, *Lucretius and Epicurus*, ch. 3, esp. 93ff.

and macrocosm, Lucretius compares the nurturing liquid in
the earth to the milk of a lactating woman (809–15) and adds
that the earth has rightly earned the name of "mother" be-
cause it is the source of life for both men and animals (5.821–
24, especially 822–23). The collocation of human and animal
softens the contrast between the *genus humanum* and the *ge-
nus animale* in 221–34: both are the recipients of nature's cre-
ative energies.[24] As his argument unfolds, however, Lucretius
shows how the processes included in *natura* necessarily in-
clude the death of many species (5.855–77), although the co-
operation between men and animals (or certain animals in this
passage) also determines the conditions under which survival
or destruction occurs. As civilization develops, men help the
useful animals to survive by giving them *larga pabula* ("abun-
dant fodder") as a reward for their labors (869–70); but be-
fore this stage is fully attained, men themselves may provide a
horrible living *pabula* to the wild beasts (5.991).

Our passage, 5.1308–49, continues this triangular interac-
tion between man, animal, and the creative/destructive forces
of *natura* that are continually active in our world. These lines,
like the grisly account of wild beasts eating men in primordial
times (5.990ff.), turn away from the unity between man and
animal life. Instead they pit man against beast in the state of
warfare that marks the negative side of human "progress."
Appropriately, the act of giving birth belongs not to "earth
and Nature" in their generosity and varied abundance
(5.233), but to "grim Discord" (5.1305–7):

> sic alid ex alio peperit discordia tristis,
> horribile humanis quod gentibus esset in armis,
> inque dies belli terroribus addidit augmen.

(Thus grim strife gave birth to one thing from another, which
would be fearful for the race of men in arms, and daily added
increase to the terrors of war.)[25]

---

[24] Cf. also the generalizing *mortalia saecla* in 5.791.
[25] Cf. too *religio* "giving birth" to crime and wickedness in 1.82–83 (*quod
saepius illa / religio peperit scelerosa atque impia facta*). On the other hand,

In the proem Lucretius remarked on the abundance of wild beasts and the "trembling terror" that they bring to men over grove, mountain, and forest (5.39–41):

> ita ad satiatem terra ferarum
> nunc etiam scatit et trepido terrore repleta est
> per nemora ac montis magnos silvasque profundas.

(Thus even now the earth bubbles up in full abundance with wild beasts and is filled with trembling fear among its groves and great mountains and deep forests.)

This spontaneous "bubbling up" of horrors from nature, however, is in fact less dangerous than man's own production of horrors through the offspring of *discordia*.[26] Such places in nature can be avoided, but the "battles" (*proelia*) that arise from an impure spirit are man's own imposition on nature. Epicurus's philosophical battle against the "monsters" of the heart is therefore a truer heroism than the forcible extermination of fabulous monsters in the poets.

This "birth" of horrors in 1305–7 stands under the sign not of Venus, Earth, or Nature but Mars. In the previous line Mars is the personification of the warfare for which the Phoenicians (Carthaginians) trained their battle-elephants (1303–4). The "terrors of war" in 1308ff. belong to the "fearfulness" that Discord bears for the human race and also foreshadow the bulls and lions used "in war's service" (cf. *belli terroribus*, 1307, and *in moenere belli*, 1308). Viewed in the light of the negative meaning of Mars in the work as a whole, the "progress" marked by 1308–49 is the perversion of just those life energies that have been present in the origins of the world described in the introduction to this segment of the argument (cf. 5.656–79, 737–50, 783–825). When man seems most triumphant over the harmful species of animals that *natura* has

---

the metaphor of "birth" has a happier use for the invention of music in 5.334 (*peperere*).

[26] Cf. also *auget* 5.220, "Why does nature nurture and *increase* on land and sea the fearful race of wild beasts hostile to the human race?" and note the use of *augmen* (5.1307).

placed around him (5.219–20), he in fact turns their destructive qualities gratuitously against himself, serving not Venus but Mars.

THE MAGNA MATER

As Lucretius moves from the bulls and boars in 5.1308–9 to lions, he echoes his account of the Magna Mater in book 2:

> turbabant saevi nullo discrimine turmas
> terrificas capitum quatientes undique cristas.

(With no distinction drawn, in their savagery they throw the squadrons into confusion, shaking the terrifying manes of their heads on all sides.) (5.1314–15)

> [Curetes] ludunt in numerumque exsultant sanguine laeti
> terrificas capitum quatientes numine cristas.

([The Curetes] play and keeping rhythm leap wildly about delighting in blood, shaking with divine force the terrifying crests of their heads.) (2.632–33)

Here the Phrygian priests ecstatically celebrate the Great Mother with this bloody and horrific rite. But what they are celebrating is the maternal power of the earth that conjoins men and animals under a single nurturant life force. What leads up to the Magna Mater is Earth's abundance and generosity to men and animals, which we have noted also in book 5 (cf. 2.594–99; 5.232–34 and 821–24).[27]

The priests of the Magna Mater yoked lions to their goddess's chariot because they wished to show that any creature, no matter how savage, was "softened" by the duties of *pietas* toward a mother (2.604–5):

> adiunxere feras, quia quamvis effera proles
> officiis debet molliri victa parentum.

[27] Note too the motif of the mountains in 5.824, of the animal *genus* that "exults wildly over the great mountains" (*in magnis bacchatur montibus passim*) and earth's generous bestowal of food (*pabula laeta*) on the "mountain-wandering race of wild beasts" (*montivago generi ferarum*, 2.597).

Besides asserting the potential unity of man and animal under the all-embracing life force signified by the Magna Mater and "the name of mother" given to Earth, this passage also has reverberations in the culture history in book 5, in which Venus "breaks" the harshness of early man's rude life (5.1017–18).

To trace all of the filiations of the Magna Mater passage through book 5 would be a long and absorbing task; but the indications offered above point to important connections in the themes of creative energy, birth, and the potential unity of man and animal under the sway of Earth and *natura*. In this perspective the echo between 5.1315 and 2.633 has at least one major implication. The lions of the Great Mother symbolize the potential "softening" of earth's creatures by the tasks of parenthood, i.e., the feelings consequent on the birth and rearing of young (2.604–5, cited above). But the point of our passage in book 5, as Lucretius goes on to explain in the next line, is that no "soothing" of the wildness of beasts is possible, for not even the domesticated animals are softened by their riders, and the "breasts" of the horses remain terrified by the lions' roaring (*nec poterant equites fremitu perterrita equorum / pectora mulcere*, 5.1315–16).

In the proem to book 6, the culmination of the progress of human culture is the birth of Epicurus himself (6.1–6):

> primae frugiparos fetus mortalibus aegris
> dididerunt quondam praeclaro nomine Athenae
> et recreaverunt vitam legesque rogarunt,
> et primae dederunt vitam legesque rogarunt,
> et primae dederunt *solacia dulcia vitae*,
> cum genuere virum tali cum corde repertum,
> omnia veridico qui quondam ex ore profudit.

(Athens long ago was the first to give forth fruit-bearing crops for wretched mortals and to renew life and establish laws, and she was also the first to give *the sweet solaces of life* when she gave birth to a man found of such a heart and mind, who once poured forth all things from a mouth that spoke truth.)

The combination of Athens's "fruit-bearing crops" (with the root of "birth," *pario*, in *frugi-paros*), renewal of life, law, and the "sweet solaces" brought by the birth (*genuere*) of Epicurus sets us as far as possible from the life-destroying horrors that discord "brings to birth" in 1304ff.

These contrasts help the reader to see 1308–49 as an emblematic foil to the Magna Mater and to other passages (like the Venus proem and other passages on the origins of life cited above) that present men and animals as joint creations of *Natura* and joint beneficiaries of the vital energies symbolized by the Magna Mater. Book 1 showed Venus's "eternal wound of love" defeating "Mars powerful in arms," ruler of "the savage tasks of war," *belli fera moenera* (1.32–34). But here Mars rages unchecked by this counterforce. The "savagery" (*fera*) now appears in the literal form of the "wild beasts" (*genus omne ferarum*, 5.1338), and the "task of war" introduces the passage (*in moenere belli*, 5.1308; cf. 1.32). Instead of being put to rest by Venus as in 1.33–40, Mars is "stirred up," albeit in an indirect way: the Carthaginians teach their war-elephants to "endure wounds and to disturb the great bands of Mars" (*magnas Martis turbare catervas*, 5.1303–4).

If Venus's quieting of Mars in the sleep of love symbolizes the triumph of Epicurean *ataraxia*, then these "stirred-up bands of Mars" are the negation of the life force of the goddess and of all the philosophical aims of the poem. In the same way we may understand the close association of *discordia tristis* in the next verse with the "birth" of all of war's horrors. *Discordia tristis* is in fact a poetically colored translation of Empedocles's νεῖχος, "strife." This νεῖχος is the principle that opposes the unifying force of "love," φιλότης, personified as Kypris, who is analogous to Lucretius's peace-bestowing Venus of his first proem.[28] The joining of Mars and *discordia* here, therefore, overdetermines the forces of destruction. Viewed against its Empedoclean background, *discordia*'s "giving birth" is virtually an oxymoron whose internal contradiction expresses the imbalance between life and death at

[28] For the contrast of dissolution versus union, νεῖχος and φιλότης, see Empedocles 31 B17, B22, B25, B26 in Diels-Kranz, eds., *Fragmente der Vorsokratiker*, vol. 1. For his identification of φιλότης with Aphrodite or Kypris, see B17.24, 22.5, 75, 95, 98.

this moment. Now Venus's "peace" gives way entirely to war (contrast 1.40, *funde petens placidam Romanis, incluta, pacem*), and "birth" and "increase" mean death (1305–7).[29]

With the power of death thus in the ascendant, even the devisers of this "invention" have abandoned hope of victory or survival and "themselves wish to perish" (*ipsique perire*, 1348). That small phrase in the penultimate line of the passage casts a heavy shadow backward. This self-destructive motivation is all the more unnatural if we recall a few lines in the previous book that (rather abruptly) touch on some of the themes of the culture history (4.843–47):

> at contra conferre manu certamina pugnae
> et lacerare artus foedareque membra cruore
> ante fuit multo quam lucida tela volarent,
> et vulnus vitare prius natura coegit
> quam daret obiectum parmai laeva per artem.

(But to join battle in hand-to-hand fight and tear the limbs and befoul them with blood existed long before the bright javelins flew about; and nature compelled [men] to avoid the wound before the left hand skillfully raised the barrier of the shield.)

Bloody fighting may lie deeply and perhaps irremediably in man's past, but even the rudest savage has a "natural" instinct for self-protection. The self-destructiveness of the end of book 5 also has analogies with books 3 and 6, where men surrender to death out of the very fear of death.[30] In fact, the description here of the lionesses pulling down their victims from behind by surprise, *et nec opinanti a tergo deripiebant* (1320), verbally echoes the movements of Death herself in book 3 as she stands unexpectedly by the head of the hapless banqueter in Natura's diatribe (3.959–60):

---

[29] On Venus's role in the struggle for life against death, peace against war in the poem, see Sellar, *Roman Poets*, 350ff.; Elder, "Lucretius 1.1–49," passim; Clay, *Lucretius and Epicurus*, 93ff.; and recently Asmis, "Lucretius' Venus," passim, with a useful discussion of previous scholarship.

[30] Saylor, "Man, Animal, and the Bestial," p. 315 with n. 41, juxtaposes 3.79–83 and 6.1208–12.

> et *nec opinanti* mors ad caput adstitit ante
> quam satur ac plenus possis discedere rerum.

(And death stood by your head *unexpectedly* before you could depart sated and full.)

Just as the lions that once served the Magna Mater are now in the service of death, so the elephants that in book 2 instanced the limitless abundance of creative energy in a world of infinite atoms are now the instruments of violence. Elephants, *boves lucae*, wounded and wounding, frame the savage fighting of our passage (1302 and 1339). The exotic epithet *anguimanus*, "serpent-handed," occurs only in 5.1303 and in 2.537, where the many thousands of these creatures defend India as with a wall of ivory (2.537–40):[31]

> anguimanus elephantos, India quorum
> milibus e multis vallo munitur eburno,
> ut penitus nequeat penetrari: tanta ferarum
> vis est, quarum nos perpauca exempla videmus.

(Snake-handed elephants, from whose many thousands India is fortified by an ivory tower so that it cannot be entered. Such is the force of those beasts, of which we see very few examples.)

In this passage these creatures have a defensive function: their vast "strength" (*vis*) protects the land. In book 5, however, as befits the ascendancy of *discordia tristis*, the tower, potentially defensive, belongs to their offensive equipment (*turrito corpore*, 1302). The contemporary parallel that they offer (*ut nunc saepe*, 1339) is not with abundance but with a savagery that destroys rather than protects its users (5.1340).

The periphrasis "Lucanian oxen" (instead of *elephanti*, as

[31] On the parallel between books 2 and 5 here, see Nethercut, "Conclusion of Lucretius' Fifth Book," 99; also De Grummond, "Interpretation," 54, and Saylor, "Man, Animal, and the Bestial," 312, who suggests a connection between the unnaturalness of the epithet *anguimanus* and the "unnaturalness of the users of such beasts." I would add too that the aggressive people defended by the elephants in book 2 are the remote and relatively innocuous Indians (*Indi* only here in the poem), whereas in book 5 their users are the aggressive Carthaginian invaders of Italy.

in 2.537 and 5.1228) sets off the "savage deeds" that war re-
leases from those carefully domesticated creatures. These
great beasts are "oxen" of a sort, now transformed back to
"savage" animals, *ferae*. The collocation of "Lucanian oxen"
and "savage deeds" in 1339–40 thus makes a fitting climax
for the inversions of civilization and savagery throughout this
section.

It is part of Lucretius's double-edged reflection on human
"progress" and its relation to war that these monstrous, hy-
brid creatures (as *anguimanus*, "snake-handed," implies),
though introduced as horrible (*taetrae*) at the beginning of this
passage (5.1302),[32] are victimized as "miserably slaughtered"
(*male mactae*) at the end (1339). Even at the beginning, how-
ever, they are more victims than agents, for they are the "pu-
pils" of men (1303–4; cf. 1313). The instruction that they re-
ceive is as much to endure as to inflict wounds (1302–4). *Male
mactae* at the end proves the instruction sadly accurate: the
beasts, like the men, are caught up in their self-destruction (cf.
ipsique perire, 1348). Their "teaching," then (*docuerunt*,
1303; cf. *doctoribus*, 1311), is self-destructive, and in the end
worse than useless. It is thus just the opposite of the peaceful,
pleasurable, and life-enhancing "teaching" of the poet and the
philosopher. *Doceo* is one of Lucretius's common words for
his own activity.

Male mactae in 1339 has still another implication: it inter-
weaves the folly of war with the folly of superstitious rites,[33]
for the phrase brings the suffering of these animals into rela-
tion with the cruelty of sacrificial murder. *Male mactae*, in
fact, may imply something like "wrongly or cruelly sacri-
ficed"; and one may compare Iphigeneia in 1.99 (*mactatu*

[32] Elsewhere Lucretius uses *taeter* to describe particularly ugly and painful
bodily injury, e.g., the mangling by wild animals in 5.995 or (four times) the
fetid smell, effluvia, or ulcers of the plague (6.1154, 1200, 1205, 1271). The
adjective can also have the more neutral sense of merely "bitter" (1.936, re-
peated at 4.11). Cf. also 4.685 ("bitter poison," *taetrum venenum*) and 6.22
(*taetro quasi conspurcare sapore*, "to befoul with ugly taste"), where both
bitterness and foulness are involved.

[33] For this combination, cf. also 2.40–46 and 5.1218ff.

maesta parentis, "saddened in the sacrificing by a parent") or the calf separated from its mother by sacrificial death in 2.353 (*mactatus*).[34] The scattering of these "miserably slaughtered" elephants in 1339–40 shows the killers turned into the killed.

For the human agents there is still a more far-reaching reversal. The terrible end of the victims of the lionesses, torn apart as the beasts hold them with teeth and claws (*morsibus adfixae validis atque unguibus uncis*, 5.1322), is a reversion to the helplessness of primitive man in his earliest condition (cf. 990–93). Even in that state of archaic impotence, however, human life was in some sense better; for, as Lucretius observes, animals killed fewer men than did the great battles of modern warfare (999–1001). Such is the refined savagery of fully developed civilization.

As war releases the animalism hidden in man, so it undoes his repression of the beasts' savagery. To this repression of savagery, in fact, many species owe their survival, for they have come to depend on their peaceful coexistence with man and the usefulness (*utilitas*) of a life of peace and work (cf. 860, 870, 873). In this reversal man betrays the trust that animals had in him. The domesticated animals were preserved because they entrusted themselves to man's guardianship (*tutela*) and protection (*praesidium*). Lucretius repeats this point three times (5.861, 867, 874). But now, in man's perverted notion of "usefulness," this class of animals (865) is exposed to that very destruction from which man's guardianship (*tutela*) had presumably offered refuge.

Now man treats war as the realm of *labor* and attempts to extract *utilitas* from creatures whose only "service" can be to inspire fear and inflict ghastly wounds. The beasts "eagerly flee" savagery to "pursue peace" (5.868); man cultivates the savagery of the beasts to pursue the arts of war. In agriculture man provided *larga pabula* (869) to domesticated beasts in

---

[34] On this last passage and its implications for the major themes of the poem, see Segal, "*Delubra Decora*," passim. Cf. also 3.52 and 5.1201–2. Though *mactus* itself is not used in an explicitly sacrificial context, it is likely to have the same connotations as *mactatus*, of which it is probably a back-formation: see the *Oxford Latin Dictionary, s. v.*

return for tilling the soil; in war he recreates the chaotic time when he himself provided *viva pabula* to savage predators (991, and cf. 1320–22).

In his earliest past, man had no view of the common good, no ability to be bound by common laws and customs. Instead, life followed the rule of the stronger. Chance and force governed (958–61):

> nec commune bonum poterant spectare neque ullis
> moribus inter se scibant nec legibus uti.
> quod cuique obtulerat praedae fortuna, ferebat
> sponte sua sibi quisque valere et vivere doctus.

(Nor could they discern a common good nor did they know how to use any social customs among one another or any laws. Whatever booty fortune brought to each, he carried off, as each was trained to be strong and to live by his own random will.)

Lines 1308–49 return man to the same state of chaotic, random violence, but the more pictorial account makes the scale seem larger.

AGRICULTURE

We are now in a better position to understand why the transition between the development of metals and agriculture should be the ambiguous "increase" (*augmen*) over which *discordia tristis* presides (1305–7) and the savage battle that follows (1308–49). Agriculture makes only a brief appearance among the uses of metals (bronze), but its fruitful earth is soon submerged, figuratively, beneath the "waves of war" (5.1289–91):

> aere solum terrae tractabant, aereque belli
> miscebant fluctus et vulnera vasta serebant
> et pecus atque agros adimebant.

(With bronze only did they work the fields, and with bronze did they mingle the waves of war and sow crops of vast wounds and take away cattle and fields.)

The rhetoric of this passage dwarfs agriculture and magnifies war. "Sowing" wounds rather than grain (*vulnera vasta sere-bant*) (mis)appropriates the power of metals for death rather than life. This dark metaphor anticipates the reversal developed later in "grim discord's" birth and "increase" of the horrors of war for mankind (1305–7). The same process is repeated with iron a few lines later. The "plowing" of the earth seems to yield neatly "evened out" rows not of crops but of battle (1294–96, especially *exaequataque sunt creperi certamina belli*, "the contests of wavering war were levelled out"). In 1308ff., however, the uses of metals undergo still further regression. In place of weapons of bronze and iron stand "claws" and "teeth," *ungues* and *dentes* (1322, 1326, 1330).

As these two passages indicate (1294–96 and 1305–7), the contrast between warfare and agriculture is a specific form of the larger contrast between savagery and civilized life.[35] That contrast, in turn, ramifies into the poem's large-scale dialectic between creation and destruction. Lucretius tends to associate the earth with the creative forces of the universe.[36] As *daedala tellus*, earth is mother of crops and animals. Thus the positive development of mankind resumes, after our passage, with agriculture and *natura creatrix*, nature herself, as the teacher (5.1362). Man's efforts here are directed at "taming" the "wildness" of the uncultivated fruits in the earth (1367–69):

> inde aliam atque aliam culturam dulcis agelli
> temptabant *fructusque feros mansuescere* terra
> cernebant indulgendo blandeque colendo.

(From there they kept on trying then one, then another cultivation of the sweet land, and they observed that the *wild fruits became tame* in the earth through kind treatment and cozening cultivation.)

---

[35] Cf. the contrast of plow and sword in 1297–1307 and 1308–40, briefly noted by Minadeo, *Lyre of Science*, 97 and 131 n. 50.

[36] Cf. 1.7–8, 1.228–29, 5.233–34. On the association of earth and life, see Anderson, "Discontinuity," 5–11. Note too the association of the sea with war and death in 5.1226–40 and 1290, as in 2.551–54 and 5.218ff., on which see ibid., 21–22.

The victory of the "tame" over the wild in agriculture becomes concrete in the cultivated landscape of the following lines (5.1370–78): the vineyards and olive groves gird the hills in the ordered abundance that still delights the traveler in Umbria or Tuscany. Phrases like *dulcis agelli* ("sweet little field," the diminutive only here in the poem), *blande, laeta, vario lepore*, and *felicibus* all enhance the mood of joyfulness, pleasure, and fertility combined.[37]

Man's participation in the cosmic movement between destructive and creative processes in the universe, the *motus exitiales* and the *motus genitales auctificique* of 2.569–72, takes the form of cooperating with the life-sustaining forces both in the earth (1361ff.) and in animals (860–77). In both cases he encourages what pulls away from savagery in order to follow the path toward peace.[38] The transference of agricultural imagery to warfare in 1290 and the account of the beasts of battle in 1308–48 show man choosing the side of death; but the shift to agriculture, whose "origin" is *rerum natura creatrix* herself (5.1362), leaves open the other possibility (1362–78).

Natura herself holds both creative and destructive energies. She nurtures the savage beasts, who in fact possess large tracts of her realm (cf. 5.201–2). This passage early in book 5 (195–234) is directed against the teleological or providential view of the world and insists on its flawed character. Natura nurtures the "fearful race of wild beasts" hostile to mankind (218–19), whereas that same Natura furnishes animals with all their needs at birth (228–34). Even here, however, men can choose the side of life, birth, and light; and this choice too takes the form of an implicit contrast between the hostile wild beasts (218–19) and the "useful" domestic animals by whose

---

[37] Commentators often note the beauty of the description. Giussani finds 1359–76 "pieni di verità e di idillica soavità" (*T. Lucreti Cari*, 3:160); similarly Bailey, *T. Lucreti Cari*, ad 1373–75; Munro, *T. Lucreti Cari*, ad 1378. With *dulcis agellus*, cf. the association of *dulcis* with life and children elsewhere (e.g., 2.997, 3.66, 3.895–96, 5.889); and cf. the "sweet laughter" (*dulces cachinni*) of 5.1397. Cf. also *in-dulg-endo* in 5.1369.

[38] Cf. 5.868, of the domesticated animals eagerly fleeing the wild beasts and pursuing peace.

efforts "human force" resists the chaotic growth of nature that would cover the fields with thorns (206–7).

Cultivating the earth "for the sake of life" (*vitai causa*, 208), men "turn up the fruitful clods with the plow" and "lift up the earth's soil toward the [sun's] risings," for otherwise the crops would not "come forth into the clear winds" (210–12). So too the success of man in "compelling the forests day by day to retreat to the mountain and the area below to yield to cultivated places" (*succedere, concedere*, 1370–71) is a direct response to the persistence of "mountains and the forests of wild beasts" in 201–2. Here, at the end of book 5, Natura is the teacher, not the obstacle (contrast 1361–62 and 206–7), and the "enemy" is not fellow man in war but the wild places that the farmers compel to "yield" and "surrender" (1370).

The setting of the battles of 1308–49 is undefined. There is scarcely a word of natural description or a hint of a landscape. It is as if these scenes of carnage take place in an abstract, nightmarish zone of unlimited violence, like the bare setting (save for the lone, spectral tree) in the great Alexander mosaic from Herculaneum (now in the Naples Archeological Museum) or the battle scenes of Paolo Uccello. In contrast to this quasi-abstract vagueness of place stand the carefully ordered fields and orchards of 1361–69, where man is led by *natura creatrix* herself (1362). Soon after come the soft grassy places and springtime floral setting of early man's rustic leisure (1384–1402; cf. 2.29ff.), and later the secure towers of the urban life of 1440ff.—settings that are thematically and verbally associated with Lucretius's metaphors for the serene life of Epicurean philosophy (cf. 2.29–33 and 2.7–8).

If 1308–49, then, shows mankind as sinking back to the level of feral nature, the passages that immediately follow—the descriptions of agriculture in 1361–78 and of rustic leisure in 1387–1411—show him as approaching the life-giving creativeness of *natura* adumbrated in the Venus proem and reiterated here in *natura creatrix* (5.1362). The "divine leisure" (*otia dia*, 5.1387) of this simple life is also a harbinger of the serenity of the sage and of the idealized calm of Epicurean divinity (cf. 2.1–33, 3.11–30). These leisurely, musical pursuits "soothe the minds of men," *haec animos ollis mulcebant* (1390; cf. 5.20–21).[39] The proem to book 5, we recall, has evoked the divine Epicurus as the truly civilizing hero (5.5–54).

In the georgic and musical setting of 1361–1411, life is a thing of joy and pleasure, of play and sweetness, of the laughter of men and the smiling face of nature (*ridebat*, 1395; *risus dulcesque cachinni*, 1403). In the battle scene of 1308ff., life is gripped by terror, engulfed in whatever *horror* "grim Discord" can bring forth for mankind. The later scene, too, reestablishes a happier relation between man and animals. By imitating the voices of the birds, man learns the delights of music (1379–87). Now he uses the animal world not for the regressive savagery of claws and teeth but for a civilizing art that adds to his contentment with life and to his more refined pleasures. The sounds of the peaceful rustics are happy and musical; those of the war scene are discordant and threatening (1316, 1336). These contrasting tableaux of war and peace, violent death and rustic jollity, then, serve as emblems of the divergent paths that human life can take and of the choices that lie open to man. They contain the contrasting value systems at the core of the poem's message.

Both the placeless scene of nightmarish savagery and the carefully landscaped setting of musical leisure interrupt the historical, evolutionary account (1308–49, 1379–1411).[40] Both draw explicit analogies between "then" and "now" (1339, 1408, 1423). They thus interweave the historical and the exemplary and suggest an atemporal dimension to these contrasts, which form an indispensable moral commentary on the evolutionary account. This implicit commentary, in turn, enables us to distinguish between true and apparent progress.

[39] Contrast 5.1316–17, where the horsemen are "unable to soothe the horses' breasts," amid the fury of the roaring (*nec pectora mulcere*).

[40] Thus Bailey, *T. Lucreti Cari*, 3: 1539, calls 5.1379–1410 "a discursive section . . . in which [Lucretius] follows his fancy."

Peace and War

In proving the mortality of the world in 5.326–37 Lucretius begins with the great wars at Thebes and Troy. These are indications of the lateness of the world's origin (5.326–27), as if war and death were the sure sign of great civilizations. His first personal intervention in the work is his prayer that Venus hold Mars in check in order to obtain *placidam pacem* for Rome. The current wars destroy the "favorable time" and the "even temperament" (*aequum animum*) that foster philosophical contemplation and *ataraxia* (1.28ff., especially 38–43; cf. *tempore iniquo*, 1.41).[41] Civil war, with the bloodshed, fear, and hatred that it brings, recurs as one of the greatest disturbances to happiness (3.65–73) and one of the surest signs of man's need for philosophical illumination in order to overcome the darkness and false terrors into which he can sink (3.77 and 87ff.).[42]

In its accumulation of bloody detail and emphasis on self-destructive violence, this passage at the beginning of book 3 has close affinities with the beasts of battle in book 5, especially in its highlighting of blood (3.71–73):

> caedem caede accumulantes;
> crudeles gaudent in tristi funere fratris
> et consanguineum mensas odere timentque.

(Heaping slaughter upon slaughter; in their cruelty they take joy in the grim death of a brother, and they both hate and fear the table of kinsmen.)

In their graphic, almost surreal description of bloodshed, lines like 5.1313 and 1328 are also akin to lines of a similar mood later in book 3, particularly the gory description of limbs severed by a scythe-armed chariot in 3.642–56. Scythe-bearing

---

[41] On peace in the poem, see Regenbogen, "Lucrez," 368; Clay, *Lucretius and Epicurus*, 266.

[42] On the negative value of war in the poem, and particularly in book 5, see Sellar, *Roman Poets*, 290–91; Schrijvers, *Horror*, 304–8; Bonelli, *I motivi profondi*, 243–44; De Grummond "Interpretation," 53–54.

chariots in fact occur shortly before our passage in book 5 (5.1301). In book 5 the victim is a hamstrung horse, in book 3 a man who has had a leg sheared off (5.1330–33, 3.650–53).

In the proem of book 5, Epicurus (like Venus at the beginning of book 1) sponsors the arts of peace. His benefactions consist in having placed life in "so calm" a condition (*in tam tranquillo*, 5.12). His victories, by words not arms (*dictis non armis*), are more valuable than Hercules', for they enable us to avoid "battles" and "dangers" (*proelia, pericula*) even more dangerous than confrontations with exotic monsters (5.43–44). Lucretius is here close to one of Epicurus's own formulations (though not to its language), which urges that the "purest security" (ἀσφάλεια) comes from serenity (ἡσυχία) rather than from physical force or wealth (*Kyriai Doxai* 14).

The contrast between Epicurus and Hercules in the proem of book 5, then, establishes a set of contrasts that extends to our passage near the end of the book:

Epicurus versus Hercules
Peace versus war
Pure life of calm versus violence and passions
Philosophy versus fighting mythical creatures
Battle against passions versus battle against beasts
Words versus arms
Real usefulness versus that which is spectacular but impractical for lived life
True divinity versus myth of divinization

Viewed in the light of the proem, the use of wild beasts in 1308–49 is a double negation of Epicurus's gains: it throws mankind back simultaneously to war and to wild beasts.

At the furthest possible remove from the "pure peace" of Epicurus in the proem of book 5 stands the general, with his legions and elephants, in 5.1226–35. Surrounded by the paraphernalia of battle, he has yielded completely to ambition, fear, and false notions about the gods (cf. 3.68–73). One who leads such a life cannot look on the gods and nature "with a mind set at peace" (*pacata mente*, 1203). Thus he offers misplaced prayers to the gods for "peace" (*non divum pacem vo-tis adit* . . . 5.1229; cf. 1.39–40). The next line unmasks this "peace" by juxtaposing it to "fear": *ac prece quaesit / ventorum pavidus paces animasque secundas,* ("And does he not in terror seek the winds' peace and favorable breezes?" 5.1229–30). *Paces* and *animae* (the latter also reminding us of the inner state of the "soul") suggest that the true source of the violence is not the weather, nor is the true solution prayer.

THE AMBIGUITY OF PROGRESS: HISTORY AND EXEMPLUM

As we have seen, the account of the beasts of battle reverses the upward progression of civilization, man's separation from primordial lawlessness (958–61) and helplessness in the face of wild beasts.[43] The next stage of civilization introduces family life, friendship, and the inhibition of aggression (1009ff.). Now neighbors agree neither to do injury to nor to suffer it from one another (*nec laedere nec violari,* 1020). Even in his rudimentary, stammering language, early man is able to make known the need to "pity the weak," the women and children (1022–23). The very fact that the human race survived proves that the larger part of mankind must have followed that "treaty" (*foedera*) with pious observance (*caste,* 1025).

This is an important point, for it makes man's very survival dependent on his ability to inhibit aggression: "Otherwise the entire human race, already at that moment, would have perished" (*aut genus humanum iam tum foret omne peremptum,* 1026). In the next section of the culture history, which discusses language, not aggression or society, the wild beasts that are so fierce and deadly in 982–98 and again in 1308–49 appear in a gentler, more benign mood. The young of lions and panthers use "claws" and "teeth" in play (1036–38). Huge Molossian mastiffs lick their puppies, and when they bite only

---

[43] Cf. 5.984–98; also 990 and 1320–21. For the "war against wild beasts" as an index of human progress in the Greek culture histories see, for example, Plato, *Protag.* 322b. See also Thomas Cole, *Democritus and the Sources of Greek Anthropology,* American Philological Association Monographs 25 (Cleveland, 1967), 123–24.

pretend to use their teeth (*morsuque petentes . . . suspensis teneros imitantur dentibus haustus,* 1068–69; cf. 991 and 1319–25). Animals, then, are subject to the same "softening" by their young as humans (cf. 1013–18). Unlike the wild animals, however, man's survival depends more on checking his capacity for violence than on using force. The acme of human development is the point at which it shades into the divine and achieves a "life" that is really tolerable for man. This is attained by victories of mind, not strength. *Dicta, non arma,* "words not arms," marked the victories of Epicurus in the proem (5.50).

The principle of peace over force has a nascent form in the "stuttering" plea for pity, *vocibus ac gestu,* in 1022. This is an early victory of *dicta* over *arma.* Even primitive man, it would seem, has the innate perception, or *notities,* of the value of the peaceful life. This perception would provide a still firmer basis for the validity of Epicurus's teaching and its eventual success among Lucretius's contemporaries.

Lucretius next turns to the invention of fire and the founding of cities (1090–1116). He "digresses" on the greed, ambition, and envy that now, as much as in the past, cause misery and unhappiness (1117–35), and then he returns to his main theme with the invention of law (1144ff.). Laws arise when the human race is "weary of leading a life of violence" (*defessum vi colere aevum,* 1145; cf. 1150), and is in decline because of mutual hostility (*inimicitiis,* 1146; cf. *amicitiem,* 1019). Amid so much *vis* and *iniuria* it is impossible to lead a life of calm and peace (*placidam ac pacatam degere vitam,* 1154), especially for the man who "by his deeds violates the treaties of peace held in common" (*qui violat factis communia foedera pacis,* 1155). *Foedera* and *amicitia* return us to the earlier but kindred stage of 1019–27. But the repetition of *pax* in two consecutive lines also anticipates the hopeless prayers of the leader of violence, the ambitious general of 1226–32, who, with his legions and war-elephants, is subject to the full *vis* of nature (1226; cf. 206, *natura sua vi*).

Our passage (1308–49), then, completes the zigzag movement in the second half of the book between progress and de-

cline, subjection to animals and control of animals, peace and
violence.[44] The checkered quality of this progress continues in
man's "splattering the altars with the abundant blood of four-
footed beasts" because he is unable to look on the world with
a heart set at peace in 1203 (*pacata posse omnia mente tueri*).
Lines 1308–49 finally prove that, for all of his Hercules-like
conquests of beasts, man still has not conquered the most dan-
gerous form of savagery (cf. 18, 43ff.). His use of wild beasts
in war at the relatively advanced stage depicted in 1308–49
reveals that he is not in fact "weary of leading a life of vio-
lence" (1145, 1150) and that in certain fundamental respects
he still "manages his life in the manner of the beasts" (cf. *vul-
givago vitam tractabant more ferarum*, at the beginning of this
stage of the culture history, 932). Despite its intellectual and
material progress, the human race remains "unhappy" (*O ge-
nus infelix humanum*, 1194).[45]

In 5.335–37, arguing that everything in the world has an
origin, Lucretius lists Epicurean philosophy as an "invention"
of recent date (*repertast nuper*, 335), parallel in its historicity
to the invention of sailing, music, and the other arts (332ff.).
But at the same time he takes the opportunity to point out that
this "invention" continues into the present writing of the *De
Rerum Natura* (335–37):

> denique natura haec rerum ratioque *repertast*
> nuper, et hanc primus cum primis *ipse repertus*
> nunc ego sum in patrias qui possim vertere voces.

> (Finally this nature and science of things *has been discovered* just
> recently, and in particular I too *was just discovered* as one ca-
> pable of translating it into the language of our fathers.)

The parallelism of *ratio repertast* and *ipse repertus* / *nunc ego*
presents Lucretius himself as the final "invention" in the prog-
ress of human history. Like Epicurus, he becomes both a part

[44] Cf. 5.860ff., 982ff., 1019ff., 1034ff., 1063ff., 1141ff.
[45] On the false values of contemporary materialism pervading the culture
history, see Taylor, "Progress and Primitivism," 190.

of the movement from the past to the present and a fact of man's life in the present moment.[46]

This shift between the historical and the contemporary characterizes Epicurus himself in the two most emphatic descriptions of his achievements. In the proem of book 1 Lucretius places him into the culture-historical perspective of the "first discoverers" or πρῶτοι εὑρέται (*primus Graius homo*, 1.66). But after a series of historical tenses (*ausus, compressus, irritat, pervicit, processit, peragravit*, 67–74) he moves back to the contemporary effects of his "victories" that leave *religio* forever in a stage of subjection (1.75–79). Here he uses the present tense: *unde refert nobis victor* (1.75); *religio . . . obteritur, nos exaequat victoria caelo* (1.78–79) ("brings back to us victoriously," "superstition is crushed," makes us equal with his victory"). Lucretius here anticipates the later, figurative victory of Epicurus over Hercules, for his language adapts the motif of the Roman general's victory procession to the intellectual "triumph" of the Greek philosopher of the pacific life.[47]

In the proem of book 5, Hercules's victories over lions, boars, and bulls (as well as over mythical beasts) belong to the remote past, whereas Epicurus's victories of the spirit are alive "even now" (*nunc etiam*, 5.20). Hercules' initial victories over bestiality involve the first three animals named in the release of savagery in 1308ff., namely bulls, lions, and boars. The superiority of spiritual conquests to the gifts of Ceres and Liber (14ff.) introduces agriculture, and indeed the origins of agriculture (cf. 15 and 1361). Yet without Epicurus's gifts, even the pacific arts will not guarantee the life of a serene heart (*at bene non poterat sine puro pectore vivi*, "But without a pure breast the good life is not possible," 18). The "soothing" that Epicurus brings to the hearts of men, even now, is at the opposite extreme from the inability of the trainers in war to "soothe the breasts" of the terrified horses (*pectora mulcere*,

---

[46] On 5.335ff., see Clay, *Lucretius and Epicurus*, 52–53; cf. also 6.1–8.

[47] On Lucretius's adaptation of the language of the *triumphator*, see Buchheit, "Epikurs Triumph," esp. 305; also P. H. Hardie, *Virgil's Aeneid: Cosmos and Imperium* (Oxford, 1986), 194–95.

1316–17; *nunc etiam per magnas didita gentis / dulcia per-mulcent animos solacia vitae,* "Now too his sweet consolations of life, spread forth among the great peoples, soothe the minds" 20–21). The glance ahead to analogies with "now" in 1339–40 (*ut nunc*) does not show the "sweet" consolations that Epicurus has spread over the human race in 20–21 (*nunc etiam*) but rather reveals that disposition to savage warfare which cries out in desperate need for Epicurean ministration.

The efflorescence of Epicurus's divinity occurs among men at a specific moment of the past: *deus ille fuit* (5.8). Ten lines later these past tenses change to the present: *hic merito nobis deus esse videtur* (5.19, "He seems to us deservedly to be a god"). And soon afterwards this divinity moves even to the future: *nonne decebit / hunc hominem numero divum dignarier esse* ("Will it not be deemed suitable for this man to be held worthy of the gods?" 50–51). Here too, as in 335–37, Lucretius himself exemplifies the continuation into the present moment of Epicurus's past discourse about the gods and nature: he moves from the Master's past *dicta* (53) to his own now (*cuius ego ingressus vestigia dum rationes persequor ac doceo dictis . . .* , "treading in his footsteps while I pursue scientific reasoning and teach by sayings," 55–56; cf. 3.3ff.).

Hercules, foil to Epicurus in the proem, has the same double status. Existing at a particular moment of time, he exterminated specific violent creatures. But he also exists outside of time, in a quasi-mythical reality, as the author of *facta* of enduring fame; and he is the exemplar of a life of physical heroism, parallel but inferior to Epicurus's spiritual and intellectual heroism. Epicurus himself, as a mortal man, was born in a specific place at a specific moment (6.5) and met death at a specific point in time (3.1042–44); but his *dicta* are worthy of immortal life (3.12f.; cf. *dictis* in 5.50 and 56).

Epicurus simultaneously occupies both the diachronic and the synchronic axes of the poem. As a "god," he is the ever-renewed exemplum of a serenity outside of time (cf. 3.16–27); but he is also the goal of men in this life and on this earth. His "invention" of philosophy, both literally and metaphorically, lifts men "out of the waves" (5.9ff.), where, in a more particularized context, the disturbed, misguided passions of ambitious generals lead men to a watery grave (5.1226–32, especially 1232, *ad vada leti*, "to the shoals of doom").[48] His "discovery," at a particular point in human history (1.62–74, 5.9–10), is the final stage of man's progress out of savagery and thus completes the conquest of the mythical beasts begun by Hercules in the remote past. At the same time his invention remains of permanent value, not to be superseded by subsequent "progress." It remains an absolute, timeless benefit (cf. 3.12), to be judged of greater value than Hercules's efforts.

The release of wild beasts in war in 1308–49, then, is also an event at a specific moment of human history. As the inversion of the work of Epicurus, as we have seen through numerous parallels, it is also an exemplar of a de-civilizing process. It historically embodies and paradigmatically illustrates the unenlightened, impure soul's surrender to the violence and bestiality of man's earlier stages and its ever-present potential.

These considerations help explain why the exemplary and the historical (the synchronic and diachronic axes) intersect so frequently as Lucretius seems to "digress" from his chronological scheme to moral generalization. The battle against savagery, both inward and outward, has been fought, and won, in the past, in history: otherwise the human race would have long since perished (1026). But that battle must be fought again and again insofar as the dangers of violence and bestiality remain alive in the human heart, even after the beasts themselves have been exterminated from the forests and mountains (cf. 5.1370–78). Wild beasts once made the humble *quies* of the cave inimical to its nude human inhabitant (982–83). Modern man, with all his power on land and sea, has still to learn how to find an inner *quies* (cf. *parere quietum*,

---

[48] This account of death at sea is also related to the diatribe in 3.1029–33, where Lucretius notes that even the great general who led his legions over the waves met his death like all other mortals. In the passage of book 5, Lucretius has deepened the irony by having the death occur at sea. We may wonder whether he is drawing on an Epicurean source here, as Philodemus, *De Morte* 33.10–23, juxtaposes the naval deaths at Artemision and Salamis with death on land at Plataea to show that, for the dead person, there is no difference.

5.1129). Otherwise he destroys not merely physical life (cf. 1000ff., 1226ff.), but the very basis for a good life: *at bene non poterat sine puro pectore vivi* ("But without a pure breast the good life is not possible," 5.18).

Lucretius resumes the chronological thread of the culture history in the next section, on weaving. But here too the exemplarity of his account intrudes in two sets of details, both of which are related to the description of the wild beasts in 1308–49: the cultivation of the earth (1361–1411), which we have already discussed above, and the coat of skins that once caused havoc by the jealousy it aroused (1416–33). This latter passage concludes with Lucretius's generalization about the lack of knowledge as the cause of this misery (1432–33).

Chronologically, this passage continues the forward movement of time and so concludes with the rapid survey of discoveries in astronomy, cities, writing, commerce, and international treaties in the last section of the culture history (1436–47). The coat of animal skins in 1418–22, however, also takes us back to the beast world, literally in the word *ferinae* (1418) and figuratively in the bloody battle that leaves this garment "torn apart amid much bloodshed" (*distractam sanguine multo*, 1421).

This specific detail places us, once more, amid the violence and savagery that intrude, synchronically, into the apparently upward course of human history. It echoes the "sprinkling of altars with much blood" in the apostrophe to the "unhappy human race" (1194) in line 1201 (*aras sanguine multo / spargere*). It also recalls the spears broken off and covered with blood in the account of the wounded boars in the bestial battle of 1308ff. (*tela infracta suo tingentes sanguine saevi*, of the wounded boars in 1328). "Quarrelling with much bloodshed" also has an emblematic, exemplary significance for the poem as a whole, for it is with the degradation and folly of this detail that Lucretius will end his poem. The kinsmen of the deceased fight to put the corpses on pyres that do not belong to them, *multo cum sanguine saepe / rixantes potius quam corpora deserentur* ("With much blood often quarreling rather than let the bodies be abandoned," 6.1285–86). This scene, at the high point of the plague's destructive power over Periclean Athens, also marks a regression to helplessness and primitive violence (cf. 6.1–8 and 1140–44).

This closing section of the culture history balances progress with regress, forward movement with circularity, in order to emphasize, as the lines on envy do (1418–19), the constants of ignorance, folly, and violent passion operating throughout human history.[49] Thus the description of early man's joyous dancing, "in hard fashion and with hard foot hitting mother earth" (5.1402), ends with an echo of the "hardness" of the human condition at the beginning (5.925–26). The generalizing attention to the desuetude of acorns for food and foliage for shelter as part of the cycle of changing preferences and values also recalls those earlier phases of the culture history when "the acorn began to be loathed and those couches strewn with grasses and made larger with leaves were abandoned" (5.1416–17; cf. 5.939, 965, 987).

"Civilized" man, Lucretius points out, derives no greater pleasure from his skills and inventions than did early man (1409–11).[50] Here he combines his historical perspective with the Epicurean universal that pleasures can be varied but not increased. This failure to reach any greater *fructus* than earlier men (1410 and 1422) also neutralizes the upward progress from savagery to agriculture, by means of which men made "the wild fruits grow tame in the earth" (*fructus feros*, 1368).

The continual change in what men and women value underlines the universality of the philosophical doctrine. This very universality, paradoxically, pulls evolutionary development

---

[49] On the complexities and ambiguities in Lucretius's view of history as progress or regress, see Taylor, "Progress and Primitivism," 189ff.; Nethercut, "Conclusion of Lucretius' Fifth Book," 97–98, with attentions to earlier literature; Beye, "Lucretius and Progress," 166–68; Borle, "Progrès ou déclin," 174; and Bernd Manuwald, *Der Aufbau der lukrezischer Kulturenstehungslehre, Abhandlungen der Akademie der Wissenschaften in Mainz*, Geistes-und sozialwiss. Klasse (Wiesbaden, 1980), Heft 3, pp. 51ff.

[50] See Furley, "Lucretius the Epicurean," 12–17 and 24. Cf. also the echo between the destructive *invidia* of 5.1419 and that of 1126–27, also in a moralizing context that stresses the constants in human life (*nec magis id nunc est neque erit mox quam fuit ante*, 1135).

back toward the exemplary and the circular. Hence, as a generalizing sequel to the disastrously coveted pelt, Lucretius echoes his completely moralizing, non-evolutionary dictum about the simple life in the proem of book 2 (cf. 5.1427–29 and 2.34–36), a passage whose universalizing, emblematic force he had already drawn upon in describing the happiness of rustic leisure in 5.1392–96 (cf. 2.29–33). Both the account of agrarian leisure and that of the fur pelt start out as part of the evolutionary scheme but end by shading into the moral constants of Epicurean exemplum. In both cases the close imitation of the moral generalizations in the proem of book 2 reinforces this shift from history to paradigm.

The constant factor that dooms the human race to anxiety and frustration "always" (1431) is ignorance: not knowing the true nature of happiness and pleasure (*vera voluptas*, 1433). The correlative *tunc . . . nunc* here, as elsewhere, tightens this knotting together of the historical and the philosophical (*tunc igitur pelles, nunc aurum*, "then skins, now gold," 1423). Shortly before, Lucretius gave the process a generalizing formulation: *nunc iacet aes, aurum in summum successit honorem. / sic volvenda aetas commutat, tempora rerum* ("Now bronze is low, gold comes to the highest honor. Thus life in its turning changes the moments for things," 1275–76).[51]

The concluding observation of this section in 1435, that the "seething tides of war" result from man's moral ignorance, resumes the recurrent theme of war as the regressive force in human life and thus also harks back to 1308–49. The effect of these echoes is to bracket this whole final phase of human evolution, from the discovery of metals up to the final listing of astronomy, cities, sailing, etc., in 1436ff., with the reminders of man's regressive fierceness and animality.

The very last lines of the book also recall the context of 1308–49: men see one thing receive illumination from another until they reach the top by their arts (*namque alid ex alio clarescere corde videbant*, "for they saw in their heart one

---

[51] Cf. also 5.1135, 1339, 1408.

thing grow bright from another," 1456). These verses echo the end of book 1, where Lucretius expressed confidence in the victory of light and truth over darkness and ignorance (1.1114–17, especially 1115, *namque alid ex alio clarescet*). A much closer parallel, however, is the pessimistic transition to the increase in the "terrors of war" and the use of beasts in battle, 1305–7: *sic alid ex alio peperit discordia tristis* ("thus one thing from another has grim strife brought to birth," 5.1305). "Coming to the top" in the last line of the book also reminds us of the struggle "to reach the top" in the dangerous ambition of powerful men (*ad summum succedere honorem*, 5.1123).[52] Close at hand too is the endless cycle of ups and downs in what men value as time revolves (1275–78): "now bronze lies in low esteem, and gold comes up to the highest honor" (*aurum in summum successit honorem*, 1275, and cf. *ad summum donec venere cacumen*, 1457, and also *nunc aurum . . .* , 1423).

The continuation of the culture history across the division between books 5 and 6 adds still another qualification to upward progress.[53] Athens, "of glorious name" (6.2), is the site of the invention of agriculture and the renewal of life (6.3). But its true pinnacle of progress is the birth of Epicurus (6.4–6), who, however, developed his "divine discovery" and his "sweet consolations" precisely because he found life-darkening anxiety, aggression, and savagery (cf. *saevire*, 6.16) in the midst of those very achievements which gave Athens its renown (6.9–34). Hence his "fame" for these "divine discover-

---

[52] Cf. also 5.1141–42: *res itaque ad summam faecem turbasque redibat / imperium sibi cum ac summatum quisque petebat*, "Thus affairs returned to the utmost dregs and to the mobs when each one sought for himself rule and the post of highest." Note also the sinister results of the desire "to reach the top," *ad summas emergere opes*, in 3.63. On the ironies in this motif of "reaching the top" here, see Müller, "Die Finalia," 214–15. See also Green, "Dying World," 58–59. For Lucretius's critique of the Roman value system implicit in such moralizing, see Minyard, *Lucretius and the Late Republic*, 66.

[53] On this bridging of the two books and its implications, see Townend, "Original Plan," 105; Minadeo, *Lyre of Science*, 45ff.; Clay, *Lucretius and Epicurus*, 258–59.

ies" in philosophy balances Athens's "illustrious name" for progress in civilizing arts (cf. 6.7 and 6.2). This collocation, when viewed in the light of the continuing spiritual and psychological woes of men in the following lines (6.9–23), effects another flattening of diachrony into synchrony. Ongoing historical development is pulled back into the constant, levelling fact of the weaknesses of human nature (cf. the "flawed vessel" in 6.17–23).

At the end of the book, then, Athens fully enters the paradigmatic order of the argument, exemplifying the most terrible degradation to which even so high a level of civilization can sink. The literal infection and contagion of the plague, in fact, resume and develop the metaphorical contamination of the "weak vessel" of human nature in 6.17–23 (cf. *corrumpier* in 18, *conspurcat* in 22, *purgavit* in 24). Thus viewed, the plague that ends the book and the poem has both a historical and a paradigmatic aspect, corresponding to the twofold function of Athens at the beginning of book 6. It is a specific event at a precise moment of historical time; but it is also a vast exemplary projection of the corrupted vessel of flawed human nature stated in general terms in the proem of book 6.

This circularity within the forward direction of human history does not negate Lucretius's appreciation of the reality of progress from earliest times to the present, but rather underlines his sense of its tragic complexity. Just because he enjoys better material conditions, modern man bears even greater responsibility for the sufferings that he inflicts on himself and his fellow men.[54]

Material progress over the course of history has in fact increased man's need for the *artes* "invented" by Epicurus and for the healing knowledge that they hold (cf. 5.9ff.).[55] Progress is a feature of man's historical past. From a different perspective, Lucretius points out that many arts are still, even now, being developed, and that the *vera ratio* of Epicurus is only a

[54] Cf. 5.1006–10 and 6.9–13. On this point, see Taylor, "Progress and Primitivism," 194; Borle, "Progrès ou déclin," 174–75.

[55] Note the terminology of "invention" and "discovery" applied to Epicurus in 1.66, 5.9–10, 5.13–14.

recent invention (5.332–36). With a striking intrusion of the first person, he adds "I myself have only recently been discovered [invented, *repertus*] as able to translate this [philosophy] into our native tongue" (5.336–37). Like the juxtaposition of the mythical Hercules and the historical Epicurus in the proem, these lines too shatter the "then" with the "now." Just as modern man must continue his primitive ancestor's struggle against the beasts and the bestial, so Lucretius, on the plane of moral rather than social or material history, "follows in the tracks" of his great predecessor (5.55ff., 3.3ff.), continues his "battles" and "victories" (cf. 5.22–51, 1.75–79), and in his own personal existence and his work of translating Epicurus marks the continuing line of "progress" and discoveries (*ipse repertus*, 5.335–37).

In drawing on the age-old struggle between light and darkness as a framing image for the book (5.11ff. and 1455–56), as also in recasting Epicurus as the successor to the ancient hero who battles fabulous monsters, Lucretius does not merely allegorize. He fabricates a new mythology of his own. Through his vivid images and his emblematic descriptions, from Venus's life force in the first proem to the surrealistic battle scene in 5.1308–49 and on to the closing scene of the poem, he re-creates the ancient mythical conflict between chaos and order, death and life, that ramifies in ever-expanding analogies through the natural and social worlds represented in the poem. He is thus able to turn the abstractions of Greek philosophy into concrete, quasi-personified beings that have an involving life of their own.

In the famous ninth chapter of the *Poetics* Aristotle remarks that poetry is more philosophical than history because it reflects the universal, what might have happened rather than what actually happened. Lucretius's description of the wild beasts loosed in war belongs, in part, to a historical perspective. At the end of that passage (1341–49) he shifts from what actually happened to what might have happened. In this passage, as elsewhere in book 5, he is more a poet than a historian; he works in that zone of universals where (as Aristotle suggests) poetry is truly philosophical.

To the Romans, even (or especially) after Pyrrhus and Hannibal, elephants in war were both historical and exotic.[56] In moving from the historical fact of war-elephants as part of man's ambiguous progress (5.1311–17) to the bulls, boars, and lions of 5.1308–49 (with the transitional "also," *etiam*, in 1308), Lucretius draws on the experience of history. Yet his vivid imagination transforms the specific events of the past into the universality of poetry.

As Schrijvers suggests in his valuable study of the passage, Lucretius employs the classical technique of ἐνάργεια, making clear and vivid. By accumulation, enumeration, and intensification of detail Lucretius uses the elephants to signal what is coming and to produce the effect of a climactic summation of the horrors of war.[57] Extending Schrijvers's approach, I would suggest that the elephants and the wild beasts that follow contribute to something like a *Verfremdungseffekt*, alienating us from the real in order to show another dimension of reality, something strange, uncanny, surreal. As "snake-handed Lucanian oxen" (1302–3), the elephants appear as monstrous *Mischwesen*, reminding us of Hercules' fabulous monsters in the proem (5.29–38). Like Hercules' monsters, they are ultimately only a foil to the deeper monstrosity and savagery of spirit within men, ostensibly their "teachers" (1304, 1311).

The outrageousness of Lucretius's details highlights the strangeness, the outlandish otherness, of a primitive violence that we are nevertheless forced to accept as a concomitant of

[56] See, in general, H. H. Scullard, *The Elephant in the Greek and Roman World* (Cambridge, 1974). In Lucretius's time, elephants were used in the civil war between Caesar and Pompey (ibid., 194ff.). Lucretius's detail of the "towered body" in 5.1302 suggests that he had seen representations of the "howdah" often mounted on the backs of war-elephants. Such scenes appear in Latium and elsewhere in Italy on the so-called *pocula* of the late fourth or early third century B.C.

[57] Schrijvers, *Horror*, 296–308, esp. 303. On the elephants, see also De Grummond, "Interpretation," 54.

civilized progress. The very harshness of the contrast recalls to us the fact that all war is and contains animalism and savagery and that these become stabilized as recurrent, indeed exalted, parts of human life.

The whole passage might be compared in its effect to paintings of Goya or Bosch. Through its exaggerated but vivid images the madness and bestiality of war become both real and surreal. The wild horror is in fact set off by the reasonable, speculative calm of the philosopher's distanced perspective of 1341–43: "But I am scarcely led to believe that they could not foregather in their minds and see that this would happen before the woe and the bane on both sides took place."

This very contrast between the normal and the abnormal is one of the recurrent devices of poets and other writers who try to grasp the terrible and elusive conjunction of reason and madness, normality and abnormality, in the phenomenon of war and similar violence, from the battle scenes of the *Iliad* and *Aeneid* to the Holocaust and other acts of mass destruction today. Freud's death instinct or contemporary sociologists's warnings that "only part of us is sane" are analogous, non-literary attempts to clarify this conjunction of opposites.

In his essay of 1972, Kenney ventured to ascribe "a certain prophetic quality to [Lucretius's] historical imagination" and mentioned nuclear armaments, the stockpiling of atomic weapons, and *Dr. Strangelove*.[58] Two decades later, as weapons in outer space threaten to move from science fiction to fact, Lucretius, explorer of "the certain dark force," *vis abdita quaedam*, seems more tragically contemporary than ever; and we may look back with desperate nostalgia to a time when unleashing lions and boars seemed the worst that man could do in the art of war.

---

[58] Kenney, "Historical Imagination," 23; see also Saylor, "Man, Animal, and the Bestial," 312.

Chapter Ten

THE PLAGUE RECONSIDERED: PROGRESS, POET, AND PHILOSOPHER

As WAR SHOWS Lucretius's society, like our own, perverting its energies and best talents from creation to destruction, so the plague shows us a society that has completely capitulated to death. Here the last offices of tending the dead are corrupted into violence and bloodshed through ignorance of the true nature of death (6.1276–86). This closing vision of death and plague is (among other things) an emotional rendering of what is at stake if we are persuaded by Ennius's "immortal verses" on the existence of Hades's *Acherusia templa* (1.120–21) rather than by the philosopher's view of infinite atoms and void. The falsehoods of the poets enclose us in the terrors of the dark underworld, which, like all darkness, needs to be dispersed by the light of philosophical *ratio* (1.146–48).

The philosopher's gaze opens our vision outward beyond the world's flaming walls (1.73–79, 3.25–30). The nightmare ending of the poem, on the other hand, corresponds to the false visions of the poets, in which darkness and violence prevail over light and peace. Born in the city where the plague had raged a century earlier (6.5ff), Epicurus diagnoses the invisible, spiritual corruptions and proposes cleansing and healing measures in "truth-speaking sayings" (*veridicis dictis*, 6.24; cf. *veridico ex ore*, 6.6). The falsehoods of the poets, by contrast, only increase our anxieties and unhappiness (cf. 1.110–11, 132–35).

The contrast between the spiritual victory of the philosopher at the poem's beginning and the superstition of mankind at the end has often been noted and discussed.[1] If this is the

---

[1] See, for example, Klingner, "Philosophie und Dichtkunst," 151ff. It is instructive for the degree of disagreement among interpreters to contrast his

ending that Lucretius intended, as I believe it is, why conclude on so dark a note? He might easily have ended with a restatement of the ultimate indestructibility of life and its endless renewal as each new generation passes on the "torch of life" (2.67–79; cf. 1.248–64, "nothing returns back to nothing," *haud igitur redit ad nilum res ulla*).[2] It is a shock, for example, to glance from Lucretius's bleak finale to the heartening conclusion of Epicurus's own ethical treatise, the *Letter to Menoeceus* (D.L. 10.135): "Day and night meditate on these things and things akin to these with yourself and with one like to yourself, and you will never suffer disturbance sleeping or waking, but as a god shall you live among men. For one who lives among immortal goods in no way resembles a mortal being." The thought itself is not foreign to Lucretius, who early in his proof of the soul's mortality affirms our capacity to triumph over the traces of nature in us "so that nothing prevents us from living a life worthy of the gods" (*ut nil impediat dignam dis degere vitam*, 3.319–22). But here at the end of the poem he withholds any such solace from his reader.

Lucretius's ending brings us back from the natural world, whose mortality, flaws, and disturbances have been the main theme of the last two books, to mankind and man's responses to the imperfect, doomed world in which he lives. Thus the poet returns us not only to the reality of nature, but to the reality of human character in its reactions to this world. We must accept our own end not only in the terms of our personal mortality, which was the perspective of book 3, but also as part of the processes of the universe, in which death is the inevitable concomitant of life.[3] Hence the movement of the poem from the end of book 3 to the end of book 6 takes in the mortality of the world in book 5 and the massive destructions

---

view of the ending (emphasizing the lack of full artistic integration, p. 155) with that of Müller, "Die Finalia," 221, for whom the present ending is "not the least significant token of [Lucretius's] genius." Müller (217ff.) also gives a useful review of earlier discussions of the problem.

[2] See Klingner, "Philosophie und Dichtkunst," 150.

[3] See Minadeo, *Lyre of Science*, 108: "One makes his peace with mortality as an impartial reflex in the lawful movement of the universe."

caused by natural phenomena in book 6, including the de-structibility of nature itself. We do, of course, feel the tragic waste in the gratuitous loss of life thanks to human folly in the poem's closing scene; but Lucretius's attitude, as often in the poem, is one of both compassion and distance.

We come to our fullest portrayal of war within the long temporal span stretching from the world's beginning to the towered cities of the present. So too we come to the poem's fullest display of human folly in the face of death through the vast spatial field of the faults in the construction and operation of the natural world, reaching from the subterranean depths of the earth to the clouds and the winds. As in the case of man's evolution, the account serves as both process and paradigm, as both history and exemplum. The power of death and dissolution in the human body, as we have seen, is both analogous to the decomposition forever going on in the universe as a whole and also continuous with the advance of death in our individual organisms. The end of book 5 has re-created both the preciousness and the precariousness of a social and moral order built up over millenia. The end of book 6 shows us the fragility of that order from the physiological point of view. While the perspective of the latter third of book 5 is overtly moral, even moralizing, that of book 6 is physical and, as in the first two-thirds of book 3, concentratedly corporeal. But, having progressed this far in our Epicurean education, the reader is better able to perceive the inseparable links between the moral and the physical. That coincidence of perspectives is nowhere clearer or more forceful than in the closing scenes of book 6. Here the moral order and the physical order are one and the same; and the key to their coherence is death and the "bodies," *corpora*, with which the poem ends.

Combining our readings of the end of book 3 and the end of book 5 in the two preceding chapters helps us toward an understanding of this last scene. Like the account of the beasts of battle studied in Chapter Nine, the plague belongs both to the diachronic and paradigmatic order of the poem. We arrive at it via disease in the world and the impersonal physical processes that bring disease. But we also move from these large-scale deaths of atomic compounds to the personal deaths of men and women, whose final agonies we have been watching with horror and pity. In the very last scene of the work we witness the collapse of the social order that we saw gradually built up in book 5, combined with the release of aggression that, as we have seen, was inhibited as a necessary stage in the development of civilization but is never fully extirpated from human history.

The choice of Athens as the site of the plague is neither entirely arbitrary nor just the result of Thucydides's influence. Athens is remote enough from Lucretius's Roman audience to be exemplary, but real enough to be terrifying. As an image of the disintegration of society, the plague shows what the ultimate cataclysm would be like in the immediate experience of individual men and women. It thus balances and completes the more detached account of the end of the world from a purely physical point of view at the end of books 1 and 2. In this respect too, it exemplifies Lucretius's tendency to move from remote perspectives to sympathetic engagement. At the same time, prophets of cosmic doom need a little maneuverability, and the Athens of Thucydides is far enough away in time and space to be mythicized for the purpose.

The closing triumph of death at the end of book 6 harks back to the triumph of "death eternal" at the end of book 3, but extends it from the individual to society. At this point of closure it also qualifies the picture of human progress, itself shot through with the ambiguities that we have examined in the previous chapter. For all his advances in technology, man remains subject to death and its terrors. Lucretius here draws not just on Epicurean philosophy, but also on the literary tradition, for example, on the great Ode on Man in Sophocles's *Antigone*. There man has subdued the sea and the earth, harnessed the beasts to his purposes, made laws, and conquered disease, but this "all-devising man" has devised "no way to flee Hades" (360–62). Lucretius sharpens this contrast between power and futility by continuing the history of human progress across the division between books 5 and 6—the only place in the poem to have such an explicit thematic linking between books.

The proem to book 6 opens with a eulogy of Athens for its invention of agriculture, but then defines its greatest contribution to human progress as the birth of Epicurus (6.4–8)— Epicurus whose death figured prominently at the end of book 3 (3.1042–44). Epicurus's fame for his "divine discoveries" in philosophy (6.7) balances Athens's "glorious name" (6.2) for its invention of the arts of civilization. In the taut structure of paradoxes underlying this argument, however, Lucretius implies that just this success in material progress has made Epicurus all the more necessary (6.9–34). Progress in one area has meant regress in another. Epicurus's birth at the beginning of book 6, continuing the material culture history of book 5, begins to emerge as the true pinnacle of human progress.

Therefore, when the end of book 6 makes Athens the site of human helplessness and a place of death and darkness rather than birth and light (as it is in 6.1–8), we are again reminded of the impotence of civilization against death. Death's power swiftly undoes millenia of human discoveries. As the closing lines of the poem suggest, death leaves us again and always in the savagery, ignorance, and superstition of primitive man. The plague in fact bears out Epicurus's own observations in that same city (6.9–19):

> For when he saw that nearly everything that need demands for sustenance was provided for mortals and that, as far as possible, life was safe, and that men had an abundance of riches and were powerful in praise and honor and were eminent in the good repute of their children, and yet that each had a heart no less anxious and that, despite their intelligence, they were harassing life without any cessation and were compelled to rage savagely in destructive lamentations, then he understood that the vessel itself created the flaw (*vitium*) and that by the flaw of that [vessel] all those goods which were gathered and came inside were corrupted inside (*illius vitio corrumpier intus*).

This inward "corruption" that Epicurus discerns "befouling all things with its rancid taste" (*taetro quasi conspurcare sa-*

pore / omnia cernebat, 6.22–23) becomes externalized and visible in the physical disease of the plague at the end, with its literal "corruptions" and "foulness" (cf. 6.1200–17, 1235–45, 1267–71).

As the proem goes on, the formulaic phrase *mortalibus aegris* of the book's opening line, an adaptation of the Homeric formula δειλοῖσι βροτοῖσι, takes on a deeper significance. It can mean both "wretched mortals" and "sick mortals" (6.1–6):

> primae frugiparos fetus *mortalibus aegris*
> dididerunt quondam praeclaro nomine Athenae
> et recreaverunt vitam legesque rogarunt,
> et primae dederunt solacia dulcia vitae,
> cum genuere virum tali cum corde repertum,
> omnia veridico qui quondam ex ore profudit.

(Athens of surpassingly glorious name was first long ago to spread forth the fruit-bearing crops for *miserable mortals* and renewed life and instituted laws, and first too gave the sweet solaces of life, when she bore a man endowed [literally, found] with such a mind, who long ago poured forth all things from his truth-speaking mouth.)

Mortals are "sick," *aegri*, in both body and in mind, and the plague shows both diseases at their worst. The only hope lies in Athens's other and truer gift, not material progress, but Epicurus himself. The careful repetitions of "first . . . first," "long ago . . . long ago," "life . . . life" (*primae . . . primae, quondam . . . quondam, vitam . . . vitae*) establish the parallels between Athens's and Epicurus's boons to mankind. The greatest "discovery" or "invention" of human culture is, in a sense, Epicurus, with his "discovered" mind (*tali cum corde repertum*, 6.5) and his "divine discoveries" (*divina reperta*) that win him a glory equivalent to Athens's (6.7–8).[4]

And yet, we must ask, do we, in this darkest hour of Athens at the end of the book, remember its role as the birthplace of

---

[4] I take *repertum* in 6.5 more seriously than does Bailey, *T. Lucreti Cari*, ad loc., especially in view of the repetition of the word in line 7.

civilization and the birthplace of Epicurus at the beginning, twelve hundred lines before? The answer, I think, is yes. These horrors show us an Athens before Epicurus and his "divine discoveries." Read diachronically (historically) as well as paradigmatically, the plague is both a demonstration and a warning of a pre-Epicurean world. It is a moral allegory of the bad death, and also a kind of historical allegory of the (moral) life of mankind before Epicurus. It shows us the true "sickness" of the *mortales aegri* of the book's first line. And, by implication, it also shows us the nightmarish world that is ours if we have only the false images of the poets that "terrify us when we are afflicted with *disease* (*morbus*) and are buried in sleep" (1.133–34). That "disease," book 6 suggests, is of the spirit as well as of the body. As such, it needs the healing θεραπεία of Epicurus.

Viewed in another perspective, the widespread death of men and animals in the plague gives us a foretaste of what the natural collapse of our world would be like—if Athens, city of the plague, had not also, in a kind of *isonomia*, also given us Epicurus and the "sweet solaces" of his truths about both man and nature (6.1–6, 24–34). The Athens that we see here is the pre-Epicurean city. But the concluding picture of the "quarreling with much blood" over the burial of dead bodies (6.1286, *rixantes potius quam corpora desererentur*) intimates what *religio* holds in store for those who have not benefited from Epicurus's presence on earth.[5] These are the unenlightened, who cannot "see that there is a fixed end to their sufferings" and who therefore have no *ratio* by which they can "stand up against the threats of seers" (1.107–9; cf. 6.25–26).

In the closing lines of the poem, "everyone" is in a state of disturbance, anxious dread, and aggressive violence: *perturbatus enim totus trepidabat, et unus quisque / . . . maestus hu-*

---

[5] The ugliness and brutality of the scene are further enhanced by Lucretius's use of the verb *rixantes*, "quarreling," which suggests brawling and low-life behavior. The verb has only one occurrence in hexameter poetry up to the end of the Augustan age, and that in a self-consciously colloquial context: Horace, *Epistles* 1.18.15. For the tone of the word, cf. Cicero, *De Oratore* 2.59.240 and Tacitus, *Histories* 1.64.

mabat (6.1280–81). The scene is the realization of Lucretius's warnings to the unnamed "you" (Memmius?) about the poets' false imaginings (*somnia*) early in book 1:

> somnia quae vitae rationes vertere possint
> fortunasque tuas *omnis turbare timore.*

(Dreams that can overturn life's orderly patterns and *stir up all* your fortunes *with fear.*)   (1.105–6)

The plague's universal terror and misguided violence, then, are a paradigm of what human life can be—unless the *vera ratio* leads us to the serenity that Epicurus and Democritus achieved in the face of death (cf. 3.1039–44).

The very abruptness of the ending of the book and of the poem indicts the irrational passions that the fear of death inspires. In the proem to book 3 (3.37–86) Lucretius stated in general terms how "that fear of Acheron . . . *disturbs* human life from its depths" (*humanam vitam qui* turbat *ab imo*, 3.38). Now in the detailed picture at the end of the poem men fight bloody battles to place on the pyres bodies empty of life. Their folly is the violent emotional and physical involvement with what death leaves behind.

In marking the closing stage of his argument in his last proem, the poet does not entirely abandon his concern with the praise that he will leave behind (6.95). But he has no need to seek the comfort of immortality against a death that he no longer fears. Earlier in this same proem, as we have seen, Lucretius gives us another model for eternal fame. This is the glory of the sage Epicurus, which, "even when the man himself is extinguished, is borne to the heavens" (*cuius et extincti propter divina reperta / divulgata vetus iam ad caelum gloria fertur*, 6.7–8). The ancient Homeric formula of "glory carried to the heavens" (κλέος οὐϱανὸν ἵϰει) now describes neither warrior nor poet, but the philosopher. The mortal "vessel," whose corrupted nature Epicurus clearly discerned (6.17ff.), is "extinguished," but the fame for this discovery survives, and Lucretius is its poet.

Praising Epicurus, Lucretius is a poet of truth, singing the true fame, just as Epicurus, not Hercules, is the true hero (the praise of Epicurus in 5.22–54 is recalled here in the echo between 6.24 and 5.43). Lucretius is the "Homer" or the "Ennius" of a renown that rests not on bloody deeds but on a quiet exit from life (*extincti*, 6.7), on "discoveries" and "intellect" (6.5–8), not battles. The combination of the philosopher's "extinguished" mortal existence and celestial glory is exactly symmetrical with the combination of his death and celestial luminosity at the end of book 3. There, we recall, the dying Epicurus "extinguishes" all other mortals as the sun surpasses the stars (*restinxit*, 3.1044).

Smitten by the Dionysiac thyrsus of desire for fame in book 1, Lucretius boasts of his journey to "pathless places" in the language of the old poets (1.922–30). In the proem of book 3, however, his model is the philosopher, not the poets. Here he disavows that "desire" of rivalry with poetic predecessors and feels a "love" not of the Muses (1.924–25) but of imitating the example of Epicurus himself (3.3–8, especially 5–6, "not so much desirous of contest as out of love [*propter amorem*], because I am eager to imitate you"). By the proem of book 6, self-praise has shrunk to a single verse (6.95).[6] Now he is interested not in his own superiority in traversing the "pathless places" of the Muses untrodden by others (*avia loca*, 1.926–27) but in glorifying Epicurus for "showing the path by which, on a small track," we can reach the true happiness that life offers to us (*viam monstravit, tramite parvo . . .*, 6.27).

If in book 3, then, Epicurus's luminosity in his tranquil quietus is a ray of hope in the dark kingdom of "death eternal," so too in book 6, in the midst of Athens's physical and spiritual collapse, we know that that city already contains the "birth" of its future savior (6.5, *genuere*). In accordance with the endless cycles of creation and destruction that Epicurus has taught us to recognize in our understanding of death, Ath-

---

[6] We may perhaps add the reference to the "glorious chariot" (of song?), to which Lucretius seems to refer in 6.47, with its probable echo of the proem of Parmenides' poem *On Nature*; but the lacuna after this verse makes it uncertain if Lucretius expatiated on the "fame" (*insignem conscendere currum*, 6.47). See Bailey, *T. Lucreti Cari*, ad loc.

ens is an ancient source of life (cf. *primae frugiparos fetus*, 6.1; also *recreaverunt vitam*, 6.3). It has now become an emblematic place of universal destruction, but it will again "give birth" to a universal source of light and life (6.5ff.). Epicurus's birth, however, in one sense breaks the cycle, for his teachings offer a way out of the madness and folly that the plague embodies.

Ending with the plague, Lucretius invites us to read both life and the poem in a way that leads up to death as the climactic experience and the ultimate fear facing humankind. But he has also suggested a downward reading, from the Big Fear, death, to the little fears that it feeds. He adumbrates this mode of reading at the beginning of book 3, where he demonstrates that all the "wounds of life are nourished by the fear of death" (3.63–64). By seeing how the smaller fears grow out of the fear of death, like branches from a central trunk, we gradually liberate our entire life from fear and from the violence, folly, and suffering that fear generates.

Epicurus perfected this process when he traced all the corruptions of life to the "flawed vessel," the human heart with its insatiable desires and therefore also its endlessly proliferating anxieties (6.9–34, especially 21–25). The plague acts out, on a gigantic scale, this metaphor of the "corrupted vessel" that taints whatever material triumphs we attain (6.17–23). We have to follow Epicurus, as Lucretius himself did in the proem of book 3, and repeat his discovery. He pointed the way, but the track is "small" (*tramite parvo*, 6.27) and, as the end of the poem implies, not easy to regain.

Chapter Eleven

THE FEAR OF DEATH AND THE GOOD LIFE

IN STUDYING THE INTERPLAY between Lucretius's poetic strategies for the most vivid possible portrayal of the fear of death and his therapeutic attempt as an Epicurean to soothe those fears, I am not reviving the "anti-Lucretius" or the morbid pessimist but rather trying to show that *both* as poet and as philosopher Lucretius appreciates the dread that death inspires in all living creatures. Although the logic of his argument in book 3 is directed at breaking the hold that the fear of death has over our minds, his fidelity to the mortal condition and his understanding of the feelings of his fellow men lead him to take a fuller account of the power of these fears than is usually recognized. Had he merely denied these fears, he would not have confronted the full difficulty of his task.

To overcome our denial of death and thus bring the fears of it into the light where they can be dealt with therapeutically, Lucretius must make death real and present to us as a process. Hence, alongside the picture of death as a value-neutral atomic process, he also presents death as the loss of vital functions and as a "tearing away" from life as the "force" (*vis*) of disease penetrates the vital organs or as the lifeless "chill of doom" invades our limbs. Death is not only present in our bodies as the concomitant to their growth, maturation, and decay; it is also present everywhere in our world, from the earth beneath our feet to the stars and planets over our heads. But Lucretius also recognizes, implicitly, the uniqueness of man's special consciousness of his own death, for the human response to death, both individually and collectively, dominates the poem. A recent sociological study of death (which, incidentally, never mentions Epicurus or Lucretius) reports a statistical study in which the fear of death has the following typology:

1. fear of the dissolution of the body
2. fear that all experiences will end
3. fear of the pain of dying
4. fear of an unknown future
5. fear of affective consequences for survivors.[1]

Lucretius would thus seem to be abreast of the most recent developments in thanatological sociology, for, as we have seen in the preceding chapters, he discusses all of these issues in one way or another.

By bringing the regular processes of the atomic world into close relation with the terrifying or degrading physical symptoms of illness or injury, Lucretius hopes to prepare us for death by leaving us "instructed," *perdocti* (3.473), so that we too, like Democritus and Epicurus at the end of book 3, may be able to see beneath the surface of the ugly and painful bodily decay and overcome fear through intellect and understanding. This is the process that he describes in his repeated simile of bringing into the light things that are terrifying in the dark.[2]

Lucretius's intense attention to the physical details of the body's subjection to decay and vulnerability to violence is not to be explained away, as is sometimes done, by an *ad hominem* appeal to his allegedly morbid personality or pessimistic outlook. The vivid accounts of pain, mortal wounds, and dying in books 3 and 6 are integral parts of the poem, for death is itself an integral part of the atomic processes of aggregation and dissolution that, visibly or invisibly, constitute the fundamental rhythms of the life around us and within us.

By insisting throughout book 3 on the gruesome details of bodily injury, physical suffering, and decay, Lucretius not only fulfils the explicit purpose of proving the soul's mortality; he also helps us to accept our place in nature's vast, inevitable

[1] Victor W. Marshall, *Last Chapters: A Sociology of Aging and Dying* (Monterey, Calif., 1980), 71, citing J. Diggory and D. Rothman, "Values Destroyed by Death," *Journal of Abnormal and Social Psychology* 63 (1961): 205–10.

[2] In 3.87–93, repeated in 2.55–61 and 6.35–41.

succession of life and death, growth and decline. He formulates this principle in a notable passage early in book 2:

> sic rerum summa novatur
> semper, et inter se mortales mutua vivunt.
> augescunt aliae gentes, aliae minuuntur,
> inque brevi spatio mutantur saecla animantum
> et quasi cursores vitai lampada tradunt.

(Thus the totality of things is always renewed, and living creatures live by mutual exchange among one another. Some races increase, others decline, and in a short span of time the generations of animals are changed and, like runners, hand on the torch of life.)   (2.75–79)

Epicurus is both the teacher and the exemplar of accepting the finite limits of one's "course of life," for Lucretius uses the same image of the Master's tranquil death at the end of book 3 (*decurso lumine vitae*, "when he had run through the course of his life's light," 3.1042). Yet the very language that conveys his exemplary status in that passage (3.1042–44), with its encomiastic conventions and self-conscious echoes of the glory of the epic hero, simultaneously bespeaks man's urgent desire to survive, his reluctance to admit the total negation of his being, his delight and solace in contemplating, even as he sees his end approaching, those "monuments of unageing intellect" that guarantee his continuity into the future, and his desperate need for some sign that he has run his "course of life" in a way that leaves a lasting imprint on the mortal soil. Lucretius himself, in the sweetness of his love for the Muses (1.924), is stirred by thoughts of how the future generations who are to compose these *aliae gentes* ("other races") will view and admire his work. He feels his heart smitten, as by a Dionysiac (and hence irrational) force, when he contemplates that "praise" that his very un-Dionysiac poem will earn (*sed acri / percussit thyrso laudis spes magna meum cor*, 1.922–23). At a later stage of his argument, however, he will remind us that these "monuments of men" or "of eternal fame" are just as perishable as the earth on which they stand (5.311, 328–31; cf. 6.239–45).

To these considerations drawn from within the poem must be added a broader sociological reflection on the extent to which a writer of Lucretius's time may have been able to scrutinize death in so public a fashion. In this matter the tastes and standards of decency vary enormously, as Herodotus amusedly observed long before Lucretius and modern anthropology. One need only juxtapose our embarrassment before virtually any direct confrontation with death and the custom in Greek villages today of exhuming and lovingly handling the bones of the deceased several years after the burial,[3] or the gravediggers' scene in *Hamlet*. What to the modern North American or West European seems morbidity may in fact be the result of a more open and public acknowledgment of death in Lucretius's society and in the ancient world generally. In fifth-century Athens, plays concerned with burial and funeral rituals were regularly presented to the whole body of citizens at the Dionysiac festivals: such are Sophocles's *Ajax* and *Antigone* or Euripides's *Alcestis* and *Suppliant Women*. In Rome the elegiac poets, writing a generation or two after Lucretius, could revel in detailed imaginings of their own or their beloved's death and depict death-bed scenes far more vivid than those of Lucretius's third book.[4] To Lucretius's contemporaries, *pallida Mors* beating at the gates (Horace, *Odes* 1.4) comes as less of a stranger than she does to the men and women of our own day.

While we contemporaries steadfastly deny death in one way by confining it to the behind-the-curtain invisibility of hospitals and nursing homes, we permit it as the almost daily diet of television and the movies. Yet this trivialization of death in the mass media is only a more subtle form of denial. The re-

[3] On the exhuming and handling of the bones as part of the mourning rituals, see Loring M. Danforth, *The Death Rituals of Rural Greece* (Princeton, 1982), 15ff., 48ff., 84ff.

[4] See, for example, Tibullus 1.1.59ff., 1.3.53ff.; Lygdamus 2.9ff.; Propertius 1.19, 2.8.17ff., 4.7, 4.11; in general, Georg Luck, *The Latin Love Elegy*, 2nd ed. (London, 1969), 126ff.

pressed returns, often with gory sadism, but on the margins of reality, as fantasy or as nightmare (in horror films). When televised newscasts or popular news magazines like *Time* or *Newsweek* show the dead or dying, it is generally only in a fleeting glimpse, more to tantalize than to inform. And in such cases anyway, death is comfortably removed from *our* reality. It belongs to the Other, whether that is the conventionalized television or movie villain or the faraway Third World victim of political chaos or natural catastrophe that does not happen "here." In Lucretius's world, and his poem, death is not so defamiliarized or trivialized. It retains its power to shock, terrify, and instruct.

We late-twentieth-century readers also stand at the end of a long process of denying or camouflaging death that can be traced back to the eighteenth century.[5] Montaigne is consciously following in the footsteps of the ancients in his essay, "That to Philosophize Is to Learn to Die" (*Essays* 1.20):

> It is uncertain where death awaits us; let us await it everywhere. Premeditation of death is premeditation of freedom. He who has learned how to die has unlearned how to be a slave.

> So I have formed the habit of having death continually present, not merely in my imagination, but in my mouth. And there is nothing that I investigate so eagerly as the death of men: what words, what look, what bearing they maintained at that time; nor is there a place in the histories that I note so attentively.[6]

In the last essay of his collection, a long meditation on aging, illness, and death, Montaigne contemplates the misery of dying from disease, which he considers worse than dying in battle, and counters with an image of the strenuous life of the soldier and a snappy quotation from Seneca: "Death is more abject, more lingering and distressing, in bed than in battle; fevers and catarrhs are as painful and fatal as a harquebus shot. . . . *To live, my Lucilius, is to fight*."[7] "Dying," he con-

[5] See Ariès, *Western Attitudes toward Death*, 85ff.
[6] Montaigne, *Essays* (trans. Frame), 1:81, 84.
[7] Montaigne, "Of Experience" (*Essays*, 3.13), Frame translation, 3:347.

tinues later, goes on all through life, so that at the end "it will kill only half or a quarter of a man."[8] "Death mingles and fuses with our life throughout," he adds in a very Lucretian spirit.[9]

In most societies prior to our own, the approach of death was a socially recognized experience; and the process of dying, for both the victim and the survivors, was carefully organized by rituals, family gatherings, the reading of testaments, confessions, prayers, and lamentations, and the like.[10] Death was felt to be an organic part of life. The dead virtually coexisted with the living through the prominence of cemeteries, tombs, funeral inscriptions, epitaphs, formalized celebrations like the Parentalia and Lemuria, and other visible and self-conscious memorializations of the deceased.[11] The funeral stelai of fifth- and fourth-century Greece also show the dead in full life, still sharing the world and the activities of the living, caught in the tenderness of motherhood or the spirited gestures of the hunt or battle. Here, as in the graveside scenes of white-ground lekythoi, the living are closely connected with the dead, either by direct physical contact (the clasping of hands is common on the stelai) or by ritual offerings at the grave or contemplation of the tomb. The loss of the commemorated person is fully recognized, but little anxiety about death itself is expressed.

Lucretius too shows death in the context of the living. In one of his most vivid passages he describes the family members anxiously gathered by the bedside of a stricken sufferer

[8] Ibid., 3:352.

[9] Ibid., 3:353. Characteristically modern, however, are the specific and personal references to his portrait at ages 25 and 35 that follow, and the abrupt beginning of the next paragraph: "I am not excessively fond of either salads or fruits, except melons." Cf. also the preceding essay, "Of Physiognomy" (3.12), where Montaigne quotes and paraphrases Lucretius on the succession of life and death in the universe, citing Lucretius 2.75, *sic rerum summa novatur* (Frame translation, 3:298–99).

[10] Ariès, *Western Attitudes toward Death*, 11–14.

[11] For Roman practices, see J.M.C. Toynbee, *Death and Burial in the Roman World* (Ithaca, N.Y., 1971), chs. 2–4, with further bibliography. On the continuity and coexistence felt between the communities of the dead and the living, see also Hopkins, *Death and Renewal*, 233–35.

(3.467–69). In describing the plague he gives a brief but powerful account of the friends and relatives who visit, or refuse to visit, the infected victim (6.1239–46). And, of course, he ends the poem with the horrific scene of the *consanguinei* of the dead, the relatives fighting to place their corpses on the pyre (6.1281–86).

In the classical world, thanatology does not exist as a separate realm of inquiry. The discussion of death, like that of sexuality, is not an autonomous domain, but belongs to the examination of a person's total existence in the household and in society. Dying, therefore, is inseparable from the conduct of life; dying well is part of living well. For the poets and moralists of antiquity, therefore, death is the recurrent, indeed the inevitable, subject of ethical thought. From Achilles in *Iliad* 9 to Herodotus's Solon and on to the Socrates of the *Apology, Crito, Phaedo,* and the pseudo-Platonic *Axiochus,* the noble and wise man knows how to die well.[12] Cicero adapts Socrates' remark in the *Phaedo* (67D), *tota enim philosophorum vita, ut ait idem, commentatio mortis est* ("The entire life of the philosophers, as [Socrates] says, is a strenuous meditating on death," *Tusculan Disputations* 1.30.74). Alongside the Greek example of Socrates, Cicero places the contemporary Roman example of M. Porcius Cato, who chose a noble death by suicide after Pompey's defeat by Caesar at Thapsus.

Although he does not welcome death, man in ancient society wrestles with it as the touchstone of his existence and as the fundamental defining quality of his nature as a mortal creature (cf. Homer's famous simile comparing men in their mortality to "the generation of leaves" in springtime, *Iliad* 6.146–49). The manner and quality of the dying reveal the peculiar stamp and quality of the individual life and enable it to be seen and evaluated as a whole, from the moment of birth to the final death. One must always "look to the end" in de-

---

[12] For such attitudes, see, for instance, Emily Vermeule, *Aspects of Death in Early Greek Art and Poetry,* Sather Classical Lectures 46 (Berkeley and Los Angeles, 1979) chs. 1 and 4. Sophocles, *Ajax* 379–80 is a concise statement.

ciding whether a life has been happy, as Herodotus's Solon advises (1.32).[13]

In his respect for every creature's instincts for survival and struggle for birth, food, growth, and reproduction, Lucretius does not deny the gripping reality of the opposite forces, nor does he deny the terrors that this necessary complement to life inspires. By revealing that most dreaded of all events in the clarity and necessity of its atomic reality, *naturae species ratioque*, he hopes to irradiate with light the "dark goad beneath the heart" (*caecum aliquem cordi stimulum*, 3.873–74) that drives man to mar with strife, bloodshed, and hatred the preciousness of life while it is his to have (3.63–64): *haec vulnera vitae / non minimam partem mortis formidine aluntur*, "These wounds of life are nurtured to no very small degree by the fear of death."

[13] Cf. also Sophocles, *Oedipus Tyrannus* 1528-30 and *Trachinian Women* 1–3. See the extended discussion in Aristotle, *Nicomachean Ethics* 1.10, 1100 a10ff.

SELECTED BIBLIOGRAPHY

Amory, Anne. "*Obscura de re lucida carmina*: Science and Poetry in Lucretius' *De Rerum Natura*." *Yale Classical Studies* 21 (1969): 145–68.

Anderson, William S. "Discontinuity in Lucretian Symbolism." *Transactions of the American Philological Association* 91 (1960): 1–29.

Ariès, Philippe. *Western Attitudes toward Death: From the Middle Ages to the Present*. Trans. Patricia Ranum. Baltimore 1974.

————, *The Hour of Our Death* (1977). Trans. H. Weaver. New York, 1981.

Arrighetti, Graziano, ed. *Epicuro, Opere*. Turin 1960.

Asmis, Elizabeth. "Lucretius' Venus and Stoic Zeus." *Hermes* 110 (1982): 458–70.

Bailey, Cyril. "The Mind of Lucretius." *American Journal of Philology* 61 (1940): 278–91.

————, ed. *T. Lucreti Cari De Rerum Natura Libri Sex*. 3 vols. Oxford, 1947.

Baltes, Matthias. "Die Todesproblematik in der griechischen Philosophie," *Gymnasium* 95 (1988): 97–128.

Beye, Charles R. "Lucretius and Progress." *Classical Journal* 68 (1962/63): 160–69.

Bollack, Mayotte. *La raison de Lucrèce*. Paris 1978.

Bonelli, Guido. *I motivi profondi della poesia lucreziana*. Collection Latomus 186. Brussels, 1984.

Borle, Jean-Pierre. "Progrès ou déclin de l'humanité?" *Museum Helveticum* 19 (1962): 162–76.

Boyancé, Pierre. "Lucrèce et la poésie." *Revue des Etudes Anciennes* 49 (1947): 88–102.

————. *Lucrèce et l'épicurisme*. Paris 1963.

Bradley, Edward M. "Lucretius and the Irrational." *Classical Journal* 67 (1971–72): 317–22.

Bright, David F. "The Plague and the Structure of *De rerum natura*." *Latomus* 30 (1971): 607–32.

Buchheit, Vinzenz. "Epikurs Triumph des Geistes." *Hermes* 99 (1971): 303–23.

Clay, Diskin. "Epicurus' Last Will and Testament." *Archiv für die Geschichte der Philosophie* 55 (1973): 252–80.

———. *Lucretius and Epicurus*. Ithaca, N.Y., 1983.

———. "The Cults of Epicurus." *Cronache Ercolanesi* 16 (1986): 11–28.

Commager, Henry Steele, Jr. "Lucretius' Interpretation of the Plague." *Harvard Studies in Classical Philology* 62 (1957): 105–18.

Conte, Gian Biagio. "Il trionfo della morte e la galleria dei grandi trapassati in Lucrezio III, 1024–1053." *Studi Italiani di Filologia Classica* 37 (1965): 114–32.

———. "*Hypsos* e diatriba nello stile di Lucrezio: *De Rer. Nat.* II 1–61." *Maia* 18 (1966): 338–68.

Costa, C.D.N., ed. *Lucretius, De Rerum Natura V*. Oxford, 1984.

De Grummond, William W. "On the Interpretation of De Rerum Natura V 1308–49." *Atene e Roma* 27 (1982). 50–56.

DeLacy, Phillip. "Process and Value: An Epicurean Dilemma." *Transactions of the American Philological Association* 88 (1957): 114–26.

———. "Distant Views: The Imagery of Lucretius 2." *Classical Journal* 60 (1964–65): 49–55.

Desmouliez, A. "Cupidité, ambition et crainte de la mort chez Lucrèce (*de R. N.*, III, 59–93)." *Latomus* 17 (1958): 317–23.

Diels, Hermann and Walther Kranz, eds. *Die Fragmente der Vorsokratiker* 5th ed., 3 vols. Berlin, 1950–52.

Douglas, Mary. *Purity and Danger*. London, 1966; reprint, London, 1979.

Elder, J. P. "Lucretius 1.1–49." *Transactions of the American Philological Association* 85 (1954): 88–120.

Ernout, Alfred, and Léon Robin, eds. *Lucrèce, De Rerum Natura*. 3 vols. Paris 1925–28.

Farrington, Benjamin. "The Meaning of *Persona* in *De Rerum Natura* III 58." *Hermathena* 85 (1955): 3–12.

Fondation Hardt. *Entretiens sur l'antiquité classique*. Vol. 24, *Lucrèce*, ed. Olof Gigon. Vandoeuvres—Geneva, 1978.

Friedländer, Paul. "The Pattern of Sound and Atomistic Theory in Lucretius." *American Journal of Philology* 62 (1941): 16–33.

Frischer, Bernard. *The Sculpted Word: Epicureanism and Philosophical Recruitment in Ancient Greece*. Berkeley and Los Angeles, 1982.

Furley, David. "Lucretius the Epicurean: On the History of Man." In Fondation Hardt, *Entretiens, Lucrèce*, pp. 1–36 (1978).

———. "Nothing to Us?" In *Norms of Nature*, ed. Malcolm Scholfield and Gisela Striker, pp. 75–91. Cambridge, 1986.

Garland, Robert. *The Greek Way of Death*. Ithaca, N.Y., 1985.

Gigante, Marcello. " 'Philosophia Medicans' in Filodemo." *Cronache Ercolanensi* 5 (1975): 53–61.

Giussani, Carlo, ed. *T. Lucreti Cari De Rerum Natura Libri Sex*. 4 vols. Torino 1896–98.

Green, William M. "The Dying World of Lucretius." *American Journal of Philology* 63 (1942): 51–60.

Heinze, Richard, ed. *T. Lucretius Carus De Rerum Natura Buch III*. Leipzig, 1897.

Hopkins, Keith. *Death and Renewal: Sociological Studies in Roman History*. Vol. 2. Cambridge 1983.

Ingalls, Wayne B. "Repetition in Lucretius." *Phoenix* 25 (1971): 227–36.

Jope, James. "Lucretius' Psychological Insight: His Notion of Unconscious Motivation." *Phoenix* 37 (1983): 224–38.

Kenney, E. J. "Doctus Lucretius." *Mnemosyne*, ser. 4, vol. 23 (1970): 366–92.

———, ed. *Lucretius De Rerum Natura Book III*. Cambridge, 1971.

———. "The Historical Imagination of Lucretius." *Greece & Rome*, 2nd ser., vol. 19 (1972): 12–24.

Klingner, Friedrich. "Philosophie und Dichtkunst am Ende des zweiten Buches des Lucrez." In *Studien zur griechischen und römischen Literatur*, 126–55. Zurich, 1964; originally published in *Hermes* 80 (1952): 3–31.

———. "Lucrez." In *Römische Geisteswelt* (1965). 5th ed., pp. 191–217. Stuttgart, 1979.

Konstan, David. *Some Aspects of Epicurean Psychology*. Philosophia Antiqua 25. Leiden, 1973.

Kuiper, Taco, ed. *Philodemus over den Dood*. Amsterdam, 1925.

Logre, Dr [sic] J. B. *L'anxiété de Lucrèce*. Paris, 1946.

Lortie, Paul Eugène. "Crainte anxieuse des enfers chez Lucrèce: Prolegomènes." *Phoenix* 8 (1954): 47–63.

McKay, K. L. "Animals in War and *Isonomia*." *American Journal of Philology* 85 (1964): 124–35.

Martha, Constant. *Le poème de Lucrèce*. 4th ed. Paris, 1885.

Michels, Agnes Kirsopp. "Death and Two Poets." *Transactions of the American Philological Association* 86 (1955): 160–79.

Miller, Fred D., Jr. "Epicurus on the Art of Dying." *Southern Journal of Philosophy* 14 (1976): 169–77.

Minadeo, Richard. *The Lyre of Science*. Detroit, 1969.

Minyard, J. D. *Mode and Value in the De Rerum Natura*. Hermes Einzelschrift 39. Wiesbaden, 1978.

———. *Lucretius and the Late Republic. Mnemosyne*, suppl. 90. Leiden, 1985.

Mitsis, Phillip. *Epicurus' Ethical Theory: The Pleasures of Invulnerability*. Cornell Studies in Classical Philology 48. Ithaca, N.Y., 1988.

Montaigne, Michel de. *The Complete Essays of Montaigne*. Trans. Donald M. Frame. 3 vols. Stanford, 1957; reprint, Garden City, N.Y., 1960.

Müller, Gerhard. "Die Finalia der sechs Bücher des Lucrez." In Fondation Hardt, *Entretiens, Lucrèce*, pp. 197–231 (1978).

Munro, H.A.J., ed. *T. Lucreti Cari De Rerum Natura Libri Sex*. 4th ed., 2 vols. London, 1886.

Nethercut, William R. "The Conclusion of Lucretius' Fifth Book: Further Remarks." *Classical Journal* 63 (1967–68): 97–106.

Nussbaum, Martha C. "Beyond Obsession and Disgust: Lucretius on the Therapy of Love." *Apeiron* 22 (1989): 1–59.

———. "Mortal Immortals: Lucretius on Death and the Voice of Nature." *Philosophy and Phenomenological Research* 50 (1989): 303–51.

Perelli, Luciano. *Lucrezio poeta dell' angoscia*. Florence, 1969.

Pigeaud, Jackie. "La physiologie de Lucrèce." *Revue des Etudes Latines* 58 (1980): 176–200.

———. *La maladie de l'âme*. Paris, 1981.

Puliga, Donatella. "*Chronos* e *Thanatos* in Epicuro." *Elenchos* 4 (1983): 235–60.

Rambaux, Claude. "La logique de l'argumentation dans le *De Rerum Natura*." *Revue des Etudes Latines* 58 (1980): 201–19.

Regenbogen, Otto. "Lucrez. Seine Gestalt in seinem Gedicht" (1932). In *Kleine Schriften*, ed. Franz Dirlmeier, pp. 296–386. Munich, 1961.

Santayana, George. "Lucretius." In *Three Philosophical Poets*, pp. 25–67. Cambridge, Mass., 1910; reprint, Garden City, N.Y., 1953.

Saylor, Charles F. "Man, Animal, and the Bestial in Lucretius." *Classical Journal* 67 (1971–72): 306–16.

Schiesaro, Alessandro. *Simulacrum et imago: Gli argomenti analogici nel De rerum natura.* Pisa, 1990.

Schmid, Wolfgang. "*Lucretius Ethicus.*" In Fondation Hardt, *Entretiens, Lucrèce,* pp. 123–65. (1978).

Schrijvers, P. H. *Horror ac divina Voluptas. Etudes sur la poétique et la poésie de Lucrèce.* Amsterdam, 1970.

———. "Sur quelques aspects de la critique des mythes chez Lucrèce." In *Syzētēsis: Studi sull' epicureismo greco e romano offerti a Marcello Gigante,* vol. 1, pp. 353–71. Naples, 1983.

Segal, Charles. "Lucretius, Epilepsy, and the Hippocratic *On Breaths.*" *Classical Philology* 65 (1970): 180–82.

———. "*Delubra Decora*: Lucretius II. 352–66." *Latomus* 29 (1970): 104–18.

———. "Ovid: Metamorphosis, Hero, Poet." *Helios* 12 (1985): 49–63.

———. "War, Death, and Savagery in Lucretius: The Beasts of Battle in 5.1308–49." *Ramus* 15 (1986): 1–34.

———. "Poetic Immortality and the Fear of Death: The Second Proem of the *De Rerum Natura.*" *Harvard Studies in Classical Philology* 92 (1989): 193–212.

Sellar, W. Y. *The Roman Poets of the Republic.* 3rd ed. Oxford, 1889.

Sikes, E. E. *Lucretius Poet and Philosopher.* Cambridge, 1936.

Snyder, Jane. *Puns and Poetry in Lucretius' De Rerum Natura.* Amsterdam, 1980.

Stork, Traudel. *Nil igitur mors est ad nos: Der Schlussteil des dritten Lucrezbuches und sein Verhältnis zur Konsolationsliteratur.* Bonn, 1970.

Taylor, Margaret. "Progress and Primitivism in Lucretius." *American Journal of Philology* 68 (1947): 180–94.

Townend, G. B. "The Original Plan of Lucretius' *De Rerum Natura.*" *Classical Quarterly,* n.s. 29 (1979): 101–11.

Usener, Hermann, ed. *Epicurea.* Leipzig, 1887.

Wallach, Barbara Price. *Lucretius and the Diatribe against the Fear of Death: De Rerum Natura III, 830–1094. Mnemosyne,* suppl. 40. Leiden, 1976.

Waszink, J. H. "Letum." *Mnemosyne,* ser. 4, vol. 19 (1966): 249–60.

West, David. *The Imagery and Poetry of Lucretius.* Edinburgh, 1969.

INDEX OF PASSAGES

254   INDEX

272 INDEX

GENERAL INDEX

Acheron, 171, 172, 176, 181, 235.
See afterlife; Hades; myth; under-
world
Achilles, 172, 177, 244
Admetus, 68
Aegium, 111
Aeneas, 36
Aeneid, by Virgil, 36, 65, 227
Aeschylus, 171, 178
Aetna, 107
afterlife, 17–19, 22, 25, 165. See
Acheron; death; Hades; myth; *re-
ligio*; underworld
age, 169
aggression, 42, 187, 188, 223, 231
Agricola, 68
agriculture, 112, 194, 207–11, 221,
223. See birth; earth; farmer;
Golden Age; *locus amoenus*; vi-
talism
air, 91, 130
Ajax, by Sophocles, 241
Alcestis, by Euripides, 68, 241
Alcman, 178
Alexander, 210
Alexandrianism, 86
allegorizations, 166, 171, 194
ambition, 37, 196
Amphinomus, 65
amputation, 128. See mutilation
anaisthêsia, 14, 145
analogy, 97–99, 107, 108, 111,
113, 132, 197, 225. See macro-
cosm; microcosm
Ancus Martius, 171, 172, 174
Andromache, 68
angor, 69, 116, 153–55, 157, 160
anima, 32, 46, 60, 62, 130, 132,
142, 149, 152, 157

animals, 119, 189, 198. See agricul-
ture; savagery; wild beast
animus, 32, 60, 61, 62, 130, 132,
141, 157
anthropology, 38
anti-Lucretius, 8, 59, 183, 238
Antigone, by Sophocles, 231, 241
Apollo, 8
Apology, by Plato, 244
Apuleius, 42
Ariès, Philippe, 26, 27
Aristotle, 74, 225, 226, 245n
arma, 192, 193, 213, 215
ataraxia, 10, 19, 33, 41, 50, 185,
202, 212
Athens, 12, 38, 39, 44, 99, 110,
112, 114, 124, 159, 161, 186,
191, 201, 221, 223, 224, 231,
232, 233, 234, 236
Attica, 39
Axiochus, 27, 33, 145, 244

Bacchic, 186. See Dionysiac
Bailey, 44, 142, 190
Baudelaire, 150
beast. See wild beast
Bignone, Ettore, 44
birth, 16, 57, 80, 83, 106, 186, 193,
195, 197, 198, 199, 201, 202,
209, 232, 236, 237. See agricul-
ture; death; Epicurus, birth of;
Natura
blood, 52, 150, 220
body, 26, 30, 32–33, 40, 52ff., 84,
94–114, 116, 144ff. See mutila-
tion; putrefaction; separated parts
Bosch, 121, 227
boundaries, 94–114, 115–70.
boundary anxiety, 21, 25

history, 203, 214–27
Holocaust, 227
Homer, 6, 36, 46, 50, 57, 64, 68,
   75, 78, 100, 130, 172, 173,
   175–87, 244. *See Iliad; Odyssey*
Horace, 241

Iliad, 68, 172, 177, 178, 227, 244.
   See Homer
imagery, 12, 15, 26, 123, 130, 156,
   157, 167, 177, 191, 197, 209,
   225
immersion. *See* drowning
immortality, 108, 179–84, 228,
   235. *See* epic poetry; fame; monu-
   ment
India, 107, 204
infinity, 7, 15, 16, 17, 72, 74–83,
   92, 93, 94, 96, 98, 103
inspiration, 184
Iphigeneia, 191, 192, 205
iron, 189, 190, 194, 208
irrationality, 9, 10, 24, 40, 86, 135,
   188, 192
isonomia, 101, 195, 234

Jerome, St., 4, 189
Juvenal, 42

Kafka, Franz, 23
Kant, Immanuel, 77, 78
Kenney, E. J., 142, 227
Konstan, David, 22
Kypris, 202

labor, 206
Lacan, Jacques, 142
Lattimore, Richmond, 17
Lemuria, 243
Leonidas of Tarentum, 173, 176–79
Leopardi, Giacomo, 75
letum, 63, 67, 68, 69, 90, 92n, 98,
   109, 115
life. *See* birth; death; vitalism

light, 19, 124–25, 130, 132, 156–
   59, 163, 165, 169, 176, 197, 223,
   225, 236, 237, 239, 240. *See*
   darkness
limit, 15, 72, 81
locus amoenus, 184. *See* agriculture
Logre, Dr., 9, 87, 124
Longinus, 77, 176
lorica, 109
love, 9, 24, 35, 86, 111, 153, 160,
   161, 173
lyric poetry, 85. *See* Catullus; Sap-
   pho

macrocosm, 94, 97, 99, 198. *See*
   analogy; microcosm
maggots, 149. *See* putrefaction;
   worms
Magna Mater, 102, 107, 191, 192,
   194, 200–207. *See* agriculture;
   birth; earth; Natura
Mars, 7, 107, 173, 187, 188, 194,
   196, 199, 200, 202, 212
Martha, Constant, 9
mathematical sublime, 77. *See* sub-
   lime
medicine, 11, 40
Memmius, 235
metals, 189, 207, 208
Metamorphoses, by Ovid, 21, 42,
   142
metaphor, 27, 114, 115, 128, 136,
   137, 157, 164, 166, 167, 191,
   192, 237
microcosm, 94, 98, 99, 105, 160,
   197. *See* analogy; macrocosm
Midas, 179, 180
moenia mundi, 95, 106, 154, 155
monument, 98, 100
Montaigne, Michel de, 13, 28n, 242
monument, 179, 240. *See* epigram
morbus, 42. *See* disease
mors, 42. *See* death
mosaic, 210